ALSO BY JANE BRODY

Jane Brody's
GUIDE TO THE
GREAT BEYOND

Jane Brody's
GUIDE TO THE
GREAT BEYOND

A Practical Primer to Help
You and Your Loved Ones
Prepare Medically, Legally,
and Emotionally for the
End of Life

JANE BRODY

RANDOM HOUSE | NEW YORK

As of press time, the URLs displayed in this book link or refer to existing websites on the Internet. Random House, Inc., is not responsible for, and should not be deemed to endorse or recommend, any website other than its own or any content available on the Internet (including without limitation at any website, blog page, information page) that is not created by Random House.

Published in the United States by Random House, an imprint of The Random House Publishing Group, a division of Random House, Inc., New York.

RANDOM HOUSE and colophon are registered trademarks of Random House, Inc.

Illustration and permission credits can be found beginning on p. 285.

The prologue was originally published as "Facing Your Own Mortality" in *The New York Times Good Health Magazine* on October 9, 1988.

ISBN 978-1-4000-6654-4
eBook ISBN 978-1-5883-6774-7

Printed in the United States of America on acid-free paper

www.atrandom.com

9 8 7 6 5 4 3 2 1

First Edition

Book design by Jo Anne Metsch

So live, that when thy summons comes to join
The innumerable caravan which moves
To that mysterious realm, where each shall take
His chamber in the silent halls of death,
Thou go not, like the quarry-slave at night,
Scourged to his dungeon, but, sustained and soothed
By an unfaltering trust, approach thy grave
Like one who wraps the drapery of his couch
About him, and lies down to pleasant dreams.

From "Thanatopsis" by William Cullen Bryant

The mere thought of death somehow makes every blessing
vivid, every happiness more luminous and intense.

Tony Snow, a columnist, the year before he died
of cancer at the age of fifty-three

I want you all to know that I am terribly happy and
am not in the least bit afraid to die. Death is nothing
and life everything. That's all.

Brooke Astor, 1902–2007, written at age ninety

No one wants to die . . . And yet death is a destination
we all share. No one has ever escaped it.

Steve Jobs, Apple CEO, following surgery for
pancreatic cancer

"Before I go over your test results, can we agree no one lives forever?"

PREFACE

Most readers know me as a staunch advocate of a healthy life—a life filled with nutritious food and regular physical exercise designed to help people live life as fully as possible. But even the healthiest of lives eventually must come to an end. In this book I hope to help my readers make that end—for themselves and for those they love—as peaceful and, yes, as enjoyable as it can be.

We live in a death-denying, death-defying culture. I am as guilty as the next person in not wanting *ever* to lose the chance to enjoy the many rewards life can offer. I want to see my four grandsons graduate from college. I want to dance at their weddings. I want to be a great-grandma someday.

But I know full well that any number of circumstances can keep me from experiencing these joys. I could suffer life-threatening injuries in an accident. I could be hit be a car. I could be hit on the head by a falling brick. I could fall down the subway stairs and never regain consciousness. Or I could develop an incurable disease, as my own mother did at the tender age of forty-eight, and fade away in less than a year.

There are many, many circumstances over which we have no

control, circumstances that can bring us unwillingly to the brink of life's end. I should say it like it really is—to the brink of death.

And so I have prepared for these possibilities as best as I can while I am still fully in control of my faculties. Decades ago, when my twin sons were infants, I began by assigning guardians for them should I and my husband become unable to care for them. Some years later, I completed a last will and testament and wrote out a living will, outlining as best as I could what I would and would not want to be done for me medically should I be rendered unable to articulate my wishes at the time.

Then, when New York State passed the appropriate legislation, I assigned my husband to serve as my health care proxy—to speak for me when and if I cannot speak for myself. And if he, too, were unable to speak, I assigned one of our sons to take on this responsibility.

Preparing for the end of life goes far beyond willing your estate to those you love or signing an organ donor card or picking out a burial plot. And for those millions of people who will have to help their parents and other relatives and friends exit gracefully from this life, preparation goes beyond finding the best doctors or hospital. It involves knowing what to say, and how and when to say it. It involves doctors who do not abandon their patients once cure becomes a lost cause. It involves getting adequate treatment for pain and other debilitating symptoms that rob dying people of their dignity. And it involves knowing what to do—and what *not* to do—when death is imminent so that you or your loved ones can die in peace.

And so, dear reader, please do read on. However old you are now, don't be afraid to face the inevitable, which I hope will be as distant from the present as possible. Because once you've taken care of the end of life, you'll be in a far better position to fully enjoy the time you have left.

JANE E. BRODY

CONTENTS

PROLOGUE:
End-of-Life Issues Are Not New for Me

I did not just start thinking about end-of-life issues when I reached my sixties. They've been with me nearly all my life, starting at age sixteen when my mother died, which prompted me to write a speech in college titled, "When You Come to the End of Your Days, Will You Be Able to Write Your Own Epitaph?" My concern with these issues has resurfaced periodically through the intervening years whenever relatives and friends developed life-threatening diseases and/or died.

When my friend Betty Marks heard I was writing a book about end-of-life issues, she recalled that nearly two decades earlier, when I was in my midforties, I had written a long article on the subject that was published on October 9, 1988, in the *New York Times Good Health Magazine*. Reading it in 2007, I was struck by how relevant the topics discussed in that article were to this book. And so, with the permission of the *Times*, it is reprinted here as a most telling prologue.

FACING YOUR OWN MORTALITY
By Jane E. Brody

Anna Engquist had just turned 80. Four hundred friends and relatives gathered at a "This Is Your Life, Anna" party at Elim Evangelical Lutheran Church in Scandia, Minn., to celebrate her indomitable spirit and dedication to the community. Barely a week after this glorious event Anna learned she had ovarian cancer and would need major surgery. She was told that the surgery would be risky because of various medical problems, including high blood pressure, 80 or so extra pounds and a heart condition. Anna spent the week before the operation getting her affairs in order—lining up caretakers for her pets, checking on her will and bank accounts. She also had prescient conversations with close friends and relatives, telling them in different ways how much they meant to her and how much she had enjoyed her life. The day before she went into the hospital, she left a long note on the kitchen table about bills coming due, repairs needed on the house and where all of her important papers could be found. Anna was prepared to die. Her surgeon wavered between concern over her seemingly fatalistic attitude—he feared she might give up too easily—and admiration for her calmness. As she was being wheeled into surgery, she gave voice to her thoughts: "I'm in God's hands."

But Anna did not die. She came out of anesthesia fighting for life, and resolved to do everything possible to rid herself of cancer. Her doctors recommended chemotherapy. Although Anna knew that the six-month drug regimen could be devastating, she was willing to go through with it. Four months into the treatment, she was plagued by such debilitating side effects that the oncologist suggested ending the therapy. But Anna, convinced that the medicine was working, chose to continue. She was determined to go on with life. That summer, she had her barn reconstructed. Now 83, Anna remains a vital member of her community, showing visitors around the two museums she founded and helping house-bound senior citizens. She talks openly about her concern that her illness may recur. The openness seems to make things easier.

Anna Engquist is my mother-in-law. By some strange turn of fate, she had the same disease that ended my own mother's life 30 years ago, when chemotherapy was little more than an experiment. It was also a time when cancer was a family secret (sometimes not shared even with the victim). Unlike Anna, my mother had no chance to come to terms with her impending death; although she must have known she was dying, she could not really use the occasion, as Anna did, to face up to her own mortality. Thinking that we were sparing her undue anguish and despair, her close relatives never mentioned the words "cancer," "incurable" and "dying" in her presence, and she played the same game with us. In our determination to protect each other, we never permitted ourselves to cry together. But the pain that the family suffered watching my mother die was no doubt more than matched by the agony of her loneliness and inability to say good-bye.

If any good came from my mother's death at age 49, it was my recognition, at age 17, of my mortality and my decision, like Anna, to live each day as though it might be my last. I work hard but I leave room in every day for having fun and seeing friends. No matter how hectic my schedule gets, I try to stop often to watch the birds and admire the trees, and create opportunities to travel to exotic places. Perhaps one is less afraid to die if one is not afraid to live. Still, I'm sure I will not go gently into that good night, not even at 80. There is an important difference between intelligently, sensibly, learning to accept the inevitable—and surrendering. Surrender, or the refusal to surrender, actually has much more to do with attitudes toward living than dying. Indeed, being hard-nosed about death can bring about a positive, healthy, energized attitude toward life, for the young or old, healthy or ill.

Betty Marks, a 60-year-old New York literary agent, has been stricken by two life-threatening ailments—insulin-dependent diabetes and breast cancer—yet she stares death down every day. Despite the odds against her, she accepts the possibility of her imminent death with astonishing serenity. When she was diagnosed with cancer, she did not ask, as many patients do, "Why me?" Instead, she thought, "Why not me? Rather than crying about your affliction, you have to live every minute you have as a gift."

She agreed to undergo an aggressive form of chemotherapy. But she stayed determined not to let her illness deny her the pleasures of life. She took up tap dancing and cut back on her workaholic tendencies. She sets aside time each day for her friends and for activities she likes, such as taking photographs and hiking.

Clearly, the nearness of death, and her way of dealing with it, have enriched the quality of her life profoundly. "There's been a reward to my illness—discovering how much people care for me," she says. "What has moved me to tears has not been my disease, but each time I talked to a friend and one of us said, 'I love you.' "

By contrast, I know of one man in his 60's, a gynecologist in Florida, who has been unable to overcome his anger at being crippled by amyotrophic lateral sclerosis—Lou Gehrig's disease—a progressive and ultimately fatal neuromuscular condition that causes the muscles to disintegrate, but leaves the mind excruciatingly aware of what is happening. When his illness was diagnosed, he, like many physicians, refused to acknowledge his encroaching impairment. He became hostile toward those around him. As his condition forced him to give up his practice, his anger often exploded. His wife, his full-time caretaker, bears the brunt of his fury. She has confided to friends with great sadness that she awaits the time when both of them will be released from the prison of terminal illness.

INTELLECTUALLY, we all know that death is a fact of life. But most people tend to avoid thinking about their own mortality, especially when they are young. For healthy young people, death seems so remote. But with a life-threatening experience—a serious illness, for example, or an accident—the confrontation is upon them. Anger, depression or panic are typical responses. But some people, young and old alike, remain calm when death suddenly presents itself, and this calmness may, on occasion, be life-saving. People who have begun to develop a sound philosophy of life, and the lust for life that grows out of it, seem best able to stay calm when the image of death flashes on the horizon.

A friend of mine, as a college student, was skiing down a steep, icy slope in preparation for a downhill race when he fell, sliding at breakneck speed toward the overhanging branch of a jagged tree stump. He knew that unless he stopped, he would smack headlong into the branch and probably be killed. But he could not stop. "I said to myself, 'This is it, it's all over,' " he recalls. "Somehow, having said that, I lay back and relaxed, and that's probably what saved me." IIe slid under the branch and was unharmed: "If I had been taut and my head had been an inch higher, it would have been over."

This lack of fear is also characteristic of some people who mistakenly believe they are in great danger, according to Dr. Richard S. Blacher, a psychiatrist at Tufts–New England Medical Center in Boston who works with patients facing cardiac surgery. "Most people think cardiac surgery is more life-threatening than other operations, even though it's no more dangerous than gallbladder surgery," he says. "However, paradoxically, patients typically go into cardiac surgery much calmer, much less anxious, than those having gallbladder surgery. Behind the difference is denial."

The denial of death is usually just temporary. Eventually, denial gives way to acceptance. To ease this transition, many psychotherapists believe that it is important for people to feel free to discuss their anxieties and other emotions concerning death with friends and relatives. Such openness helps dispel the fear of dying.

Taken to the extreme, fear of death can rob people of life, keeping them from taking the kinds of risks that can yield rich rewards— rafting down a river, for instance. By contrast, my friend quickly got back on his skis after his fall, and decades later remains an avid racer.

AT no time is honest communication more crucial than when death draws near. A heart-to-heart conversation or even a loving gesture not only helps the person who is dying; it also helps the survivors deal with their grief. Anne W. Rosberger, a social worker who, with her psychiatrist husband, Dr. Henry Rosberger, directs the Bereavement and Loss Center of New York, has found that people "who prepare for death by talking about it, sharing feelings, being completely open, leave behind survivors who are less plagued by guilt." Guilt often arises because of unresolved conflicts that make people feel that they somehow caused the death of their loved ones. With less guilt, Mrs. Rosberger says, bereavement tends to be briefer, not as consuming.

Many families resist talking about death, whether or not it is near, according to Mary-Ellen Siegel, a social worker and senior teaching associate in community medicine at Mount Sinai School of Medicine in New York. Frequently, a person who is elderly or terminally ill wants to talk about his or her death, but family members are uncomfortable with the subject. Even as a professional who works with the dying and their families, Ms. Siegel says she had difficulty listening to her dying mother's wishes. "I was tempted to say, 'Don't talk like that,'" she says. But she resisted the temptation. "We finally did say what we wanted to say to one another."

It is even harder to talk about death with an elderly relative who is healthy, says Ms. Siegel. One active 83-year-old woman who lives in her own apartment in Buffalo corroborates this view: "My children try to hush me up when I talk about my preparations for death, but I feel better knowing that my funeral and burial arrangements will be as I want them and my possessions will be distributed fairly."

Families seem to have the greatest difficulty speaking openly about death when the dying person is young. Dying can be an extraordinarily lonely experience for children when their parents do not allow the subject to be discussed. Penelope Buschman, a nurse specializing in psychiatry at the Babies Hospital of Columbia–Presbyterian Medical Center in New York, often encounters parents who insist that their dying children don't realize their illnesses are life-threatening. "But I hear very different things from the children," she says. "They are very aware that they are not getting better, and they need to talk about it."

Ms. Buschman recalled the case of a 9-year-old girl who had undergone extensive treatment for cancer and knew she was dying. Toward the end she became withdrawn and despondent and said she was very frightened. She wanted desperately to convey this to her mother, but whenever she tried, her mother would change the subject. Finally, Ms. Buschman intervened and urged the mother to listen to the child without saying anything. The mother followed this advice, responding to her daughter only by holding her. Unburdened and relieved, the girl died a few days later.

At any age, Mary-Ellen Siegel says, "those who are open about what's happening can have a lot of emotionally painful times. But in the long run, family members are likely to feel less depressed, less guilty, if they have made their peace with the person who died."

THE ability to look upon death with serenity often reflects a strong belief in the hereafter. As the daughter of the woman from Buffalo describes her mother, "She's not anxious to die, but neither is she anxious about dying." The woman herself attributes her tranquility to her religious convictions and a belief in a spiritual life after death.

Secular souls can also face death with equanimity. Raphael Patai, an anthropologist specializing in the ancient and modern Middle East, has found at age 77 that death no longer seems threatening. "When I was young, death always felt like a mortal enemy," he says, smiling at the play on words. "As my physical strength diminishes, as I can do less, death appears more and more as a friend. I have the romantic notion that when I die I will come into a society of people I loved who died before me. As I get older, the attraction of society in this world gradually lessens and the attraction of society in the other world gradually increases."

Even without a belief in the hereafter, many people come to a more accepting view of death. A 61-year-old psychiatrist in Brooklyn, who has known since his late 30's that he has coronary heart disease, finds solace in the idea that when he dies he will somehow return to his beginning. "I have no religious beliefs to help me, but I sort of think that when I die I'll be going back to where I came from," he says. "My molecules will become part of the universe once again."

Encroaching disability often speeds such a reconciliation with life's end. Florence R. A. Wilde, who was widowed in her early 30's, lived a healthy, active life as an artist and a professor of art in Florida until, at age 82, cataracts made it impossible for her to continue painting. Soon afterward, her chronic intestinal problems were diagnosed as colon cancer. She kept up a fighting faith but began to live more and more in the past. During what turned out to be her final hospitalization, she confided in her grandson that she felt her "fingers being loosened" on all the things she valued in life, and said she was "ready to go."

Psychotherapists report that people who live independent lives seem to be able to die gracefully. Those who are highly dependent emotionally on other people, however, often experience great terror when they are dying. They seem to lack the inner resources to sustain themselves.

Dr. Samuel C. Klagsbrun, the medical director of Four Winds Hospital, a psychiatric facility in Katonah, N.Y., says that he witnessed many "good" deaths and "bad" deaths during the 18 years he spent as a teacher at St. Christopher's Hospice in London. In his view, "a bad death—one in which the dying person fights destructively, casting blame on others, making people feel that whatever they do is not enough—leaves behind two major pieces of unfinished business. The survivors feel guilty. And knowing all along that on some level they wished for the person to die, they feel that they may have caused the death or speeded it up."

It is far better, Betty Marks believes, to end on a positive note, appreciating "the wonders of life, which include the mysteries of death." She sees life and death as, in a sense, two sides of the same coin. "There's no emotion inherent in life or death," she says. "It's the loving that surrounds you that makes both of them meaningful."

PART 1

GET READY *NOW* FOR THE GREAT BEYOND

We live in a society of death deniers, typified by the failure of most of us to prepare for the inevitable, whenever and however our time will come to leave the world of the living. The result can be undue anguish for ourselves in the course of our dying and those we leave behind, not only during our final days, but for weeks, months, even years thereafter.

In this section, you and your family will learn what is best done well in advance of the end and how to accomplish it. Perhaps you are now young and healthy and thinking, "Why worry about something most likely years in the future?" But when you are young and healthy is the very best time to start— with minimal emotional pressure to color your thoughts. Furthermore, as you well know but probably don't want to admit, you never know when your time, or the time of your loved ones, may come to cross over to the Great Beyond.

Fear not. Nothing you do or say now will be etched in stone. You can always make changes as your life circumstances, feelings, and beliefs alter. But without an initial template, waiting until the bitter end will make the task that much harder and perhaps even impossible to accomplish.

"Actually, I preferred 'Heaven,' too, but then the marketing guys got hold of it."

CHAPTER **1**

Death Is Inevitable:
So Be Prepared

There's only one certainty in life, and that is sooner or later it will end. No matter how good a person you are, no matter how important your contribution to society, no matter how healthfully you eat and faithfully you exercise, you will not—you *cannot*—live forever. That is an incontrovertible fact from which you cannot—and *should not*—hide. Despite the best that modern medicine can offer, there is no cure for mortality.

Yet the overwhelming majority of people are ill prepared for their final days, or the final days of the people they love. Some people are superstitious. They harbor an irrational belief that thinking about death is inviting trouble. But the real trouble comes from *not* thinking about death well in advance. Others simply haven't bothered. Why not put off until tomorrow what you don't have to do today? But what if tomorrow is too late . . . ?

No matter what your age or the age of your loved ones, the time to prepare yourself for the inevitable is now. You never know when the end may come and whether you will be able to speak for yourself as it approaches.

Too many people wait until it is too late to determine how they wish to spend their final days.

Too many people have neither discussed nor recorded their

end-of-life wishes with the people most likely to have a say in the matter.

Too many people are at risk of ending up like Terri Schiavo, locked in a vegetative state for years while their families fight over how to proceed.

Too many people spend their dying days suffering needlessly with intractable pain or plagued by futile medical interventions.

Too many people assume incorrectly that having written a living will, they are protected from unwanted interventions when death is near.

And too many families are unprepared for the sudden, unexpected death of a loved one—young, old, or in between.

The terrorist attack of September 11, 2001, claimed 2,996 lives, nearly all healthy people and many in their thirties and forties with young families. A more commonplace tragedy occurred in August 2006 when a flatbed truck loaded with bricks slammed into a car carrying the young Christmas family of Queens, New York. Charles, age forty, and Theresa Ann, age forty-one, and their two-year-old daughter, Victoria, were killed, leaving their four-year-old daughter, Theresa, an orphan. The truck then overturned and crushed an SUV, taking the life of thirty-seven-year-old Norma Ryan but sparing her two children, Peter, age twelve, and Samantha, six months old.

All of these, to say the least, were horrid, unexpected deaths. For most people nowadays, the Grim Reaper approaches with far more warning. In 1990 cancer overtook heart disease as the leading killer among Americans under age eighty-five, which means the majority of Americans now die slowly.

Yet even when there are weeks, months, or even years to prepare for the inevitable, relatively few people acquire the knowledge and take the steps needed to be sure that the end of life is as peaceful and comfortable and, yes, as celebratory as it can be, and that those who will be left behind are not overly burdened with medical and financial responsibilities, unanswered questions, and unresolved guilt.

In days of yore when deaths, other than accidental ones, occurred mainly at home, entire families—even young children—were familiar with it. People died at all ages—in infancy, childhood, childbirth, as well as in old age—surrounded by their loved ones, not strangers in white coats. Death was a part of life and, sad though it may have been, most everyone accepted it as such. There were no respirators, feeding tubes, needles, and fluid-filled pouches keeping people alive for weeks or months. No one had to decide when to turn off life-prolonging machinery or stop treatments for an incurable disease.

The case of Terri Schiavo, the twenty-six-year-old who lingered for fifteen years in a vegetative state sustained by a feeding tube while her family fought over the right to end her so-called life is perhaps the most dramatic illustration of the need for everyone—young, old, and in between—to be prepared:

- To make your wishes known about how you want to be treated if you are unable to communicate them at the time.

- To officially designate someone you trust to speak for you when you cannot speak for yourself.

- To know how to find doctors who treat the whole person, not just the disease, and who will not abandon patients when cure or meaningful prolongation of life is no longer possible.

- To know how to enlist the aid of the medical profession so that comfort and dignity, not agony and terror, are the hallmarks of your loved one's final days.

- To know how to respond appropriately when someone is dying so that the final hours, days, weeks, or months of life are not needlessly traumatic and financially exhausting for you or your loved one.

- To recognize and understand what happens, physically and mentally, when death is imminent, when hand-holding and reassurance, not food or drink or an oxygen mask or CPR, is the proper course of action.

- To have a properly executed will so that your heirs will know how you wanted your assets distributed and will not become enemies battling over inheritance rights.

- And perhaps most important of all, to assign guardians for your underage children, along with a means to support them, if possible, should they become orphaned by the death of both parents.

It has been nearly forty years since Dr. Elisabeth Kübler-Ross's best-selling book, *On Death and Dying,* turned this long-taboo subject into a socially accepted topic of conversation. Once the door had been opened, other books for the general reader followed: *Final Gifts* by Maggie Callahan and Patricia Kelly in 1992, *How We Die* by Sherwin Nuland in 1994, *The Good Death* by Marilyn Webb in 1997, *Peaceful Dying* by Daniel R. Tobin in 1999, *The Needs of the Dying* by David Kessler in 2000, *On Grief and Grieving* by Elisabeth Kübler-Ross and David Kessler in 2005, *Last Rights* by Stephen P. Kiernan in 2006, and *Final Conversations: Helping the Living and the Dying Talk to Each Other* by Maureen P. Keeley and Julie M. Yingling in 2007, among others.

Since Dr. Kübler-Ross opened the floodgates, many who work in the health care industry—nurses, physicians, social workers, chaplains—have written widely on the subject of death and dying in articles published in leading medical journals. Indeed, the *Journal of the American Medical Association* published an entire issue on the subject in 2000 and regularly runs articles under the rubric "Perspectives on Care at the Close of Life."

The *American Journal of Nursing* ran a yearlong series on caring for patients at the end of life. And many other leading journals—the *Archives of Internal Medicine,* the *Annals of Internal Medicine,* the *New England Journal of Medicine,* and the British journals the *Lancet* and *BMJ,* among others—have collectively published scores of research studies and discussions intended to enlighten physicians and other health care professionals about how best to cope with the myriad medical, ethical, and humane concerns that emerge when patients approach the end of life.

Still, there is so much ignorance about and resistance to this subject, much to the disservice of people who are dying and those who love and care for them. Avoidance and denial, not acceptance, are the states most commonly associated with the end of life, among physicians as well as laypeople like you and me.

For example, none of this information managed to penetrate the psyche of the leading oncologist who treated my friend Frank Crewdson in 1998 following a diagnosis of a relatively rare lung cancer unrelated to smoking. When it became obvious that the treatment the doctor had prescribed in hopes of "buying time" for his patient was not working, he sent in one of his henchmen— a physician who had had no prior contact with Frank—to tell him, "There's nothing else we can give you."

It was as blunt a death sentence as could be delivered, and Frank, who was alone at the time, had no one to help soften the blow. Furthermore, his physician never saw Frank again, never came in to say, "We tried our best, but I'm very sorry that our best was simply not good enough. We can promise, however, to make you as comfortable as possible."

Nonetheless, changes are taking place in how dying patients are treated, thanks largely to the hospice movement and to the ongoing debates about physician-assisted deaths. A new medical specialty called palliative medicine, which focuses on alleviating patients' symptoms and delivering humane medical care to patients whether they are expected to live or die, is gaining ground in hospitals nationwide. If properly executed, palliative care can obviate the need for laws to permit assisted suicides. Patients facing a protracted, fatal illness can spend their last days in comfort, saying their good-byes, imparting their wisdom, healing wounded relationships, and expressing their love and appreciation to family and friends.

Ordinary people today are speaking more openly about loved ones afflicted with diseases like cancer, AIDS, and dementia. It is less and less common in newspaper obituaries for people to die "after a long illness."

Now the task at hand is to help millions of people like you to face up to the inevitable long before it will be necessary to put those preparations into action. You just never know. Remember Terri Schiavo was only twenty-six years old.

You can—you *must,* for your own sake and the sake of those you love—help to change the culture of denial and avoidance to one of acceptance and preparation. You and your heirs will be glad you did.

FOR FURTHER READING

Kiernan, Stephen P. *Last Rights: Rescuing the End of Life from the Medical System.* New York: St. Martin's Press, 2006.

CHAPTER 2

A Good Death: There's More Than One Right Way to Die

"**D**eath gives life meaning. Without death every birth would be a tragedy," Dr. Richard Smith wrote as editor of *BMJ*, the British medical journal. He recalled Jonathan Swift's writing in *Gulliver's Travels*:

> *Gulliver was vastly excited when he traveled to Laputa and heard of the Strudbruggs, the immortals. He imagined them with their "minds free and disengaged, without the weight and depression of Spirits caused by the continual Apprehension of Death." In fact, they were the most miserable of people. One of their "prevailing Passions" was envy of the deaths of the old.*

Some people would say there is no such thing as a "good death"—that all deaths, except perhaps the deaths of terrorists and violent criminals, are necessarily unwanted and unwelcome. That may well be true when you are young, healthy, physically and mentally intact or, if not all of the above, at least still able to enjoy the good things and people in your life.

But what if you are very old and sick and no longer able to care for yourself? What if you become demented and no longer recognize or care about the people you loved? What if you have an incurable, untreatable illness that has progressed to the point where death is, as Hamlet put it, "a consummation devoutly to be wished?"

At such points, death might be a welcomed exit from an existence that has become intolerable or meaningless.

But I've discovered from people I've known and others I've read about, there is no one definition of a good death. Just as we have followed different paths in life, each of us must decide for ourselves how we want to be treated when death is near—where we want to be and with whom, and feeling, thinking, and doing what best suits us as individuals.

Some people, like my late friend Frank Crewdson, prefer the "security" of being in a hospital surrounded by equipment and medicines that can assuage any crisis, at least temporarily. Others, like my late friends Jessica Wing and Mickey Martinez, prefer to die at home surrounded by familiar, caring faces and caressed by their tender, loving hands and kisses.

Some, especially those with a deep, abiding faith, are ready to "meet their Maker" whereas others may refuse to acknowledge the approach of the Grim Reaper and insist that everything possible be done to treat their illness and keep them alive for as long as possible.

The five stages of death—denial, anger, bargaining, depression, and finally acceptance, so brilliantly described in 1969 by Dr. Elisabeth Kübler-Ross—are universal only in the sense that different people choose to die at different stages. In death as in life, there are different strokes for different folks. There is no one "right way" to die.

What can make dying especially painful for both the dying and those they will leave behind is when the two are at different, incompatible stages and neither is willing or able to budge:

- The patient is in denial while the family has accepted the inevitable and only wishes the patient would prepare for it as well.

- The patient has accepted the fact that death is near but loved ones keep scouring the Internet and insisting that this, that, or the other therapy—however outrageous—be tried when all the patient wants is to be left to die in peace.

- The family is unable to relinquish anger over what they believe to be medical mistreatment—a missed diagnosis or improper therapy—while the patient has moved beyond anger to accepting the fact that doctors are human and mishaps are sometimes unavoidable.

- The family is so grief-stricken that no one can "hear" the patient's attempts to settle unfinished business, express previously unsaid feelings, and bring life to a peaceful closure.

While it may not always be possible to reconcile such differences, when loved ones are at least able to accept the patient's choice in how to approach the end of life, the parting is likely to be less painful for the patient and the grieving less difficult for the survivors. It is not possible for patients to say good-bye in a meaningful way if loved ones insist that this is not the end or that they would get better if only they would "eat something," "try this new medicine," "see the doctor who helped Mrs. Wilcox," and so on.

Accepting the Patient's Terms

Dr. Joseph Sacco struggled to bring his father, Joe, to "acceptance," which he, as a medical doctor, thought was the way one should face an inevitable death. Having smoked unfiltered cigarettes for fifty of his sixty-seven years, all the while ignoring his son's repeated pleas to quit, Joe Sacco was diagnosed with an inoperable advanced lung cancer.

But Joe kept insisting to his more knowledgeable son, "Don't worry about it, kid! I'm going to beat this thing," Dr. Sacco relates in his book, *On His Own Terms*, with the telling subtitle *A Doctor,*

His Father, and the Myth of the "Good Death." Joe refused to ac-knowledge the fact that he had an incurable cancer, insisting in-stead that once the bloody fluid was drained from his chest cavity and he finished chemo, he would be able to breathe better and be on his way to recovery.

Even as Joe's body shrunk under the onslaught of cancer and he dropped to half his former weight, he remained in denial, repeat-edly insisting he would "beat this thing." And his son, not wanting to hurt his father, felt compelled to play the same game. "For my father, what was in order was a little good-natured lying—'Hey, Pop! What do you say we visit Sicily when you get better?' " he re-called saying in an effort to meet Joe on his own terms.

Not until the last few days of Joe's life, when he asked his son if he could do something to bring his life more quickly to a close, was Joe ready to admit, at least indirectly, that he was dying.

"Had my father not been frozen by fear, he might have been able to talk openly and reaffirm his knowledge that his son really did love him," Dr. Sacco wrote. "Instead, paralyzed by the implica-tion that death was imminent, he brushed me aside with a wave of the hand and the comment that he wasn't going to die."

Nonetheless, most experts believe, it is the job of physicians and nurses as well as families to help patients achieve their unique vi-sion of a good death. Dr. Susan D. Block, a specialist in psychoso-cial oncology at the Dana-Farber Cancer Institute in Boston, identified six characteristics that many patients consider central to a good death:

- Optimizing physical comfort

- Maintaining a sense of continuity with one's self

- Maintaining and enhancing relationships

- Making meaning of one's life and death

- Achieving a sense of control

- Confronting and preparing for death

When physicians can help patients meet these goals, Dr. Block has found that doctors also can benefit from a "deeper understanding about the nature of life, an appreciation of the gifts of being alive, and constantly renewed inspiration and hopefulness about human resilience."

But the importance of each of these six goals can vary from patient to patient, and it is the job of all who attend a dying person to follow that person's leads. In other words, whether you are a doctor, nurse, family member, or friend, helping someone to die "on his own terms" is a win-win situation for all concerned.

As Dr. Sacco sees it, from tending to many more dying patients after his father's demise, "The central task of those who care for the dying is to understand what they need and give it to them. Truth is only one of many possibilities. Was it really so terrible that [my father] fought death, filled with fury and terror, virtually to the end?"

He tells of another patient, Mrs. Santana, who "would not die my way"—with acceptance. Gravely ill but in total denial, she cooperated fully "with all the blood tests, X-rays, and procedures her doctors requested, never uttering the words cancer or dying so much as once," he wrote. "And, if only by the sheer weight of her grace, the doctor who was most responsible for her care came to realize that not only was acceptance not possible for her, but also not necessary. Beautiful Mrs. Santana—who combined denial with dignity, fear with a graceful calm—taught him this, and died in a way that was uniquely her own."

When the Patient Is Prepared

A more common scenario these days is one I have now witnessed a dozen times in recent years. These are the people who know the end is not far off and use the months or years remaining to prepare for the day when they will no longer be among the living.

Just one day before I started writing this book, a courageous and extraordinary woman I knew died of a cancer that had wiped out her immune system and the ability of her blood to clot. She spent the last month of her life in hospice care, where she was kept comfortable by an attentive nursing staff and visited daily by her husband and various friends and relatives, including her almost-two-year-old granddaughter.

Jan Jeffrey of Brooklyn, New York, was sixty-eight years old, wife of Bill, mother of Randy and Scott, grandmother of Rowan. A social worker by training, she used her natural writing skills to help carry her through more than two years of—as she put it—"coexisting with my disease."

More about how Jan coped with life despite a life-threatening illness can be found in chapters 5 and 10. For now, the most telling part of her tale is how she arranged in advance to spend her final days. She spoke with me for about an hour just two and a half weeks before she died.

Jan was a strong person who orchestrated her care throughout her illness and up to the moment she died. No one, no matter how much they loved her, dared to contradict her decisions for how she was to be treated medically, how she would say her good-byes, how she would die, and how she would be memorialized afterward.

"I've had such a good time to say my good-byes, including a visit a year ago with my eighty-six-year-old mother and my brother in North Dakota and my sister in Minneapolis—it was such good closure," Jan said. "I've had time to plan my memorial services—one here in Brooklyn and the other in North Dakota, where I spent the first twenty-one years of my life. I've had time to make known my wishes to be cremated and to have my husband and sons with me at the end."

Jan, who had been an avid birder and lover of flowers, also got to enjoy the first of what is likely to be a number of memorials in her honor. The year she died—2006—was her fiftieth high school reunion year, and her classmates planted a tree in her honor on July 4. In concert with her passions, she said, "It's a flowering tree that bears berries for the birds in winter."

As a great admirer of nature, Jan wanted nature to take its course with regard to her death. She chose to receive blood and platelet transfusions and antibiotics to ward off complications until her body simply gave out.

Though barely able to talk at the end, Jan was conscious and free of pain, and having taken care of all that she considered important, she was ready to die. It would be hard to see Jan's as anything but a good death that will enable her family and friends to celebrate her life with enthusiasm as they mourn her loss.

When Death Is Sudden

All well and good, you say, if you know you're going to die soon and have the time and energy to make the arrangements you desire. But what happens when death comes swiftly and unexpectedly as, for example, happened to my father, who collapsed and died of a heart attack at age seventy-one while shopping for groceries in a Brooklyn supermarket on the eve of Rosh Hashanah, the Jewish New Year?

He had been a vigorous and happy man until the moment he died, and his death was swift, and if painful, the pain would have lasted only a few moments. Easy for him, perhaps, but very, very hard on his survivors—especially his wife of twenty-two years (my stepmother) and my brother and me—who had no opportunity to say good-bye and tell him how much we loved and admired him.

Trained as a lawyer, my father had a properly executed will, leaving most of his worldly goods to his wife. But beyond that we knew nothing of his wishes. So we muddled through a funeral with a rabbi we had never met and who didn't seem to know much about my father either, although he attended temple regularly.

I spoke at the service, describing a man who loved nature— weeds and all—a man who adored children (he should have been a pediatrician), a man who was always kind to strangers, a man who died "with his boots on" doing something he loved—shopping!

Establishing memorials was easy: trees planted in Israel, a seat in the new auditorium of his beloved alma mater, a tank of aquatic plants at the Brooklyn Botanic Garden.

All in all, my father's *was* a good death—uncomplicated, no end-of-life decisions necessary like when and if to discontinue treatment, and no postmortem conflicts among his survivors.

Help from an Advance Directive

If only all deaths were like my father's! But more and more, these days, deaths are more like Jan's—slow and complicated. Too often they are marred by difficult decisions, conflicts with physicians and insurers, disagreements within the family, and sometimes conflicts between the family and the patient as to what and how much should be done to prolong life. But many if not most of these problems can be circumvented with proper preparation, preferably when you are still physically well and mentally intact (see chapter 3).

Like Jan, my mother-in-law, Anna Engquist, also had what everyone who knew and loved her called a good death. Anna, a tough Minnesotan used to overcoming adversity, had always been a no-nonsense person, and she remained so through her dying hour. She had endured a rather challenging treatment for ovarian cancer at age eighty, but four years later she developed symptoms indicating that the cancer had recurred. In the intervening years, she had labeled all her possessions of any value—sentimental or otherwise—as to who should inherit them.

Minnesota had just passed a "living will" law and she wasted no time in filling out the form stating that if she developed a life-threatening condition, she wanted no medical intervention aimed at prolonging her life. When she suddenly started hemorrhaging and was whisked by ambulance to her local community hospital, she made sure to bring her living will along. In accordance with her wishes, the admitting nurse put a "do not resuscitate" notice on the door to her room. Her family was immediately notified, and all who mattered to Anna either rushed to her bedside or spoke to her by phone—children, grandchildren, great-grandchildren, close friends, and her minister. No one dared to contradict her decision to let her life ebb away.

Anna lived twelve pain-free, fully conscious hours, saying all her good-byes and telling those who loved her that she was ready to die. Her minister said he'd never in thirty years witnessed a more peaceful death. And those who loved her were relieved that the end was short, sweet, and as dignified as Anna herself had been in life.

Even a Good Death Can Sting

Still, families sometimes have a hard time accepting even the best-orchestrated death of loved ones they are about to lose.

In a column titled "Sometimes Dying Still Stings," published on November 15, 2000, in the *Journal of the American Medical Association*, Dr. Greg A. Sachs cautioned against "painting too rosy a picture of end-of-life care" and creating unreasonable expectations of "spiritual growth" and "transcendence" for the survivors. Dr. Sachs described the "peaceful death" planned for his father-in-law, Al, by the family, Al's physician, and Al himself.

Following a diagnosis of advanced lung cancer, Al opted for no cancer-specific treatment. Without ever discussing his grim prognosis, Al spent the year "straightening out files; reconciling accounts; and labeling everything in the house, including fuse boxes and cabinet drawers, so that his wife would be able to find everything when he was gone," Dr. Sachs recalled.

At no point during the eighteen months as his illness progressed did Al spend a day in the hospital. According to the agreed-upon plan, "Our deathbed vigil was not taking place with him on a ventilator in some intensive care unit, surrounded by strangers and high-tech equipment." Al, who remained ambulatory until two weeks before he died, "was at home, with his wife, two daughters, and two sons-in-law taking turns providing hands-on care with the assistance of home hospice (see chapter 9). Four grandchildren played on the bed with their Pa Al when he felt up to it."

Al remained alert until forty-eight hours before his death, his symptoms well controlled by morphine, antianxiety medication, and oxygen. Despite all this excellent, planned care, as the family waited for Al to die, Dr. Sachs heard from various family members, "This is horrible, just horrible." "Can't we do something else for him?" "This sucks."

Why, Dr. Sachs asked, did this excellent end-of-life care still leave everyone feeling bad? His answer: "Al was still dying, he didn't want to die yet, and his family sure didn't want him to die. Death means someone is lost to us forever." For those left behind, he explained, "some of the suffering is existential or spiritual" and even the most superb end-of-life medical care cannot ease that kind of suffering.

What Most Patients and Families Want

What really counts to people who are dying and those who attend them?

Dr. Karen E. Steinhauser and colleagues at the Veterans Affairs Medical Center in Durham, North Carolina, did groundbreaking research to determine what might constitute a good death in the eyes of patients, their families, and health care providers. The eighty-five study participants had no trouble describing a "bad death"—having inadequately treated pain while receiving aggressive but futile cure-directed therapy.

The team reported that descriptions of bad deaths "frequently included scenarios in which treatment preferences were unclear. Patients felt disregarded, family members felt perplexed and concerned about suffering, and providers felt out of control and feared that they were not providing good care. Decisions that had not previously been discussed usually had to be made during a crisis, when emotional reserves were already low."

Christina Forbes, who practices elder law in Washington, D.C., notes that "nursing homes and hospitals will have a list of interventions that may or may not be desirable at various stages of decline. But staff and doctors typically do not want to make care decisions. They will intervene if no other guidance is available, often with disastrous results."

Families who are unprepared for what happens when death is imminent often panic and rush the patient to the hospital, where last-ditch and usually futile attempts at resuscitation are made, when both patient and family would have preferred a home death (see chapter 7).

Does this sound familiar? It doesn't have to end this way. In contrast to these negative scenarios, the study identified six components of a good death, described in full in the May 16, 2000, *Annals of Internal Medicine:*

- **Pain and symptom management.** Physical comfort, to the best of medicine's ability to provide it, is critical to achieving a good death. Studies have shown that 40 to 70 percent of Americans suffer significant pain in the last days of their lives. This does not have to happen (see chapters 7 and 9). A patient with AIDS described how he relieved his anxiety about a painful death: "I don't want to be in pain, and I've discussed it with my doctor. He said, 'Oh, don't worry about pain. We'll put you on a morphine drip.' That sort of eased my mind."

- **Clear decision making.** Patients want to have a say in treatment decisions. As one patient explained, "This is *my* medical problem. Sometimes I don't want to stay on the rigid schedule, and he [the physician] would say, 'I would like for you to stay on that, but you are the manager of your ship. You decide how fast you want to paddle, if you want to go backwards, sideways, or make a 360-degree turn.' "

- **Preparation for death.** Too often, health care providers and family members and friends avoid talking about the end of life with people who are dying because they are afraid it will destroy their hope. Yet many patients want to know what to expect during the course of their illness and, like Jan, they want to plan for the events that will follow their deaths. One patient said, "I have my will written out, who I want invited to the funeral. I have my obituary. That gives me a sense of completion that I don't have to put that burden on someone else. It's to prepare myself for it."

- **Completion.** When patients recognize that the end is in sight, the time has come for many to tie up all loose ends. Spirituality or meaningfulness becomes important to patients at the end of life. Completion includes not only faith issues but also reviewing one's life, resolving conflicts, spending time with family and friends, and saying good-bye (see chapter 10).

- **Contribution to others.** This can take the form of material or spiritual gifts or transmission of wisdom. For some, it means giving their healthy organs to others whose lives depend on a transplant, or donating their bodies to science (see part 3). Many people nearing death achieve clarity as to what is really important in life and want to share that understanding with others. "As death approaches," the authors wrote, "many patients reflect on their successes and failures and discover that personal relationships outweigh professional or monetary gains." One patient would tell each new nurse or physician who came to his room, "Take care of your husband [or wife]. Spend time with your children."

- **Affirmation of the whole person.** Yes, doctors, there is still a real live person in that bed! No patient, and especially not someone who is dying, wants to be treated as "a disease" or "the patient in room 103A." Study participants emphasized the importance of being seen as a unique and whole person and

"I'd like to be buried in this outfit, if I can lose ten pounds."

being understood in the context of their lives, values, and preferences. As one family member told the researchers about her
father's last days in the hospital, "The residents always approached my father as if he was a person and there weren't any
divisions between them. They didn't come in and say, 'I'm doctor so and so.' There wasn't any kind of separation or aloofness.
They would sit right on his bed, hold his hand, talk about their
families, his family, golf, and sports."

The researchers' bottom line? "There is no single formula for a good death. Many participants cautioned health care providers against implying, 'You're not dying the right way because you're not dying the way we think you should.' " Rather, they concluded, most of the time people choose to die the way they lived, "in character." They may be angry, critical, mellow, dignified, at war, or at peace.

FOR FURTHER READING

Meyer, Charles. *A Good Death: Challenges, Choices and Care Options.* New London, CT: Twenty-Third Publications / Bayard, 2001.

Nuland, Sherwin B. *How We Die: Reflections on Life's Final Chapter.* New York: Vintage Books, 1995.

Sacco, Joseph. *On His Own Terms: A Doctor, His Father, and the Myth of the "Good Death."* Ashland, OR: Caveat Press, 2006.

CHAPTER 3

Advance Directives: A Living Will Is Not Enough

While writing this book, I asked dozens of people of varying ages what preparations they have made for the end of life. Most of those under age sixty looked at me as if I were from another planet. A few with young children said they had assigned guardians for their children in case of incapacitating illness or death of both parents. The typical response from those over age sixty was: "Well, I have a will and a living will." The latter is an advance directive that is meant to tell medical practitioners how you want to be treated when your life hangs in the balance and you are unable to consent to or refuse treatment.

But there are two things you should know up front:

1. Even if you have a living will—and only one in five of us does—chances are its instructions are too vague to protect you from unwanted medical interventions at the end of life or, even worse, to save your life in a medical emergency before you are ready to check out.

2. A living will is only a piece of paper, and it may not be at hand when needed. You also need to assign a *living person* who can speak for you when you cannot say what you want—and do

not want—to be done medically. This person, who is often called a health care proxy or agent, holds dual power of attorney for your health care and, in most states, is legally considered the patient when the real patient is too incapacitated to make medical decisions.

Some fifty-nine million Americans were prompted to fill out living wills in recent decades in the wake of several well-publicized cases—Karen Ann Quinlan and Nancy Cruzan, and most recently, Terri Schiavo—in which families battled with doctors or with one another over the right to terminate life-supporting measures for patients who are in what is now called a persistent vegetative state—a kind of permanent, irreversible coma in which the heart may continue to beat or the lungs breathe on their own but higher brain functions that enable us to think, see, hear, respond, and control our muscles are dead (see chapter 6).

In those living wills, most of us specified that we wanted no effort made to prolong our lives with measures like cardiopulmonary resuscitation, mechanical ventilation, feeding tubes, and what-have-you if we should become "brain dead," near death with a terminal illness, or severely demented and unable to express our desire to be free of further medical intervention, except that which may bring comfort to our last days on earth. In relatively few cases, people who completed living wills specified that they wanted every effort made to prolong their lives regardless of how hopeless the situation may seem.

In all but three states (New York, Massachusetts, and Michigan as of this writing), these wills are legally binding if completed when you are of sound mind; properly signed; and, as required in some states, notarized.

But Will Your Living Will Help?

Experience has proved there's many a slip twixt the will and what really happens during medical crises. For one thing, the living will, filed away in some cabinet, bureau drawer, or safe deposit box, is often unavailable when the need for it arises. Or perhaps no one but the person who prepared it may know of its existence, and that person is in no position to produce it at the moment, if ever.

Second, even when a living will is accessible when needed, circumstances may have changed since the time the patient completed it. For example, you may have second thoughts about forgoing cardiopulmonary resuscitation, even at age eighty-five or beyond, if your heart could be restarted and, despite your having an incurable cancer, you would be able to attend your granddaughter's wedding a month later. Or say you are a reasonably active seventy-five-year-old with congestive heart failure and develop a life-threatening pneumonia. Do you really want the doctors to withhold mechanical ventilation that could tide you over for a week or so and antibiotics that could cure the infection and restore you to your former life?

Third, living wills are highly subject to misinterpretation. Too often their language is not specific enough to effectively guide treatment decisions. As Daniel P. Hickey, an assistant professor of family medicine and pediatrics at the Medical College of Ohio, wrote in the *Journal of Health Law,* "General language rejecting 'heroic measures' or 'treatment that only prolongs the dying process' in actuality provides no guidance at all," leading to frequent problems in interpretation.

"Medical crises cannot be predicted in detail, making most prior instructions difficult to adapt, irrelevant, or even misleading," Dr. Henry S. Perkins wrote in the *Annals of Internal Medicine* in July 2007. "Unexpected problems arise often to defeat advance directives."

Living wills are meant to be invoked if, and only if, patients are unable to say whether they do, or do not, want to undergo a potentially lifesaving procedure. However, nurses and physicians sometimes misread them as meaning "do not treat" when the patients intended them to say "do not resuscitate" when resuscitation cannot restore any semblance of meaningful life.

Finally, in the heat of a medical crisis in which seconds count, doctors often make value judgments and in doing so may purposely or unknowingly violate the tenets of the patient's living will. For various reasons, about one in four validly executed advance directives is not honored by physicians. In some cases, physicians fear lawsuits if they withhold or withdraw life-sustaining therapy, even though state laws grant them immunity from civil or criminal liability if they comply in good faith with a valid advance directive. And, as Professor Hickey noted, sometimes family members "bully physicians into continuing treatment that the patient, while competent, clearly indicated was not wanted."

This, in fact, is exactly what happened with a very famous patient, then ninety-seven-year-old Dr. Michael E. DeBakey, the cardiac surgeon who pioneered many lifesaving heart operations, including the one doctors ultimately used on him. Dr. DeBakey had a leaking aortic aneurysm, a ballooning of the body's main artery that was on the verge of rupturing. A fully conscious and mentally alert Dr. DeBakey declined his doctor's request to attempt a repair. Yet, when his condition deteriorated and he became unresponsive, his wife insisted that the surgery be performed, even though the hospital's anesthesiologists feared he would die on the table. Finally, his wife called in a willing anesthesiologist from another hospital, and his doctors decided that if their patient could vote, he'd opt for the surgery, which Dr. DeBakey miraculously survived. Despite a very rocky and costly postoperative course, Dr. DeBakey made a remarkable recovery and eventually was able to return to work with his mental faculties intact.

Not so, though, for another patient whose advance directive was ignored. Dr. Sidney Wanzer's mother was ninety-two years old and living in a nursing home with an advanced case of Alzheimer's disease. But long before this illness had robbed her of her full mental capacities, Dr. Wanzer wrote in *To Die Well* (a book he produced with Dr. Joseph Glenmullen), she completed a living will stating that "she did not want her death prolonged by medical treatment if the quality of her life ever became so poor that there was no significant intellectual activity or reward." And this was clearly the case when her heart developed an irregular rhythm that would have soon been fatal had not the doctor in charge decided to implant a pacemaker in the poor woman's chest. When Dr. Wanzer learned of this move, he was furious— furious because there had been many discussions with her doctors and nurses about her wishes, furious because the woman had no quality of life, which lasted another five years in a state of helpless debilitation "lacking all dignity totally contrary to her written request."

"I thought everything was all set," Dr. Wanzer wrote. "But we made a big mistake. We did not ask her doctor explicitly, 'Do you agree with this approach and will you promise to adhere to our mother's wishes?' He had simply listened to us, and we had erroneously assumed that he agreed."

Dr. Wanzer's mother had clearly voted with the majority. Dr. Dwenda K. Gjerdingen and colleagues at the University of Minnesota surveyed eighty-four cognitively normal men and women age sixty-five and older. Three-fourths of those queried said that if they were mildly demented, they would not want cardiopulmonary resuscitation, the use of a respirator, or to be nourished by tube, and 95 percent said they would not want these life-sustaining measures if they had severe dementia.

Doctors and the institutions they work in may also have a financial incentive for continuing with treatment that the patient indicated was unwanted. The dead, after all, don't pay, but insurance often covers attempts to keep patients alive, however futile those attempts may be in the short run.

But there can be more subtle reasons doctors fail to honor an advance directive. If the person is young (and that may mean any age younger than the doctor's), physicians are likely to make every effort to bring the patient back from the dead, as it were. And who can blame them for identifying with a patient who reminds them of themselves? A similar effort might be made to "save" an older patient who resembles the doctor's spouse or parent. Doctors, after all, are taught to save lives, not to hasten death.

Do You Really Mean "Do Not Resuscitate"?

Dr. Ferdinando L. Mirarchi, chairman of emergency medicine at Hamot Medical Center in Erie, Pennsylvania, has witnessed many instances in which a patient's living will failed to fulfill its intended purpose. Most wills, he maintains, are much too vague and non-specific to cover the myriad medical situations that may arise. Most serious are those instances in which the existence of a living will specifying no treatments that would prolong life results in a failure to treat a potentially reversible health crisis. They are sometimes interpreted by health care practitioners as DNR, or "do not resuscitate," orders.

For example, Dr. Mirarchi tells of a sixty-four-year-old woman who had surgery to reset a broken leg. Two days later she developed abdominal bleeding and began excreting and vomiting blood. But the attending nurse, noting the DNR notation in her chart, delayed calling in a physician, and when she finally did call, she told the doctor the patient was a DNR and nothing needs to be done. Fortunately, barely in the nick of time, a second physician intervened, resuscitated the woman, and rushed her into surgery to stop the bleeding. She went home a week later and resumed a normal life after her broken leg healed.

A seventy-two-year-old man was not as lucky. He had been undergoing kidney dialysis for a decade when he developed chest pain and went to the emergency room, where he was found to be having a heart attack. He was admitted to the hospital and treated, but the next morning his heart began to beat erratically, or fibrillate, which results in certain death unless a normal heart rhythm is quickly restored. But the cardiologist who rushed in to try to correct the dysfunctional rhythm with a defibrillator, was stopped twice, first by a nurse and then by the man's primary care physician, who said he was "a DNR." Instead of being resuscitated, the man was pronounced dead.

An Improved Living Will

Without a legally binding advance directive, families can face the gruesome decision to end or continue with life support and, as happened to the Cruzan and Schiavo families, battle the matter out in court, incurring great expense and untold anguish. But even with a living will, as you can see from the above cases, conflicts can arise between medical practitioners, within families, or between families and physicians.

However, there are two steps you can take to reduce the risk of such conflicts and misinterpretations. One is to create a living will that health care practitioners readily understand, one that spells out your desired "code" status. If you've watched any of the myriad medical dramas on television, you no doubt have heard of a "code blue" called when a patient goes into cardiac arrest. Doctors, nurses, and machines are rushed in to try to revive the patient.

In TV dramas, cardiopulmonary resuscitation—popularly called CPR—succeeds in reviving a dying patient in two-thirds of cases. The real-life facts, however, are quite different. Fewer than one in one hundred terminally ill patients given CPR recovers, and half of those who survive do so with profound brain damage. More than 99 percent end up as corpses with broken ribs.

If, however, you have a treatable condition and your heart stops, surely you'd want to be revived. Having a clear statement of your desired code status in your living will can decrease the risk that your wishes will be misinterpreted and potentially lifesaving treatment will be withheld when you are far from ready to greet the Grim Reaper.

By the same token, a well-thought-out and fully spelled out living will can greatly reduce the chance that you will be kept nominally alive when, like Terri Schiavo, there is virtually no chance you will emerge from a persistent vegetative state (see chapter 6). Waiting to complete a living will until you are hospitalized with a life-threatening health problem could be too late.

"I want my living will to stipulate that I spend my last hours sipping a piña colada on Maui."

And while you may think that because you are now young and healthy, you have plenty of time to prepare a living will, completing a living will that doctors are unlikely to misinterpret is especially important for younger patients because they could be kept alive for decades in a condition they would categorically reject if only they could.

Recognizing this need, Dr. Mirarchi devised such a will—he calls it the medical living will with code status advance directive—which he reproduced in his book *Understanding Your Living Will: What You Need to Know Before a Medical Emergency*. With his permission, it is included here, along with the second step you need to take—assigning someone to serve as your health care proxy, holding dual power of attorney for your health care.

Dr. Mirarchi strongly advises that you fill out your living will in consultation with your physician, so that you fully understand the instructions you are giving to health care practitioners and they, in turn, can be certain of your wishes and can carry out your instructions accordingly. Currently, most living will forms are devised by attorneys and completed by individuals on their own; as a result, they don't necessarily give physicians the detailed information they need in order to proceed according to the patient's wishes.

Once your living will is completed and your signature is notarized (a good idea, even if your state doesn't require it, since a medical emergency can happen anywhere), copies should be made for your emergency contact (usually your spouse or partner or an adult child); your personal physician; your attorney, and as you'll see in a moment, your designated health care proxy, if different from one of the aforementioned individuals. File the original with your personal records along with your last will and testament and estate papers.

You may also want to make a small investment to file your living will with the U.S. Registry of Living Wills, a private organization that stores the information electronically and provides online access to it, along with emergency contact and organ donor information, for health care practitioners twenty-four hours a day, seven days a week. The registry points out that more than a third of living wills cannot be found when they are needed.

Here are four ways to contact the registry: via the Internet, www.uslivingwillregistry.org; by mail, U.S. Living Will Registry, PO Box 2789, Westfield, NJ 07091-2789; by phone, (800) 548-9455, or by fax, (908) 654-1919.

And, as also produced by Dr. Mirarchi, you should place in your wallet a "medical living will resuscitation card" that states your desired code status in an emergency and the names and phone numbers of two people: your emergency contact and your health care proxy.

This is what is meant by the three code statuses:

- **Full code** means that every lifesaving and supportive measure should be applied in an emergency. However, if your condition does not improve and you cannot convey your wishes, then your detailed advance directive goes into effect, specifying such things as "I do (or do not) want a feeding tube or long-term mechanical ventilation or kidney dialysis or organs to be donated," and so forth.

- **Full code except cardiac arrest** tells doctors that if your heart stops beating, they should not attempt to resuscitate you. But in every other emergency, the measures spelled out in your advance directive should be applied.

- **Comfort care / Hospice care** means that in a life-threatening emergency, doctors should provide no life-prolonging measures but only treatments for pain and other debilitating symptoms. For example, morphine may be given to relieve pain and anxiety and make it easier for you to breathe. *It is important to know, however, that to control pain adequately, you may require intravenous fluids, so you may not want to refuse them in your living will.*

If you choose to be an organ donor and your organs are potentially useful when you die, your living will should also state that the "do not's" with regard to life-supporting measures that you filled out can be suspended temporarily to keep your organs healthy enough for transplantation (see chapter 16).

Most important: *Don't wait to complete a living will until you are diagnosed with a life-threatening illness or are terminally ill. Do it as soon as you become an adult.* You never know when it may be needed. Young people can suffer strokes, heart attacks, ruptured blood vessels, strangulated intestines. Young people can develop a potentially fatal cancer. Young people can suffer life-threatening injuries in an accident. Accidents happen. They can leave people in irreversible comas, and leave loved ones out on a limb, not knowing what to tell the doctors to do—or not do—for you, in accordance with your wishes.

Finally, keep in mind that as your life circumstances change, you may want to revise your living will, which you can do at any time as long as you are of sound mind. Just be sure to send the changes to everyone who has a copy of the original.

MEDICAL LIVING WILL WITH CODE STATUS ADVANCE DIRECTIVE

Here, then, is the prototype of a living will that is easy for medical personnel to interpret devised by Dr. Ferdinando L. Mirarchi. In granting permission to reproduce it here, Dr. Mirarchi emphasized that you should consult your physician and attorney before finalizing it.

Name _____

Phone _____

Address _____

City _____ State _____

Zip Code _____

In an emergency, contact _____

_____

Phone _____

Primary Care Physician _____

_____

Phone _____

Health Care Power of Attorney (Proxy) _____

_____

Phone _____

Attorney _____

Phone _____

Please honor these code status designations:

(   )   **Full Code**
I would like to receive all lifesaving and supportive measures should an emergency arise. Should my condition fail to improve and I am no longer able to make my own decisions, then I would like my advance directive to become active and be followed. Please see Sections A and B.

(   )   **Full Code Except Cardiac Arrest**
If I suffer from a cardiac arrest, you are not to institute CPR.

(   )   **Comfort Care / Hospice Care**
Please see Section C.

Patient
Signature _____ Date _____

Witness
Signature #1 _____ Date _____

Witness
Signature #2 _____ Date _____

Health Care Power of Attorney
Signature _____ Date _____

SECTION A: HOLD HARMLESS STATEMENT

I am aware that state laws vary with respect to advance directives and living wills. These are my wishes with respect to my care. Neither you, nor your health care facility, is to be held responsible, in any way, for following my wishes.

1. I __ do __ do not want cardiopulmonary resuscitation.

2. I __ do __ do not want advanced cardiac life support protocols to be followed.

3. I __ do __ do not want endotracheal intubation.

4. I __ do __ do not want long-term mechanical ventilation.

5. I __ do __ do not want defibrillation.

6. I __ do __ do not want invasive procedures to be performed in an emergency situation.

7. I __ do __ do not want invasive procedures to be performed if they will add to my comfort.

8. I __ do __ do not want intravenous fluids.

9. I __ do __ do not want antibiotics.

10. I __ do __ do not want my organs to be donated.

11. I __ do __ do not want long-term parenteral nutrition.

12. I __ do __ do not want a feeding tube.

13. I __ do __ do not want thrombolytic agents (clot busters) or angioplasty, should it be needed.

14. I __ do __ do not want blood or blood products.

15. I __ do __ do not want peritoneal or hemodialysis.

16. I __ do __ do not wish to have an ethics consultation settle controversy between my treating physician and health care power of attorney.

Check all those with whom you have discussed your living will and wishes for medical treatment.

a. ____ Family

b. ____ Spiritual adviser

c. ____ Family physician

d. ____ Physician specialist

e. ____ Friend

f. ____ Attorney

g. ____ No one

SECTION B: PERMISSION

I direct my attending physician, in conjunction with another physician who is a specialist in my life-ending condition, to withhold or withdraw life-sustaining measures that serve only to prolong the process of my dying. I give this permission if I am in a state of permanent unconsciousness and am no longer able to make my own decisions.

SECTION C: COMFORT / HOSPICE CARE

1. In the event that my condition becomes such that I need any emergency or life-sustaining interventions, you are not to institute them. If you have instituted life-saving care without the knowledge of my advance directive, you do have my permission to withdraw such interventions. *(Initial here)* _____

2. I have decided that I would like comfort measures and, if eligible, hospice care only. *(Initial here)* _____

3. I would like to be kept comfortable and free from pain to the best of your abilities, even if this requires administering intravenous fluids counter to my advance directive. Should I become addicted to such medications or should my breathing stop secondary to this intervention, you in no way are to be held responsible. I take full responsibility. *(Initial here)* _____

4. I would not want to be transferred to the emergency room for treatment unless you are unable to control my pain where I am currently located.
(Initial here) _____

In witness thereof, this living will has been executed on this ___ day of _____, 20___, as my free and voluntary act, and I state that I am over 18 years of age. (Sign here) _____ I, the undersigned, a notary public authorized to administer oaths in the State of _____,

certify that (your name here) _____, having appeared before me and having been first duly sworn, then declared to me that he/she willingly signed and executed this trust agreement and that he/she executed such instrument as his/her free and voluntary act for the purposes therein expressed.

In witness whereof, I have hereunto subscribed my name and affixed my official seal this ___ day of _____, 20___.

_____

Notary Public
Seal of Notary Public

Warning: To comply with different witnessing requirements of most states, do not have the following people witness your signature: your assigned health care agent or alternative agent; your treating physician or anyone employed by your health care provider; your life or health insurance provider or any employee of that provider; anyone related to you by blood, marriage, or adoption; anyone entitled to any part of your estate or anyone who will benefit financially from your death.

Another excellent source of guidance and forms for completing an advance directive that is most likely to be honored in almost any medical situation you could find yourself in is the booklet *Health Care Advance Directives*, produced as a collaborative effort by the AARP (formerly called the American Association of Retired Persons), the American Bar Association Commission on Legal Problems of the Elderly, and the American Medical Association. You can download a copy of this very helpful booklet from the American Bar Association website, www.abanet.org. The American Bar Association's Commission on Law and Aging has also produced a twenty-six-page *Consumer's Tool Kit for Health Care Advance Planning*, 2nd ed., which can be downloaded as an Adobe file from www.abanet .org/aging/publications/docs/consumer_tool_kit_bk.pdf.

You can also obtain advance directive information specific for the state in which you live, along with forms if they exist, from the following:

Legal Counsel for the Elderly, AARP, PO Box 96474, Washington, DC 20090-6474

Choice In Dying, Inc., 200 Varick St., New York, NY 10014-4810; phone: (800) 989-WILL

Website: www.caringinfo.org

Other Sources: Hospital associations, medical societies, or bar associations in your state or county and your local area agency on aging (AAA) may provide forms for your state.

You do not need a lawyer to create an advance directive for health care, although a lawyer can be helpful if you have a complicated or uncertain family situation.

You Must Assign a Health Care Proxy

Now to the second critical step in preparing for your care when you cannot tell doctors what to do or not do: assigning someone to be your health care agent, surrogate, or proxy (all three terms mean the same thing) if you should be unable to make treatment decisions for yourself. *Having a health care proxy is even more important than having a living will,* which can be misinterpreted or overridden to your disadvantage. Assigning a person to be your health care agent starts with a conversation in which you describe how you would want to be treated if your life hung in the balance. The more specific you can be, the better.

If, for example, you were recently diagnosed with metastatic cancer, which is usually incurable, would you want to be resuscitated if your heart stopped? Your answer may well be "yes" if restarting your heart could buy you months of quality time during which you could get your affairs in order, resolve conflicts with family members and friends, and say your good-byes. On the other hand, if your cancer was now widespread and very painful or incapacitating, leaving you with little quality of life, your choice may be to "let me die."

You can specify which life-prolonging measures are acceptable to you and which are not. For instance, you may have no problem with intravenous fluids or kidney dialysis, but you may want to draw the line at a feeding tube and long-term mechanical ventilation. You can use the list of treatment possibilities in the Medical Living Will with Code Status Advance Directive form as a guide for your discussion.

Or you can review six simple yes-or-no questions suggested by New York's Office of the Attorney General, in an excellent document called "Planning Your Health Care in Advance." Copies of this report, prepared by Rashmi Vasisht, director of policy and research for health care, are available through www.oag.state.ny .us/health/EOLGUIDE.pdf.

Q. 1. Would you want your doctor to withhold or withdraw medical treatment, if that medical treatment will only prolong dying? ❑ Yes ❑ No

Q. 2. Would you want cardiopulmonary resuscitation (CPR) to restore stopped breathing and/or heartbeat? ❑ Yes ❑ No

Q. 3. Would you want to continue mechanical respiration, i.e., use machines to keep you breathing? ❑ Yes ❑ No

Q. 4. Would you want tube or intravenous feeding and water? ❑ Yes ❑ No

Q. 5. Would you want maximum pain relief even if it hastens your death? ❑ Yes ❑ No

Q. 6. Would you want to donate your organs and/or tissues? ❑ Yes ❑ No

In discussing questions 2, 3, and 4, be sure to delineate the circumstances under which you would make these choices. For example, if at age eighty-three you suffer a stroke and have a reasonable chance of recovering enough to walk again with assistance, would you still reject tube feeding or mechanical respiration to carry you through the immediate crisis?

You can also discuss with your potential health care proxy where you would like to die, the people you want to be with you, which organs you would consider donating, and what you'd like done with your body afterward.

In considering who you would want as your health care agent, Stephen P. Kiernan, author of *Last Rights: Rescuing the End of Life from the Medical System,* recommends selecting someone who is not a sentimentalist who may, at the last moment, decide to try to keep you alive at all costs when you would have chosen to be allowed to die in peace. You should seek someone who will be forthright and uncompromising and willing to shout at doctors, if necessary, to see to it that your wishes are honored.

Your health care proxy must be someone you can trust to follow your wishes, even if they might differ from his or her own choices. Most people choose their spouse or an adult child, if they can be trusted to act in the patient's interest should the need arise. But if you are concerned that inheritance issues could influence a relative's health care decisions for you, then you'd be wise to choose someone else—a close friend, for instance—who would have no vested interest in your demise.

Keep in mind that if you choose your spouse to be your health care proxy and you later divorce or legally separate, to obviate a conflict of interest that person can no longer serve in that capacity. It is a good idea to choose an alternate health care proxy, a backup person who is as uncompromising as your primary agent and who also knows your wishes in case your first choice is unavailable when a medical crisis arises.

For example, my husband, who I know couldn't care less about inheriting my share of our accumulated assets, is my primary agent. But if we were both in comas following an accident or if he could not be contacted when a life-or-death decision needed to be made, one of my sons, who lives nearby, would serve as my alternate health care agent. Although both of my sons would realize a significant financial gain from my demise, I know that ethically they are beyond reproach and I have no hesitation in trusting either of them with my life—or my death.

Health care proxy forms are provided by your state's health department and can usually be obtained from your physician or local hospital. They can also be downloaded from the Internet at www.partnershipforcaring.org.

On the form itself, you don't have to list any specifics beyond stating, "My health care agent knows my wishes about life-prolonging measures like feeding tubes and mechanical ventilation." The form need not be notarized, but your signature should be witnessed by two people who are unrelated to you and would not benefit from your death.

Lilian Sicular, a social worker who has helped countless elderly clients create an advance directive, was nonetheless unable to convince her own husband, a physician, to do so. I suppose, like many other physicians, death was anathema to him, a subject he simply could not face. But one summer day after he had played tennis, gone swimming and sailing, and visited with his grandchildren, he suffered a hemorrhagic stroke that rendered this vibrant man into what his wife called "a vegetable," sustained by a respirator and feeding tube.

When it became apparent that "no miracle was going to happen," Ms. Sicular said she wanted him to be removed from life support. But one of their four children objected, and without any evidence of what the patient himself would have wanted in such a situation, his wife and doctors could do nothing. Seven weeks later, nature provided a solution—a fatal heart attack. But Ms. Sicular still shudders to think that he could have ended up like Terri Schiavo, living—if you can call it that—indefinitely and unconscious with the aid of modern medicine.

Once you have completed both a living will and a health care proxy, make several photocopies of the forms. Keep the originals in a safe but accessible place—not in a safe deposit box—and give copies to your health care agent and alternate agent, your attorney or other adviser, close family members, your personal physician, and anyone else you want to involve in your health care. Make sure your doctor includes the forms in your medical record, and if you have been a patient at your local hospital, have copies of both forms placed in your hospital record.

Finally, consider carrying a wallet card that states the existence and location of your living will and health care proxy. Or you can go one step further and do what my husband and I have done: place copies of our health care proxies in our wallets.

Advance directives remain in effect indefinitely unless you cancel them or include an expiration date on the forms or describe circumstances under which you would want them to expire.

Remember, too, that you can cancel or change your advance directives, including your health care agent, at any time. Periodically revisit the forms you completed and make sure they still represent your wishes about health care. If you wish to cancel a living will, simply destroy it. But be sure to tell others who know of its existence that it is no longer in effect. At any time you change your advance directives, make new photocopies for everyone who has the originals.

When Someone Refuses to Create an Advance Directive

My cousin Susan has struggled for years with no success to get her mother, my aunt Gert, now in her upper eighties, to talk about her wishes should she become incapacitated and unable to speak for herself. Mom's consistent reply: "I don't want to talk about this now," as if such a discussion would be a curse and bring about just the situation Susan is trying to be prepared for.

If you find yourself faced with a loved one who is reluctant to discuss creating a living will or assigning a health care proxy, experts at Harvard Medical School suggest the following approach in *A Guide to Living Wills and Health Care Proxies:* Explain to the person why it's important to have an advanced directive and that you would feel much better if this were done. Try appealing to the person's independence by saying "I love you and I wouldn't want to do anything you didn't agree with if a situation came up that left you unable to tell me what you wanted."

For someone like my aunt Gert who doesn't ever want to think about death or dying, you might say that you're really talking about quality of life, not death. However, the Harvard experts advise against pushing too hard. "Be ready to drop the subject if the person gets angry or upset, but explain that you'll want to discuss it later." Then be sure to follow up after a reasonable cooling off period.

FOR FURTHER READING

Doukas, David John, and William Reichel. *Planning for Uncertainty: Living Wills and Other Advance Directives for You and Your Family.* Baltimore, MD: Johns Hopkins University Press, 2007.

Gavi, Benny, MD, Jack Lombard, and Alan Meisel, eds. *A Guide to Living Wills and Health Care Proxies.* Cambridge, MA: Harvard Health Publications, Harvard Medical School, 2008.

Mirarchi, Ferdinando L. *Understanding Your Living Will: What You Need to Know Before a Medical Emergency.* Omaha, NE: Addicus Books, 2006.

CHAPTER 4

Funeral? Memorial? Why Plan Ahead for the End

Whether death comes suddenly or follows a prolonged illness, it typically renders survivors into a state of semishock. In the midst of their grieving, they must make quick decisions about what to do with the remains of loved ones and how their lives might best be memorialized. In those most stressful moments, the immediate survivors are highly vulnerable to sales pitches by funeral parlors—or even entreaties from more distant relatives—that could result in enormous expenses and elaborate rituals that the deceased, if they could have a say, would never have wanted and the survivors, in more rational moments, would never have done.

Someday, whether you choose to think about it or not, you will be that deceased person and the people who love you could be in a similar predicament. You may assume your survivors will know what you want in the way of a funeral (or no funeral). You may assume that they know what you would want to be done with your remains (Burial? Cremation with ashes kept or scattered? Donation to a medical school?). You may assume that they know what you'd want said at a funeral or memorial service or even in a printed obituary. But chances are, they do not know.

An elderly New Jersey woman, herself an invalid, was at a total loss when her husband died. The details and costs of arranging for his funeral and burial were almost more than she could weather, and the resulting stress took a terrible toll on her own fragile health. "If only he would have told me ahead of time what he wanted," she lamented.

Likewise, Douglas Kramp's mother died after a lingering illness, leaving behind few instructions for what she'd want to happen next. She did say she wanted a closed casket (which implied she wanted a funeral service) so that family and friends would remember only how she looked when she was alive. Still, Doug and his immediate family were left to make all other arrangements. As his wife, Erin, recalled, "Doug, his father, and his brother would have preferred to spend time together, sharing thoughts and memories of his mother, rather than having to manage the myriad details associated with planning her funeral service. With all the work that needed to be done, there wasn't much time for them to grieve."

Fortunately, all three agreed on how to proceed, but that is not always the case. Without guidance from the deceased, family members may squabble about what to do with regard to funerals, burials, and memorials, and sometimes these arguments result in lasting grievances.

So Doug and Erin, who was being treated for breast cancer at the time, chose a different course for themselves. They sat down and discussed their preferences. They researched the various funeral parlors near their Dallas home and obtained maps of available plots. Then they visited the cemeteries and chose two plots in an area they found appealing. The funeral directors they spoke with told them that most people wait until someone dies to make funeral arrangements, forcing them to make "immediate, detailed, sensitive, and costly" decisions while they are grieving.

In their book, *Living with the End in Mind* (coauthored with Emily P. McKhann), they offer excellent guidance about how to go about planning well in advance for what you want to happen after you die. "Being physically prepared for death is one of the most unselfish things a person can do for others," Erin wrote.

"This one comes with a complimentary last will and testament."

Controlling the Costs

As the Kramps reported, "By planning your funeral or memorial and your burial or cremation in advance, you can substantially reduce the expenses." Doug, in fact, was shocked to discover how costly it could be to die. In 1990s prices, this is what he found:

Item	Price Range
Burial plots	$1,000–$8,500
Caskets	$2,000–$8,000
Headstones	$600–$10,000

Prices today are even higher. No wonder, when tragic deaths occur in poor families, the community so often rallies to help cover the costs of a "proper" funeral!

These are some of the ways you can reduce the costs. The very best advice the Kramps and I can give is to take a trusted friend or your lawyer along when planning a funeral to help you avoid being talked into costly options you neither want nor need. If you are concerned about the expenses your survivors may face when you die, you can establish a trust fund, an insurance policy, or a dedicated savings plan to cover funeral costs.

By deciding ahead about the kind of funeral you want, you can negotiate the price with the funeral parlor, although you do not have to pay in advance. After all, the funeral parlor could go out of business before you need its services.

Burial costs a lot more than cremation. The national average cost of a burial in 2007, according to the National Funeral Directors Association, was $3,595, whereas the average cost of cremation was $1,495. The burial price includes embalming and other body preparations, the services of the funeral director and the parlor for a viewing and funeral service, and a hearse and transport to and from the funeral home but not the casket, cemetery plot, or opening and closing of the burial site. The cost of cremation does not include the cost of the container or site for its placement.

Donating your body to a medical school is the least expensive, though this must be arranged in advance with the school. Which approach would you and your survivors find most appealing?

I decided years ago that my own wishes should trump those of my survivors. I want to be cremated and my ashes scattered sometime later in the beautiful St. Croix River, where I swam daily for so many summer days and where my beloved spaniel Max's ashes were also scattered. My sons, on the other hand, who are interested in saving money *and* helping humanity even after they are dead, have decided to donate their bodies to a medical school. So I'm reconsidering my decision: I'm thinking now that I will donate my body, and when the school is through with it, my remains can still be cremated and my ashes scattered.

If you choose not to have your body present at a visitation or funeral service, you need not invest in an expensive casket. There are alternative containers that cost less than $200. Or you can rent a casket for the service and then use the inexpensive alternative for the burial. By immediately disposing of the body, you can save the costs of temporary preservation and storage as well as an expensive casket.

You may also be able to save considerably on a burial plot. Check the classified ads or ask local clergymen. There are often people selling plots they purchased years ago but now no longer want.

And do you really want a limousine-led procession to a burial ground? "By the time you have a family car, pallbearers' car, minister's car, lead car [and perhaps even a flower car], it adds up," the Kramps found. Also, a police escort is sometimes needed in dense urban areas. Better to ask family and friends to provide the transportation.

Warning: An Advance Purchase Can Backfire

In its magazine of January/February 2008, the AARP warned of "a funeral-industry scandal that's fleecing thousands of Americans." The report, written by Barry Yeoman, tells what befell Audrey and

Carl Brewer, who purchased two prepaid funeral plans from Forest Hills South, a mortuary and cemetery in Memphis. They paid for the plans, which included caskets, funeral services, and two burial plots, only to discover thirty-one years later that the company had been sold and the new owners reneged on all contracts made by the previous owners.

Mr. Yeoman warned, "Depending on state law, customers often have little recourse when their prepaid funeral policies disappear." Although lawsuits are an option, they are often unsuccessful because the company may have gone bankrupt or simply out of business and there are no funds to recoup. Thus far, the federal government has done nothing to protect consumers from funeral fraud. Until and unless proper protections are established, it is best to steer clear of such prepaid funeral contracts.

BACK-TO-NATURE BURIALS

Is conservation of natural landscapes one of your important values? You might consider an increasingly popular option: burial in a "green" graveyard. The idea began in 1998 with Dr. Billy Campbell, a dedicated environmentalist and then the only doctor in Westminster, South Carolina. As reported in the *AARP Bulletin* in 2004, he has buried patients, friends, and others, unembalmed, in biodegradable caskets—or even in no caskets—in a nature preserve that he created along Ramsey Creek. "We put death in its rightful place, as part of the cycle of life," he told the reporter, Barbara Basler. "Our burials honor the idea of dust to dust."

The concept, which has since spread to other parts of the country, including such well-to-do areas as Marin County, California, is meant to combine in-ground burials, adorned by modest ground-level plaques, with preservation of natural areas. Dr. Campbell's company, Memorial Ecosystems, sets aside 25 percent of the burial price for conservation and for projects like nature classes and plant surveys.

For further information and links to other green burial sites, consult the website www.memorialecosystems.com.

Still another option for those choosing cremation is to become part of a reef ball, a giant perforated ball of concrete that is sunk in salt water to create an artificial reef or become part of an existing one. These memorial reefs, now mostly off the southeastern coast, are gradually being developed farther north, with future locations expected on the West Coast and even in the New York City area. For further information, consult the website www.eternalreefs.com.

Planning a Service

Many people say that funeral and memorial services are not for the dead but for the living and therefore what these services should include—hymns, songs, planned, and spontaneous speakers, and so on—and their location should be up to the survivors.

Nonetheless, there are plenty of people—people like Jan Jeffrey, for instance (see pages 61–62)—who would prefer to decide for themselves how their deaths and lives should be remembered. If you are like Jan, you might want to decide well ahead of time who should write your obituary and what it should include, who should preside over your funeral or memorial service, who should deliver your eulogy, what should be included in the service (hymns, scriptures, prayers, music, singers, etc.), even who should prepare the food for those who visit after the service, and whether you want people to make donations to a favorite charity in lieu of sending flowers.

Making such decisions in advance is especially important if what

"I understand old Ferguson wrote the service himself."

you prefer is a nontraditional service—for example, a lawn party with guitar music and folk songs, good food and dancing—or no service at all!

The more such designations you make in advance of your death, the easier things will be for the loved ones who survive you and want to honor your memory as you would have liked to be honored. This is easiest to do the further away you are from the end of your life. As one daughter said about her mother who had incurable cancer, "When the end was near, my job was to be cheerleader-in-chief. In the last three months, I could not say, 'Let's talk about the end.'"

For help in deciding about *your* end, the Funeral Consumers Alliance provides a booklet through its website, www.funerals.org, called "Before I Go, You Should Know" in which you can record such information as the kind of service and burial you want, vital statistics for your obituary, phone numbers of people and places to call when you die, and where you have filed any funeral plans you have already made. Make sure your family knows about this booklet and where you keep it—*not* in a safe deposit box, which may become inaccessible as soon as the bank learns of your death.

FOR FURTHER READING

Harris, Mark. *Grave Matters: A Journey Through the Modern Funeral Industry to a Natural Way of Burial.* New York: Scribner, 2007.

PART 2

CHARTING A COURSE TO THE END OF LIFE

*D*eath is a fact of life; about that there's no denying. For some, death comes suddenly, offering no opportunity for last-minute preparation and reparations. But for most of us, the journey to the end of life is a much longer one, lasting weeks, months, or years. During that time much can happen to make the trip more painful than it need be for both the person who is dying and those they leave behind.

In this section you will discover the many ways in which this journey can be better understood, more effectively coped with by all concerned, and made, if not joyful, at least far more pleasant than it might otherwise be.

CHAPTER 5

Uncertain Future: Living with a Bad Prognosis

Arlene Wysong was sixty-five years old and otherwise very healthy when she received a grim diagnosis: stage IV lung cancer, a malignant tumor that had spread well beyond its origins. The New York businesswoman recalled, "It was a total shock, and I knew what that meant. It meant I had an incurable cancer. But I asked questions. I asked for a prognosis. The doctor said three to twelve months."

Arlene made a choice: knowing she had no chance to be cured, she decided "no chemotherapy, only palliative care"—treatment for pain and any other symptoms that might impede her ability to live out her last months as fully as possible.

"I didn't want toxic chemo," Arlene told me. "I didn't want to lose my hair and be sick. I felt I had a very short time left and I didn't want to spend it being sick. So I rented a house in the country large enough for people to visit and stay overnight, and I enjoyed the summer.

"My goal from the beginning was to make sure I saw all the friends and family I wanted to see and to spend quality time with them. I made out a new will and transferred my business, but I stayed involved with it as long as I could." She also worked through some serious issues that had caused a rift between her and her daughter and repaired their ability to talk meaningfully with each other.

Sixteen months after receiving the news of her cancer, she decided to call in hospice so she could remain at home until she died with her family at her bedside.

Had Arlene's physician hemmed and hawed and failed to tell her just how serious her disease was and not given her a realistic estimate of her remaining life expectancy, she might have chosen a route that for her would have been less desirable. She might have lived her remaining months with the fantasy that she just might beat this cancer if she subjected her body to everything modern medicine had to offer or searched for a "miraculous" alternative remedy. She might have postponed those all-important last visits and the reconciliation with her daughter until perhaps it was too late.

Tell Me, Doc, How Much Time Have I Got?

Telling patients that they have a terminal illness and giving them a clue as to how long they might live is one of the hardest jobs physicians face. How much should they say and to whom? What if patients don't want to hear bad news? What if their families don't want them to be told they have only a short time left? What if failing to tell them results in their dying with much unfinished business, with important goals unmet, or with conflicts with family members or friends unresolved?

On the other hand, what if imparting the truth to terminally ill patients strips them of all hope? And what if the doctor's prognosis is wrong and the patient lives a much shorter or longer time than the doctor predicted?

Studies of hundreds of cases in which experienced physicians were asked to estimate how long terminally ill patients might be expected to live have revealed an often serious gap between what physicians tell patients and what is realistically to be expected. More often than not, out of fear, ignorance, or a genuine concern for their patients' emotional well-being, doctors give an unduly optimistic prognosis.

In one study of terminally ill patients receiving hospice care at home, 63 percent of their doctors' survival predictions were overly optimistic. In another study among patients terminally ill with cancer and referred to hospice care, the patients survived an average of twenty-four days whereas their doctors had told them they could expect to live three months!

Arlene Wysong's physician did what most experts recommend. Asked how long she might live, the doctor gave a range—and a rather broad range at that—based on the fates of other patients similarly afflicted and how healthy she was at the time of diagnosis. The fact that she fell outside his most optimistic estimate was an unexpected but very welcome gift.

Ms. M, an eighty-three-year-old childless woman who had lived with a friend in their own home for fifty years, also outlived her doctor's prediction of three months. She, too, had advanced cancer, the origins of which were unknown. But the cancer had already spread to her intestines and surfaced as nodules on her abdomen. On a hunch her doctor checked for estrogen receptors on her tumor cells and upon finding them prescribed tamoxifen, an estrogen-blocking drug commonly used to treat and prevent breast cancer, even though Ms. M's breasts showed no evidence of cancer. Ms. M was interviewed for the *Journal of the American Medical Association*—not three months but thirty-three months after her diagnosis!

The journal authors, Dr. Elizabeth B. Lamont of the University of Chicago Medical Center and Dr. Nicholas A. Christakis of Massachusetts General Hospital in Boston, noted that Ms. M's physician had "substantially underestimated Ms. M's survival, an event which has been shown to occur in less than 20 percent of patients." They explained that because "the science of prognosis is anchored in disease diagnosis and extent," not knowing exactly what kind of cancer Ms. M had made it extremely challenging for her doctor to arrive at a more accurate prognosis.

More typically, physicians overestimate patients' life expectancy—by a factor of three to five, the journal authors wrote, possibly because they often have an emotional attachment to their patients and, consciously or otherwise, don't want to impart bad news. More accurate estimates of longevity result when patients consult "disinterested" physicians, preferably more than one doctor who did not previously know them. So if you, the patient, or your family wants a realistic prognosis, you'd be wise to seek a second opinion, preferably from a doctor who had no prior relationship with the patient, the journal authors suggested.

Two factors are especially relevant when doctors form an estimate of remaining life expectancy for someone with an illness that is expected to be fatal, whether it is cancer or chronic lung disease or congestive heart failure. One factor is how advanced the disease is at the time. For example, when cancer has spread to multiple sites like the liver, bones, and brain, survival time is likely to be much shorter than when it has spread only to a nearby nonvital organ.

A second important factor is what physicians call performance status—just how healthy the patient is apart from the terminal illness. When Mickey Martinez, at age sixty-four, was diagnosed with colon cancer that had already spread to his liver, he was in otherwise tip-top physical condition, playing tournament tennis and whipping players far younger than he. Given Mickey's otherwise excellent health and stamina, his oncologist recommended throwing the book at his disease to maximize the length of quality life.

Mickey endured three years of chemotherapy (when one drug stopped working, another was introduced, but none made him especially sick) and two debilitating surgeries, each time bouncing back and returning to the tennis court. He remained well—and lived fully—until the last two months of his life. When he had exhausted all therapeutic options and it was apparent that his health was declining rapidly, his family called in hospice, allowing him to die at home surrounded by his devoted family.

Other important factors in determining prognosis are the patient's signs and symptoms, including problems like shortness of breath or difficulty breathing, trouble swallowing, loss of appetite, mental confusion, and dry mouth. When such symptoms appear, physicians can usually tell that death is imminent—likely to occur within days or weeks, rarely more than a month.

The Value of Knowing Time Is Short

Most, though clearly not all, patients with an illness that almost certainly will ultimately be fatal want information about the expected course of their disease, including how long they are likely to survive. They use this information in many ways:

- Like Arlene Wysong, some use it to help them decide on a course of treatment, including no treatment.

- Many use this as an impetus to get their affairs in order, as Arlene did with her business.

- When rifts have occurred with family members or friends, many use the time to make amends, again as Arlene did.

- Many use the time to say meaningful good-byes to the people they love.

- And some seize the opportunity to plan for events after they are gone, including their funerals or memorials and arrangements to help their survivors live on without them.

Jan Jeffrey, who had an incurable cancer that attacked her blood-forming cells, said the diagnosis left her with two choices: "Live each day to its max or go into a deep depression. So I chose the more positive route. And I learned a lot of good coping skills along the way, like how important the little things are—the birds singing, the flowers blooming, and my darling little granddaughter."

Jan saw herself as "coexisting with my disease," not battling it, for as long as she could, which turned out to be two and a half years. "I chose not to struggle against it but rather to save my energy for living," she said.

Jan, who had studied poetry and was an excellent writer, used e-mail extensively to reconnect with a lot of people she hadn't been in contact with for years, including old high school chums, and to stay connected with her current friends. She described her lengthy e-mail communications as "the best support I had. It was so therapeutic to share my experience with others and get responses back."

Many of her e-mail recipients passed along her messages to others who they thought would benefit from them. Before long, she was exchanging e-mail with about two hundred people, leaving behind an incredible legacy of how to live well with a very bad prognosis.

Jan arranged for her elderly mother to move into an assisted living facility, which, she said, "took a huge load off me." She also used her time to plan in great detail two memorial services, one in North Dakota where she grew up and the other in Brooklyn, New York, where she had lived for many years. And with her mind sharp even as her body weakened, leaving her with little physical strength and no immune system, she arranged for hospice care in a neighborhood facility where friends and family visited daily until the end.

In general, having some idea how much longer a person with a life-threatening illness is likely to live can help them and their families cope with the inevitable. As a medical team from the University of Sydney in Australia put it, "Information itself is considered one of the general strategies that many individuals use to cope with or manage major life events, and open conversation about death and dying can bring considerable relief to patients and their families.

"However," the team added, "individual coping styles vary, and not all patients want information concerning their prognosis."

In general, though, the majority of patients prefer the truth to whitewashed information that leaves them in limbo. In one study in Ireland, for example, researchers compared the attitudes of elderly patients and their relatives toward telling the truth about cancer. While 83 percent of patients wanted to be told the truth, only 55 percent of their relatives wanted the patient to be truthfully informed. The researchers concluded that doctors should not rely on relatives to determine what a patient does and does not want to know.

Talking the Talk

Some experts recommend that before imparting bad news or offering a prognosis, doctors should talk to their patients first and find out just what and how much they want to know. And when a doctor is asked by a patient "What is wrong with me?" "How serious is it?" or "How much longer do I have?" doctors are advised not to be evasive but rather to tell the truth at whatever level of detail the patient desires.

When a family member is resistant to informing the patient, doctors might try talking with the relative to find out why and to explain to the relative the emotional cost to the patient of not being informed. Sometimes the matter can best be resolved by holding a joint meeting with the patient and family to get everyone on the same page.

And sometimes the opposite situation prevails: the patient doesn't want one or more relatives to know how serious the situation is. Here, too, it is best if someone explains to the patient how important it can be to loved ones to know that the patient's time is limited, since it can affect the family's ability to care for the patient and to make needed preparations. Caregivers may need to know, for example, how much time they may have to take off from work, what is involved with caring for a dying person at home or whether other arrangements should be made, and even how to recognize when the end is near (see "When Someone Is Actively Dying," page 88), and what needs to be done after a person dies.

If you are the patient and you think it will be difficult to tell relatives about your condition, ask the doctor to assist you.

Serious matters about a patient's health should always be discussed with the physician face-to-face in a quiet, comfortable, private setting, not in a hallway, on the phone, or in the middle of grand rounds with half a dozen strangers listening. Such conversations should take place when there is ample time and opportunity for you and your relatives to vent feelings and ask questions.

Whether you are the patient or the family, you must insist that the doctor sit down with you *in private* to discuss the patient's current status and future prospects. When these conversations take place, every effort should be made to have a relative or close friend along who can provide emotional support for the patient, write down important information, and ask questions that can help them and the patient better understand the situation. If there is no support person available, you, the patient, might tape-record the conversation so it can be replayed later for family members, another physician, or simply for you to review, since much of what the doctor says after the diagnosis of a serious illness is likely to be forgotten.

It is also important that the primary physician, not a nurse, assistant, or medical resident, do the job of informing patients and their families. The doctor should avoid using euphemisms like "growth" or "tumor" or "cyst" when the patient has cancer, since this can lead to misunderstandings about the seriousness of the illness.

If the doctor uses technical jargon (like "metastasis" or "infiltrate" or "infarct") that either the patient or relatives don't understand, ask for an explanation in simpler terms.

Treatment options and the reasons for further tests should be clearly described along with their likely or possible side effects so that you, the patient, can make an intelligent choice. You should also inquire about the likely consequences of no treatment, if that is an option you might consider.

Always remember: It is your body and your life. No one but you should have the final say about how you do or do not treat it.

In addition to medical information, someone on the medical staff should provide information about support services, including support groups or professional counseling that can help patients and their families cope better with the ups and downs of a terminal disease. When the time is right, information about hospice care and bereavement counseling should also be provided.

Most important of all, no matter how grave the situation, a patient should never be told that "nothing more can be done." Even if there are no further treatment options that might curb progress of the disease, there is always some treatment that can make the patient more comfortable. As two psychologists, Dr. J. T. Ptacek and Tara L. Eberhardt, wrote in the *Journal of the American Medical Association,* "Hope should always be conveyed. The goal of maintaining hope does not mean that physicians should be less than truthful. In the case of imminent death, hope may entail information about the physician's ability to control symptoms and minimize discomfort."

Hope is an essential element in human life, but it is often viewed too narrowly, as hope for a cure or remission of the disease. When an illness is terminal, hope must be redefined as, perhaps, freedom from pain and other debilitating symptoms, or living long enough to see a child get married or the birth of a grandchild, or simply having the opportunity to impart words of wisdom and say good-bye to loved ones.

Doctors Need Help, Too

When it becomes apparent that treatments have failed to contain a patient's illness, doctors often experience feelings of guilt and helplessness that prompt some of them to abandon their patient rather than face defeat. Of course, this is just the time patients most want their doctors to remain on the scene (see chapter 13).

In dealing with bad news, some doctors need all the help they can get. An understanding word from the patient or the patient's family may help the doctor overcome negative feelings and remain a source of comfort and hope for all concerned.

For example, the patient might say something like, "I know, Doc, that you tried very hard to make me better. But it just wasn't in the cards. I want you to know that I appreciate all you did for me. It's not your fault that I'm not going to survive this disease, and I don't want you to feel bad about it. We've been through a lot together, and I do want you to stay with me for the long haul."

Then the patient and the doctor might have a good cry together and go on from there.

CHAPTER 6

Coma: When the Brain Is on Hold

I n June 2006 Terry Wallis, who was paralyzed and brain injured in a vehicular wreck at age nineteen, spoke for the first time in nineteen years. The now thirty-eight-year-old said, "Mom." He subsequently added, "Pepsi" (his favorite beverage), "Dad," and many other words to his vocabulary, though his personality had changed and his memory remained stuck in 1984. Headlines proclaimed, in effect, "Man in Coma 19 Years Speaks."

A year earlier, the nation had been transfixed by family and court battles over whether to "pull the plug" on Terri Schiavo, a woman who at age twenty-six had suffered a cardiac arrest that destroyed her brain's ability to think, speak, respond, and initiate voluntary movements. She had lain in a nursing home breathing on her own but sustained by a feeding tube, with no notable change in her condition in fifteen years. Was there a chance she might one day emerge from what most people called a coma? If so, in what condition? The courts ultimately decided the answer to the first question was no and the feeding tube was withdrawn. Terri died two weeks later.

These and other famous cases of patients who seemingly did— or did not—emerge from what the public viewed as a long-standing coma have left many people thoroughly confused about the meaning of this state of altered brain function and whether it is worthwhile to keep comatose patients "alive" year after year. Knowing something about the many causes of coma, recognizing the extent of brain injury, and understanding the likelihood of a partial or complete recovery of normal brain function can help families and physicians decide whether extraordinary life-prolonging measures are desirable when patients lapse into a coma.

It may surprise you to know that, according to current neurological understanding, neither Terry Wallis nor Terri Schiavo was in a classic coma. Rather, Terry Wallis (who never had a full neurological exam) is thought to have experienced what is now called a minimally conscious state, and Terri Schiavo, who showed no activity in the cognitive parts of her brain, lingered all those years in a permanent vegetative state.

An expert on brain function at the Mayo Clinic, Dr. Eelco Wijdicks, says motion pictures have thoroughly confused the public about comas and their likely outcomes. He analyzed thirty movies in which actors portrayed patients in prolonged comas. Inaccurate portrayals showed miraculous awakenings—often within seconds and as if from a terrible nightmare—with no long-lasting cognitive or other deficits. He called it the Sleeping Beauty effect.

"Inaccuracy concerns me because the public sees an unrealistic portrayal of a neurologic disease that could lead to improbable expectations from a family of a patient in a coma, for example, that it will be just a matter of time till the patient awakens and everything will be fine and dandy," Dr. Wijdicks concluded.

Common Causes of Coma

A coma is a state of profound unconsciousness. The word is derived from the Greek word *koma,* meaning "deep sleep." But unlike sleep, a person in a coma cannot be awakened and does not have normal sleep–wake cycles. Nor can someone in a coma respond to pain, touch, light, or verbal commands, or take voluntary actions.

Coma results when a widespread brain injury disrupts the network of neurons responsible for conscious brain functions. Traumatic head injury—say, from a car accident, sports injury, child abuse, or mugging—is the most common cause of coma in young people, who, in general, have the best chance of emerging from this unfortunate state. Other physical causes of coma include strokes and brain tumors.

Metabolic causes of coma disrupt brain function by changing the brain's chemical environment. Some common causes include diabetes (when blood sugar gets too high or too low); infections like meningitis and encephalitis that cause inflammation of the membranes around the brain and spinal cord; organ failure, particularly of the liver or kidneys; Reye's syndrome, which can sometimes result from giving aspirin to a child with a viral infection; drug overdose; and extreme alcohol intoxication.

Most people who lapse into a coma emerge from it within a few weeks, though they may not recover all their former mental or physical abilities. Comas that are not due to trauma—such as those caused by in infection or metabolic disturbance—and that persist for three months or longer generally have a poor prognosis. Comas that result from a traumatic head injury and that persist for a year or more are likely to be permanent.

When visiting someone who is in a coma, experts recommend speaking in a normal voice as if the person can hear and understand you. And don't say anything you would not want the person to hear. When people emerge from a coma, they often report remembering conversations that took place while they were unconscious.

There are no specific treatments for a coma. When the cause is an injury or illness that results in brain swelling, physicians can take steps—like temporarily removing part of the skull or draining excess fluid—to reduce pressure on the injured brain. When the cause is a metabolic disturbance, the treatment involves reversing the abnormality—say, giving insulin to lower dangerous levels of blood sugar or giving a sugar solution to counteract excess insulin.

A Confusion of States

A person in a coma has his or her eyes closed, does not respond in any way to physical or verbal stimuli, lacks sleep–wake cycles, and cannot be aroused. The person may have spontaneous body movements like jerking, shaking, trembling, eye opening and closing, and irregular breathing.

However, there are several other conditions of altered consciousness with which coma is often confused.

- **Stupor.** This describes a person who is unresponsive but can be aroused briefly, say, by sharp pain, but then immediately falls back into a state of unconsciousness. Someone who is very drunk or spaced out on drugs might be in a stupor.

- **Vegetative state.** Individuals in a vegetative state are unconscious and unaware of their surroundings but have sleep–wake cycles and occasional brief moments when they seem to be alert. They may open their eyes; wince at bright light or when startled; make noises, randomly cry or smile; withdraw from a pinch, and make random movements. They may emerge from this state after a few weeks.

- **Persistent vegetative state.** When a person remains in a vegetative state for more than a month, the condition is described as persistent. This condition, which afflicts up to thirty-five thousand adults and children in the United States, sometimes follows a coma. People rarely emerge from this state after, say, three months, and almost never after a year or more. Their brain stem, which regulates automatic bodily functions like breathing, heart rate, digestion, and sleeping and waking, remains intact, but they lack awareness of their surroundings and have no cognitive functions. As occurred with Terri Schiavo, their eyes may open in response to stimuli, and they may sometimes grimace, cry or laugh, but they cannot speak or respond to commands. Patients in this condition have survived for up to thirty-seven years with intact sleep–wake cycles and normal heart and respiratory functions but with no sign of awareness, thought, or emotion.

• **Minimally conscious state.** People with this condition are, as the term implies, barely conscious. They can breathe on their own and they retain some cognitive ability. They may occasionally respond to instructions to blink their eyes, move a part of their body, or reach for an object, though such responses are unpredictable. When spoken to about meaningful events in their lives or when they hear the voice of a loved one, a study showed patterns of brain activity similar to those of healthy people. They occasionally make intelligible sounds or gestures, smile at jokes, or cry when sad. However, they are bedridden, cannot communicate, and cannot feed or care for themselves. Terri Schiavo showed no evidence of ever having been in this state. However, in July 2007 doctors reported that a thirty-eight-year-old man who had suffered a severe head injury and spent five years in a minimally conscious state had recovered the ability to speak—albeit a few words at a time—and to move voluntarily after having his brain stimulated with pulses of electric current. Plans were made to try the procedure in eleven other patients similarly afflicted.

• **Locked-in syndrome.** People in this rare neurological condition are aware and awake, but they cannot move or speak because, except for the muscles that control eye movements, their voluntary muscles throughout the body are completely paralyzed. They typically communicate with eye blinks. There is no cure, but treatments involving electrical stimulation of muscle reflexes may help them move some paralyzed muscles.

- **Brain death.** This is an irreversible condition in which the brain shows no electrical activity. It is synonymous with death. In fact, it is now the universally accepted definition of death, used, for example, in determining when it is appropriate to disconnect a patient from life support and retrieve organs for transplantation (see chapter 16).

CHAPTER 7

Living Well to the End: Where and How

You may wonder about the title of this chapter: Is it *really* possible to live well when you're dying—even, say, when the end is but days away? The answer, based on a number of studies of patients and their families, is a resounding yes.

But the studies also show that while there are some factors in common, the definition of "living well at the end of life" differs depending on whom you ask. It is often different for doctors than it is for their patients. It is sometimes different for patients than for their families. And it is sometimes different for African American and Hispanic patients than for whites.

What these differences suggest, then, is the overwhelming need for patients (or their close relatives) to understand what does and does not help to smooth the transition between life and death and then to make their preferences known to their families and health care providers while they still can (see chapter 3).

Do You Really Want to Die at Home?

The studies also have had some surprising findings. For example, if you ask the man on the street where the best place to die is, most would answer, "At home." However, a study of 340 seriously ill patients, 332 recently bereaved relatives, 361 physicians, and 429 other care providers showed otherwise. When patients nearing the end of life were asked where they would rather be, only 35 percent preferred to die at home. Likewise, only 30 percent of bereaved relatives felt it was important for their family members to die at home. On the other hand, 44 percent of physicians and 46 percent of other caregivers thought dying at home was important.

Dying at home was consistently ranked as least important among nine considerations by the study participants, regardless of whether they were patients, family members, or health care providers. (The other eight attributes were freedom from pain, being at peace with God, having family present, being mentally aware, having one's treatment choices followed, having one's finances in order, feeling life was meaningful, and resolving conflicts.)

The researchers suggested that "the notion of dying at home may be romantic among health care professionals who want to provide a good death." However, as symptoms get worse in a person's last twenty-four to forty-eight hours, some patients and families feel overwhelmed by the challenges of relieving those symptoms and, therefore, prefer a skilled care environment like a hospital or nursing home. Some families also feel very uncomfortable about the idea of having a dead person in their home.

For example, Mr. R, who had been well cared for at home by his wife while he battled unsuccessfully against pancreatic cancer, decided as the end approached that he preferred to be in the hospital. "He felt safer there," his wife explained. "He had always said he wanted to die in his own bed. But that was not in terms of this illness."

There are also often cultural differences concerning the most desirable location for end-of-life care, Polly Mazanec and Mary Kay Tyler reported in the *American Journal of Nursing*. For example, while most African American families prefer to care for dying elders at home, some believe that a death in the home brings the family bad luck. Some Chinese American families share this belief in bad luck, but others believe that the patient's spirit will get lost if death occurs in a hospital. Likewise, some Hispanic or Latino American families believe the patient's spirit will get lost if death occurs in a non-home setting. Whenever possible, in Hispanic or Latino cultures, extended family members care for loved ones who are ill.

Thus, before recommending a location for end-of-life care, physicians should ask about family and cultural preferences, respect the family's choice, and help the family arrange for the care needed in the preferred location, regardless of what may be required—supplemental oxygen, intravenous pain medication, the assistance of a home health aide, or home-based hospice care.

What *IS* Important? Control of Symptoms

I can't imagine how anyone—patient, relative, friend or physician—can feel good about an end-of-life experience that is marred by uncontrolled pain, shortness of breath, nausea and vomiting, poor personal hygiene, and disregard for one's emotional and spiritual needs. None of this needs to happen *if* patients and their families make their wishes and needs known to health care providers and insist that those needs be met. For further end-of-life guidance, see chapter 9.

Pain. As the above study suggested, control of pain leads the list as most important to all concerned. Although there have been improvements recently in the knowledge and practice of pain control for terminally ill patients, serious shortcomings still persist, much to the distress of patients and their loved ones.

Some doctors are still inclined to say, "If I give him more drugs, he'll become addicted," a meaningless issue for someone who is approaching death.

Many doctors have had little or no training in pain management. They fail to adequately assess their patients' pain and wouldn't know enough about how to treat it if they did do a proper assessment.

Other doctors are afraid (and sometimes with good reason) of being called on the carpet by the overly aggressive U.S. Drug Enforcement Administration (DEA), which has of late taken to cracking down on physicians who prescribe lots of narcotics for pain relief, as if they were drug dealers instead of well-informed and compassionate health care providers.

And some doctors fear being accused of causing the patient's death, since the high doses of narcotics *sometimes* needed to control pain can indeed hasten death. (This, however, is something of a non-issue. Although the DEA can still cause havoc for a physician who prescribes lots of narcotics, according to the doctrine of double effect outlined in Supreme Court decisions, when a treatment is used for a legitimate purpose like pain relief but has an unintended effect that would be illegal if done deliberately, like ending a patient's life, the physician is not responsible for the unintended effect.)

Sometimes families object to an increase in pain medications, fearing that it will wipe out the patient's ability to think, speak, and feel. And, yes, large doses of narcotics can do that. But a dying person in pain is not likely to think, speak, and feel very well, either, and both patient and family are unlikely to consider being in uncontrolled pain a desirable way to spend one's last days. In the experience of professionals who provide hospice care, there is almost universal relief among all concerned when pain is adequately controlled near the end of life.

Every patient, whether near the end of life or not, should have pain periodically assessed by health care professionals. The doctor or nurse should inquire about the intensity of pain—mild, moderate, or severe—perhaps by using a scale of 1 to 10, with 10 being the worst pain imaginable, or by using a rating determined by color intensity or facial expressions. Patients should be asked when the pain is worst, what may make it better or worse, and what impact it is having on the patient's life.

Based on the findings of such an assessment, the proper means of pain relief can be selected—ranging from simple aspirin and acetaminophen to long-acting narcotics—along with treatment of possible contributing factors like depression, anxiety, nerve pain, or bone pain (the latter two often respond better to treatments other than narcotics). When narcotics are needed to control pain, they can be given orally or by continuous infusion according to a predetermined dose, with a fast-acting "rescue dose" administered if pain suddenly worsens.

No patient in pain should be reluctant to ask for relief and, if the treatment given is not adequate, to request a larger dose or a stronger drug. If the patient is unwilling to speak up, a family member should do so.

Also important is not to wait until the pain becomes too much to bear. Pain relief works best when medication is used in advance to head off pain. Once pain is well established, larger doses or more potent drugs are required, and relief takes that much longer to achieve.

If the drug used to control pain causes constipation or nausea and vomiting (as narcotics often do), medication can and should be given to relieve these side effects.

Shortness of breath. Known medically as dyspnea or air hunger, difficulty breathing is a common, fear-provoking symptom in patients near the end of life. Among possible causes are anxiety, airway obstruction, thickened pulmonary secretions, fluid in the chest cavity, and pneumonia.

It may surprise you to know that administering oxygen to a patient with air hunger has nothing more than a placebo effect, if that. The best relief for breathlessness near the end of life is obtained by administering a low dose of a narcotic like morphine or oxycodone, often in combination with a drug that treats anxiety, like lorazepam or diazepam.

Nausea and vomiting. There are perhaps a dozen causes of this symptom in terminally ill patients. In addition to narcotics used for pain, they include various other medications, spread of a cancer, congestive heart failure, irritation of the lining of the digestive tract, mechanical obstruction, anxiety, excessive gastric motility, infectious illness, and dizziness.

Depending on the cause, there are at least seven classes of drugs that can treat nausea and vomiting. Oft-used treatments include scopolamine, misoprostol, meclizine, haloperidol, cannabinoids, and various antacids. Often, two or more medications taken together will work better than one alone since more than one factor may be triggering the nausea and vomiting. The treatments are best administered on a schedule around the clock, rather than waiting for this distressing symptom to recur.

For cancer patients on chemotherapy who are living at home, Anne Haughney, an ambulatory care nurse at Memorial Sloan-Kettering Cancer Center in New York, suggests that control of cooking odors is often helpful in preventing nausea. Among her suggestions: Open a window or use an exhaust fan when cooking. Warm foods in a microwave oven, which results in fewer odors than warming foods on the stove. Whenever possible, consider serving meals that require no cooking or serving bland foods that can be eaten at room temperature.

Techniques that foster relaxation may also help, like music and guided imagery.

Oral complications. Difficulty swallowing and mouth sores are common problems in patients near the end of life. Constance Dahlin, a nurse practitioner specializing in palliative care at the Massachusetts General Hospital, notes that swallowing problems can result from cancerous growths, neurological diseases like Parkinson's or dementia, the side effects of chemotherapy or radiation, and stroke.

Since most patients would prefer to be able to eat normally rather than be fed by tube, Ms. Dahlin suggests that it is possible to control swallowing problems by:

- Correcting or treating the cause

- Strengthening oral muscles

- Administering steroids to reduce tissue swelling

- Helping patients with feedings

- Having the patient sit upright to eat so that gravity can assist in swallowing

- Minimizing distractions, like the TV or visitors

- Adjusting the size and consistency of foods

If solid foods do not go down, pureed or other smooth foods might, such as applesauce, mashed potatoes, yogurt, and puddings. Some patients can handle semisolid foods like scrambled eggs, cottage cheese, and soft tofu. But it is best to avoid hard or crunchy foods, raw fruits and vegetables, and dry foods like bread and crackers. Also avoid thin liquids, which may go down the wrong pipe, as it were. Pureed soups or fruit shakes are often easier than water to swallow correctly.

For mouth sores, Ms. Dahlin suggests treating them with antibiotics and oral rinses and avoiding irritating foods and drinks— those that are sharp, hard, coarse, spicy, salty, or acidic. Swishing the mouth with a protective rinse before eating can ease the discomfort, as can sucking on ice chips or using a saliva substitute.

Foods best handled by a patient with mouth sores include "milk shakes, bananas, applesauce, mashed potatoes, cooked cereal, soft-boiled or scrambled eggs, cottage cheese, macaroni and cheese, pudding, custard, and gelatin," Ms. Dahlin wrote in the *American Journal of Nursing*. She added, "Popsicles and frozen yogurt or ice cream may be especially soothing."

Other symptoms. Various other symptoms can detract from a person's ability to get the most out of the end of life, including constipation, diarrhea, fatigue, insomnia, tissue swelling, and breakdown of the skin. Each of these discomforting symptoms has one or more solutions.

For example, the best treatment for skin breakdown, which can result in ulcers—bedsores—that never heal, is prevention.

- Keep the skin clean and dry.

- Use dressings on pressure points and on skin that may come into contact with bodily wastes.

- Place an egg-crate-style foam pad and air mattress under the patient to create at least an inch of space between the patient and the underlying bed mattress.

For insomnia, the first step is to check on consumption of caffeine and frequency of napping, which may make it more difficult to sleep at night. Other common sleep disrupters include pain, anxiety, and gastroesophageal reflux (known as GERD), all of which can be treated by medication, adjustment of sleep postures, and counseling. If sleep is still a problem once these causes are corrected, sleep-inducing medications can be used to counter insomnia.

For more information on managing end-of-life symptoms, see chapter 8.

Is There a Role for Feeding Tubes?

My friend Jo-Ann's mother had advanced Alzheimer's disease and no longer knew who she was or recognized her daughter or any other family members. She also needed round-the-clock care in a nursing home. Jo-Ann knew that, as happens with this disease, eventually her mother would stop eating and that her caretakers would naturally consider installing a feeding tube to keep her alive.

But, Jo-Ann asked herself, to what end? What would be the point of prolonging the life of someone who really wasn't living in the sense most of us would consider living. She could no longer care for herself in any way or enjoy any of the things, activities, and people who once made her happy. So Jo-Ann made sure that everyone in the nursing home knew that if and when her mother stopped eating, nothing more would be done, and in a matter of weeks her life would draw to a close. Jo-Ann reminded the nursing home personnel of this request at every visit and made sure it was prominently written into her mother's medical records. And so it happened as Jo-Ann had requested.

Another family I know of lacked Jo-Ann's knowledge and fore-sight in dealing with an older woman's Alzheimer's disease. Without an advance directive to guide the nursing home in caring for the patient, a feeding tube and other life-supporting measures were introduced when the woman's condition warranted. She lived, if you can call it that, for twenty years in a wholly demented state, a situation that proved so stressful for her husband that he preceded her in death.

Here is what families and patients should know about feeding tubes:

- They are most useful in a temporary situation, when patients are expected to recover eventually but need intensive nutritional support in the meantime.

- Except for patients in a coma who have a chance of emerging from that state, artificial nutrition offers no survival advantage in critically ill patients, palliative care experts reported in *Patient Care*. In fact, they wrote, tube feeding is associated with *decreased* survival in patients with acute respiratory failure and chronic obstructive pulmonary disease who have widespread infections.

- In patients with advanced dementia, feeding tubes can increase health risks and discomfort. Their use is associated with a host of potential complications, including diarrhea, clogged tubes, infections, and aspiration pneumonia.

"Grampa's secret of longevity is life-support."

- Some patients, especially those who are confused, try to pull out feeding tubes, which prompts hospital personnel to physically restrain the patients.

- Feeding tubes do not reduce the risk of pressure sores or infections, and they do not improve function or significantly relieve discomforting symptoms in patients nearing the end of life.

- Nursing homes, especially those that are for-profit facilities, often prefer to use feeding tubes, not for the patient's benefit but because feeding patients by hand is more costly and time consuming. And, in some states, Medicaid pays a higher daily rate for patients who have feeding tubes.

When Treatment Is Futile

Some patients—and sometimes their families—are reluctant to give up aggressive therapy, even when doctors explain that the patients can no longer benefit from treatment for their disease and would do best with palliative, or comfort, care in a hospice-like setting. A survey of 173 patients with advanced cancer was conducted a week to ten days after their oncologists had recommended that they discontinue disease-related treatment and instead receive only palliative care. Only 27 percent of the patients chose hospice care, although all had insurance that would cover such care. A surprising 63 percent requested further disease-related treatment—chemotherapy, radiation therapy, hormonal therapy, and/or experimental medications. Three percent asked for a second opinion, and the remaining 7 percent were undecided.

Those who chose hospice care survived an average of thirty-one days, and those who requested disease-oriented treatments survived an average of thirty-three days. The researchers concluded that "there was no survival benefit for those who did not choose hospice care." And, I suspect, there were significant downsides resulting from side effects of the futile treatments chosen by those who resisted their oncologists' recommendation for hospice care.

In a California report, "Managing Pain and End-of-Life Issues," experts summed up a common problem of "patients with a slim, if non-existent, chance of recovery, who continue to receive intense, invasive, and costly procedures because there is no other clear alternative. Frequently, such patients are near death, permanently unconscious, and no longer able to make their wishes known. Yet their families, uncertain of what to do or unable to accept the reality that their loved ones cannot be restored to them, continue to insist that 'everything' be done."

The report quotes Sister Judy Laffey, a nurse and chaplain for a Catholic health system in Pennsylvania: "Very often we see so much suffering with our patients because families do not understand or do not want to let go." Sometimes, she continued, families do not follow the patient's clear wishes and even disregard the patient's living will.

"On one level," Sister Laffey said, "I think we have to wait until the family gets to some point where they can let go. But when you know that nothing you are doing is going to help the patient, and the family is waiting for a miracle that just isn't going to happen, it is very frustrating. From an ethical standpoint, you are looking at both the amount of money and resources spent on this patient and also at the suffering that is caused."

Dr. Kenneth Greer, director of intensive care at Mercy Hospital in Pittsburgh, pleads with families "to try to determine what the patient would want given the situation, not what *they* would want, but what they think that person would want."

Most of the time, Dr. Greer says, when a patient has reached the point where recovery is impossible or highly unlikely, families will choose comfort care instead of insisting on treatments that are invasive and have little chance of helping the patient. However, he added, "When there are families who do not see it the way we do, we are very much obligated to continue to treat the patient according to the family members' wishes." In 1997 the American Medical

Association recommended that all hospitals develop a medical futility policy to govern when hospitals and clinicians could decide to stop treatment or not provide treatments deemed nonbeneficial. But the problem, many experts say, is that no one can decide on what "futile" really means. A life that some people would regard as not worth living might be quite valuable to others.

Thus, the first challenge is to accurately define *medical futility*. One definition calls a treatment futile if it "merely preserves permanent unconsciousness or cannot end dependence on intensive medical care." Another more encompassing definition, published in an editorial in the *Archives of Internal Medicine*, describes "life-or-death situations in which proposed treatments will fail to prolong quality life, achieve the patient's key goals for medical care, achieve a critical physiologic effect on the body, or result in a therapeutic benefit for the patient."

Patients and their families are understandably mistrustful when doctors say further treatment is futile. Some fear that insurers will use it as an excuse to deny payment for costly but potentially beneficial treatments. Some think physicians use it as an excuse to justify their reluctance to provide all the treatments patients and their families ask for.

What is the bottom line? The editorial writers concluded that "most treatments can be considered futile only within the context of an individual's goals for care. If a patient desires aggressive care, the patient is unlikely to consider many treatments futile, even treatments the physician believes are extremely unlikely to be beneficial."

In other words, we each must decide for ourselves just how far we wish to delve into the realm of therapeutic attempts (see chapter 5). After about six months of intensive chemotherapy for a deadly cancer called mesothelioma, my brother-in-law Gordon Engquist, age seventy-five, said "enough" and asked to be transferred into hospice care. He told me, "It was obvious the treatment wasn't helping. I was continuing to get worse and weaker, so there was no point in pursuing it any further."

Withholding and Withdrawing Life Support

Laura Ingersoll Johnson of Marine-on-St. Croix, Minnesota, and Big Sky, Montana, was sixty-five years old and an extraordinarily active and productive grandmother and community leader when a breathing disorder she'd apparently had for years suddenly reared its ugly head. She spent many initially hopeful weeks at the Mayo Clinic, known for its expertise in treating her disease, called interstitial pneumonitis. Despite the fact that Laura was widely known as "one tough cookie," nothing these world-renowned experts did seemed to help, and eventually she had to be intubated so that a respirator could breathe for her ever-stiffening lungs.

To reduce her body's need for oxygen and relieve the inevitable anxiety that accompanies severe breathing difficulties, Laura had to be heavily sedated. For the last weeks of her life, she was in a coma, unable to speak or communicate in any way. When it became apparent that Laura was not getting better, only worse, and nothing more could be done to maintain her failing body, James, her adoring husband of forty-two years, and their two grown children, Todd and Maclaren, made the heart-wrenching decision to remove her from life support. The decision was made a bit easier by the fact that Laura's vital organs were failing and by Laura's own recognition of her mortality. Before losing her ability to speak and while her family still had hope for her recovery, she had said to James, "I never thought I would die so young." Ten minutes after the ventilator was turned off, Laura died.

Laura, in effect, died as she had lived her life; she made things easy for her family and her doctors. Not only had she told her husband years earlier that she would not want to live dependent on life support, but her failing organs told all that she was ready to die.

However, decisions to discontinue life support are not always so clear-cut. For example, Mr. D was an elderly man with dementia and end-stage kidney disease whose family struggled over a decision to discontinue the kidney dialysis that had been keeping him alive for ten years. Finally, after much discussion with both the kidney specialist and Mr. D's primary care physician, a decision to stop dialysis was made. Mr. D died peacefully five days later, with his family in attendance. In an interview months afterward, Mr. D's son said, "If I had to go back and do it over again, I would have gotten into high gear several years earlier. One of the difficulties I had is that the doctors I talked to perhaps should have more forcefully stressed the severity of the situation and the imminence of general decline. Communication about the hopelessness of the situation would have been useful. My one regret is that we should have stopped treatment perhaps a few months earlier."

There is a serious misunderstanding among the public, and sometimes among physicians, that once patients have been connected to machines that are keeping them alive, it may require a court order to unplug them or risk being charged with murder. This is not true. Legally speaking, there is no difference between not starting life support and discontinuing it when the patient has no chance to recover. When conflicts arise, physicians can turn to ethics consultations to help curb the futile use of life-sustaining treatments for patients receiving intensive care.

Ethics consultation is a service available in most hospitals that is provided by an individual consultant, a team, or a committee to help resolve ethical issues involving a specific patient. Its purpose is to improve patient care by helping to identify, analyze, and resolve ethical dilemmas facing physicians and families.

For example, in a study published in the *Journal of the American Medical Association* in September 2003, ethics consultations were obtained for 278 randomly chosen patients in intensive care at seven American hospitals. Their fate was compared to 273 similar patients for whom ethics consultations were not obtained. The death rates in the two groups were similar, but among the patients who died, those in the consultation group spent fewer days in the hospital and on life-sustaining treatments. Fully 87 percent of physicians, nurses, and patients or their surrogates agreed that the consultations helped them deal with treatment conflicts.

Doctors have long been concerned about keeping patients alive indefinitely on machines when there is clearly no chance for recovery or improvement. Patients, too, and their families have often been in torment over decisions to either begin or terminate life-sustaining therapies that they view as unduly burdensome and usually pointless, since they are unlikely to result in return to a life they would want to live.

In 2005 endocrinologists at the Mayo Clinic reviewed the medical and ethical aspects of prolonged life support of terminally ill patients. "There is no ethical or legal difference between withholding or withdrawing life-sustaining treatments," they wrote. "Therefore, treatments should not be withheld because of concern that they cannot later be withdrawn." This view has been supported by the U.S. Supreme Court, which in 1990 affirmed the right of patients or their surrogates to refuse unwanted life-sustaining treatments. Furthermore, the Mayo team concluded, "Honoring a patient's request to refuse or to withdraw a life-sustaining treatment is not the same as physician-assisted suicide or euthanasia" (see chapter 14). Rather, "when a patient dies after a life-sustaining treatment is refused or withdrawn, the underlying disease is the cause of death."

When Someone Is Actively Dying

Given that in the last half century, most deaths that did not occur instantly took place in hospitals and nursing homes, unwitnessed by laypeople, it is not surprising that most adults today would be unable to recognize the signs that someone is "actively dying" or know what to do—and what not to do—when this happens. In fact, fear is one reason some families are reluctant to keep patients home until the bitter end. They are afraid of what may happen and that they won't know what to do.

When life as we know it ebbs, physical and mental changes occur that can confuse and frighten caregivers and often cause them to respond inappropriately to changes in the patient's condition. When a patient can no longer take in food orally, the temptation is to nourish the patient through a feeding tube. When a dying person gasps for air, the tendency is to reach for an oxygen mask. But these are not necessarily desirable tactics, say experts on the care of the dying.

In the *American Journal of Nursing*, Elizabeth Ford Pitorak, a registered nurse who directs hospice care at the Hospice of the Western Reserve in Cleveland, described what happens and what should be done—and not done—when death is imminent.

"Active dying, the process of total body system failure, usually occurs over a period of 10 to 14 days, although it can take as little as 24 hours," Ms. Pitorak wrote. She noted that patients who are dying usually become dehydrated; swallowing becomes difficult, and peripheral circulation decreases, resulting in perspiration and clammy skin that feels cold to the touch.

But, she warned, this should not be a signal to pile on the blankets since "most dying patients can't tolerate even the slightest weight on the feet or other extremities. Blankets and sheets should be left loose and untucked."

Pulmonary congestion, another common symptom when death is near, can cause breathing problems and prompt patients to gasp for air. However, supplying oxygen is not the way to relieve this "air hunger" because a dying person usually cannot benefit from it, she explained. A more effective way to relieve breathlessness is to open windows, use a fan, allow space around the patient's bed, and administer morphine or a related drug, which can reduce both breathing difficulties and the anxiety that typically accompanies them.

When a dying person can no longer swallow, the instinct of many people is to turn to feeding tubes—artificial nutrition and artificial hydration. But feeding tubes can only add to the patient's discomfort and they do little to prolong life.

Ms. Pitorak explained that "patients who are actively dying aren't usually hungry." Furthermore, without fluids or nutrition

patients often experience a kind of euphoria from a buildup of ke-
tones in their blood when the diet contains no sugar and other car-
bohydrates. Ms. Pitorak pointed out that even a small amount of
sugar administered intravenously can counteract this euphoria.

"The absence of nutrients and fluids is nature's way of bringing
gentle closure and even pain relief as the body gradually shuts
down," Jennifer Sutton Holder and Jann Aldredge-Clanton wrote
in *Parting: A Handbook for Spiritual Care Near the End of Life.*

In fact, any attempt to feed a dying person can backfire. When
beautiful Jessica Wing was nearing the end of her life at age thirty-
one, her father thought that perhaps a little applesauce would give
her more energy and keep her around longer. The unfortunate result: Jessica vomited, aspirated, and died soon after, changing what
had been planned to be a gentle, peaceful death at home into
something rather sudden and violent and very disturbing to her
survivors.

While artificial hydration can help a terminally ill patient who
becomes delirious as a result of dehydration, when intravenous fluids are administered to someone who is actively dying, it can result
in swelling, nausea, and pain.

It is not unusual for a person approaching the end of life to turn
inward and become less communicative. But families should not
confuse this apparent withdrawal with rejection. Rather, it reflects
the dying person's need to leave the outer world behind and focus
on inner contemplation.

There are other reasons why families should not wait until the
last hours of life to communicate with dying patients since that
may be too late. In a study of one hundred terminally ill cancer patients, only fifty-six were awake one week before they died. And in
the final six hours of life, only eight were awake, forty-two were
drowsy, and the remaining fifty were in a coma, which precludes
any further communication.

However, even when a dying person seems "out of it" and unable to respond to sights or sounds, it is important for those nearby
to know that hearing is the last sense to leave the body, so nothing

"*Of course I'm not dead! First I have to go 'AAARGH!' <u>Then</u> I'll be dead.*"

should be said near dying patients that you would not want them to hear.

· **As Death Approaches.** Changes that take place when death is imminent can be disturbing and frightening to family members who don't know what to expect. Muscles of the mouth relax and secretions that accumulate in the throat or chest can result in loud, gurgling breathing sounds, commonly called a "death rattle." Trying to suction these secretions can be very discomforting to the patient and is rarely successful in any case. A better plan would be to turn the patient to one side, elevate the head and, if needed, give medication to decrease the secretions, Ms. Pitorak suggested.

Dying patients may also moan or grunt as they breathe, which sometimes prompts family members to think they are in pain. Ms. Pitorak said these noises are rarely a sign of pain. But she emphasized that, if needed, appropriate pain relief should always be provided since a patient in pain cannot communicate effectively or die peacefully.

Family members at a deathbed vigil sometimes think they should say something to help patients who are struggling to hang on to instead release their hold on life. A commonly used phrase is "It's okay, you can go now." However, Ms. Pitorak suggests that it is more helpful to someone who is dying to be told that those left behind will be well even though the person will be missed.

When a loved one dies, survivors sometimes focus on the reaction of the patient's physician, who may be tempted to withdraw from the scene rather than face feelings of failure, guilt, or inadequacy and the family's grief or anger (see chapter 13). Ms. Pitorak's advice to medical personnel: Don't abandon the family. Don't leave the room without expressing your sympathy. And give the family as much time as they want with their dead relative before taking the body away.

If medical personnel fail to act appropriately when your loved one has died, consider writing a letter to the physician, department head, and head of the hospital stating what happened and describing your distress. Sometimes that's all it takes to ignite an effort to help physicians deal more effectively with families when patients die.

FOR FURTHER READING

Callahan, Maggie. *Final Journeys: A Practical Guide for Bringing Care and Comfort at the End of Life.* New York: Bantam, 2008.

Dolan, Susan R., and Audrey R. Vizzard. *From the Start Consider the Finish: A Guide to Excellent End-of-Life Care.* Parker, CO: Outskirts Press, 2007.

Kaufman, Sharon R. . . . *And a Time to Die: How American Hospitals Shape the End of Life.* Chicago: University of Chicago Press, 2006.

Tobin, Daniel R., with Karen Lindsey. *Peaceful Dying: The Step-by-Step Guide to Preserving Your Dignity, Your Choice, and Your Inner Peace at the End of Life.* New York: Perseus, 1999.

Wanzer, Sidney, and Joseph Glenmullen. *To Die Well: Your Right to Comfort, Calm, and Choice in the Last Days of Life.* Cambridge, MA: Da Capo Press, 2006.

CHAPTER **8**

Caregiving: Tending
Someone at the End of Life

Most people, when asked where they'd like to spend their last days, would say "at home, in familiar surroundings and comfortable, with my family and/or close friends nearby." But by the 1980s dying at home had become a rare event. Among those with terminal illnesses, last breaths were nearly always taken in a hospital or nursing home, in austere surroundings and in considerable discomfort, with tubes and needles and whirring machines for company.

But in recent years, thanks in part to the growth of at-home hospice care, there's been a change in this scenario. More and more people approaching the end of their lives are being cared for at home, usually by a family member who is the primary—and often the only—caregiver. There are now more than twenty-five million family caregivers for all kinds of patients in the United States, and they provide about 80 percent of home care services.

While many family caregivers serve patients with chronic disabilities or slowly progressive illnesses, the fastest recent growth has occurred among those who care for terminally ill patients during the last weeks, months, or year of life. Family or friends serve as informal caregivers to almost three-fourths of sick or disabled older adults living in the community during their final year of life, according to a report in January 2007 in the *Archives of Internal Medicine.*

Still greater increases in the informal—that is, family or friend—caregiver workforce are expected in the years ahead, as the population ages and more diseases are managed, sometimes for years, in outpatient settings.

As the former first lady Rosalynn Carter points out on her website, "There are only four kinds of people in the world—those who have been caregivers, those who currently are caregivers, those who will be caregivers, and those who will need caregivers."

In most cases, the family caregiver has taken on the job with no training or background skills, guided only by love and respect for the patient. The usual caregiver is the patient's spouse, who may be elderly and have health issues of his or her own. In one study, family caregivers for terminally ill patients ranged in age between seventy and ninety-one years old. Next in line is an adult child, usually a daughter. She is often a member of the so-called sandwich generation—physically and emotionally divided between a dying parent and a very much alive family and usually a job of her own.

Either way, caregiving can be a very daunting task, a task that can be greatly eased by knowledge: a better understanding of the physical and emotional needs of people nearing the end of life, where and how to get help when help is needed, and the critical importance of self-care for the caregiver. The most effective caregivers are those who take good care of themselves.

A Rewarding Experience

Mr. R was a seventy-year-old legally blind man with incurable pancreatic cancer. Mrs. R, his wife and longtime business partner, had severe rheumatoid arthritis, among other health issues. Yet she was determined to care for her husband at home through his last months of life. From time to time, she was assisted by a home care nurse, a housekeeper, and her grown daughter, Ms. L.

"I knew I would take care of him myself because we had always done things together. We worked together for 30 years. We played together, we did everything together since I was 18 years old," Mrs. R told an interviewer for the *Journal of the American Medical Association.* "Because he had been legally blind since the early 1970's, I had always been by his side. There was never a question that I wouldn't continue to be during this period."

She explained, "Giving care at home made me feel useful. It only became scary for me at night when there were just two of us here, and I realized that if anything untoward occurred, I wouldn't be able to do anything for him."

Although end-of-life caregivers often experience significant emotional, physical, and financial stress, more than two-thirds of such caregivers who participated in a national study reported that it was a very rewarding experience. More than three-fourths said caregiving made them feel useful and needed, and about 70 percent agreed that caregiving "makes me feel good about myself" and "enables me to appreciate life more." In fact, many caregivers said they derived benefits from the patients, who kept *them* company and helped out with finances and household tasks when they could.

Despite the many strains, families are often strengthened through caregiving at home. As Mr. R's daughter put it, "The burdens just brought us closer. I felt very privileged to be able to be helpful to him and to be helpful to my mother. And it occasioned a lot of the most precious moments of connection that I'll always remember."

A Demanding Job

Family caregivers each have what amounts to a full-time job, providing more than forty hours a week of demanding care while making little use of supportive services, the report in the *Archives of Internal Medicine* stated. Caregivers are often the last people to ask for help but they are the ones who, next to the person being cared for, need it the most. No "sick days" for the caregiver, who may be on the job 24/7 providing nursing and personal care, administering medicines, and helping with shopping, transportation, finances, and household chores. All without any training or financial compensation.

As Mrs. R, who chose to provide home care for her dying husband, put it, "It just never stopped. It wasn't the care, it was the whole commitment. It never went away."

It's no wonder that terminally ill patients often worry that their continuing existence is taking too much of a toll on the family members who care for them, a thought that prompts some patients to seek or wish for a faster exit (see chapter 14).

Caregivers, too, may wish for patients to die sooner rather than later, a thought that stems from a combination of factors: a desire for a very sick loved one to be finally at peace and a desire for the caregiver to be finally free of the awesome responsibility of keeping the patient alive and comfortable. Such a wish is a common source of guilt that adds to the emotional strain of being a family caregiver.

But the biggest burden involves the *physical* demands on family caregivers, most of whom have no special skills, training, or guidance for the job. "The home caregiver doesn't know what they don't know," Mrs. R said. Her daughter added, "It was never presented to us what it would entail, in terms of taking care of him."

Family caregivers are the representatives of the medical team while the patient lives at home. That means they have to provide the same kinds of medical services and make periodic medical assessments similar to those typically done in hospitals or nursing homes. The responsibility includes making difficult decisions about when to call the patient's doctor, when to bring the patient to the emergency room, when to call 911, and when *not* to call 911.

In addition to the ordinary tasks of feeding, bathing, and changing the bedclothes and bedding of a very sick person, the untrained family caregiver may have to change the patient's dressing and administer multiple medications, sometimes by injection. Mr. R, for example, was taking ten medications, all of them managed by Mrs. R. Several were given on an as-needed basis, which made her responsible for determining when they were needed and how much of them to give to her husband. This responsibility became overwhelming as Mr. R's health declined and he approached the end of his life.

As described in the *American Medical Association Guide to Home Caregiving*, "When there is no hope for recovery and death is inevitable, the caregiver's goal is to do everything possible to help the person die peacefully, with dignity and without pain." The main challenges at this time are knowing what to expect and how to relieve the patient's symptoms, especially pain. In addition, caregivers must be able to recognize the signs of active dying and know what to do—and, even more important, what *not* to do—when this stage of life is reached (see also chapter 7).

Relieving Symptoms

Terminal illness is often characterized by symptoms that cause considerable discomfort for patients and anxiety for their caregivers, who may not know how best to provide relief without making matters worse. The following guidelines for handling common end-of-life symptoms are adapted mainly from the American Medical Association's book.

Constipation. Although many people believe that bowels should be emptied once a day, once every three days is considered reasonable for someone who is terminally ill. Constipation is best relieved by giving the patient foods rich in fiber and high in bulk, like prune juice and bran cereal, or by adding fiber supplements to foods and drinks, and making sure the patient drinks plenty of fluids. Stool softeners are often helpful. If constipation is severe, ask the doctor about administering a laxative, and be sure to call the doctor if the patient has not had a bowel movement in more than three days.

Eating and Drinking Problems. It is natural for caregivers to fret over a terminally ill patient's inability or reluctance to eat or drink amounts most of us think are necessary to keep a person alive. It may help to cut foods into very small pieces, as if feeding a toddler. Offer soft or pureed foods to patients who have difficulty chewing or swallowing. Serve small amounts on small plates to make a meal seem less intimidating.

For patients who have no appetite, try to introduce some physical activity. Have the patient sit up in bed, get out of bed and walk around, do range-of-motion exercises in bed—anything the patient is able to do is better than just lying still. If the patient can no longer consume solid foods, or if the amount of food eaten is minimal at best, offer a liquid dietary supplement like Ensure or Sustacal.

Adequate liquid intake is important to prevent dehydration. Many patients find it easier to drink through a straw than straight from a glass or cup. If fluids aren't tolerated, offer ice chips to suck on. However, don't overdo fluids, especially for a patient near death. Excessive fluids, like those given intravenously, can cause respiratory distress in someone who is dying.

Breathing Problems. Being unable to take in enough air is one of the most frightening experiences at any stage of life, and breathing difficulties are a common source of stress for terminally ill patients. Some simple measures that may bring relief are to raise the head of the patient's bed, open a window, or turn on a fan in the patient's room. However, breathing difficulties are often severe enough to require the use of oxygen, which can be administered at home (but should not be used when a patient is actively dying). Also helpful are small doses of morphine or drugs that expand the bronchial tubes. Both of these must be prescribed by a doctor.

Nausea and Vomiting. The illness itself, or medication given to treat it or to relieve its symptoms, can cause nausea and vomiting, symptoms that are highly distressful to both patient and caregiver. Do not urge a person who is nauseated to eat or drink. The best treatment is an antiemetic drug, which can be given by a rectal suppository if the patient can't keep down anything consumed by mouth.

Hiccups. This symptom plagued my friend Mickey as he neared the end of his life after a three-year battle with colon cancer. If sipping water slowly through a straw doesn't help, try to get the patient to drink from the wrong side of the glass (the side farthest from the patient, who must be sitting upright or standing to do this). If both these measures fail, medication may be needed to stop the hiccups.

Dry Mouth and Lips. Terminally ill patients often breathe through their mouths, which adds to the dryness of both mouth and lips. Frequent sips of water or sucking on ice chips or hard candies can help moisten the mouth. Lemon glycerin swabs sold in drug stores can be used to wipe the inside of the mouth and teeth. Or you may need a doctor's prescription for artificial saliva. For the lips, try a light coating of petroleum jelly (Vaseline) or frequent use of a lip balm.

Itching. Itching can result from dry skin or sometimes from a sensitivity to substances used to wash bedclothes or linens. Try applying an alcohol-free skin lotion or calamine lotion to the itchy areas. Or gently rub the areas with cornstarch, baking soda, or baby powder. If the heat is on, running a portable humidifier in the patient's room can help to prevent or relieve dry skin. Use a scent-free hypoallergenic laundry detergent to clean the patient's linens, towels, and bedclothes.

Agitation and Anxiety. As death grows near, patients sometimes become anxious and agitated. They may pull at the bedding, fidget constantly, groan, or be unable to sleep. If reassuring words and touch do not provide relief, physician-prescribed medication like alprazolam or lorazepam can relieve the patient's anxiety and agitation. During the last few weeks of my friend Mickey's life, he became very agitated. His wife, Mary Alice, who was his caregiver, couldn't sleep either when she heard him pacing about during the night. Hospice came to the rescue, giving him antianxiety medication that enabled him to calm down.

Managing Pain

Pain, a symptom all too common at the end of life, warrants a subsection of its own because there is so much controversy, fear, and confusion regarding its relief. Patients, family members, and doctors alike often fear that potent painkillers (i.e., narcotics, aka opioids) will result in addiction and/or render the patient unable to communicate or think clearly.

Do not worry about a patient's becoming addicted to pain killers. First, when narcotics are properly administered to relieve pain, addiction almost never occurs. And even if it did, what difference would that make to someone who is terminally ill and suffering intolerable pain? Second, a patient in severe pain is not able to communicate effectively or think rationally, whereas relieving pain can actually facilitate meaningful communication. Finally, watching a loved one who is dying with uncontrolled pain is a most excruciating experience for caregivers and other family members and friends.

The widespread reluctance to administer adequate amounts of painkillers to terminally ill patients stems largely from the fact that most people, and even many physicians, do not understand the difference between physical dependence on a drug, tolerance to a given dose, and addiction.

Physical dependence occurs within a few days of taking a narcotic for pain relief. That simply means withdrawal symptoms will occur if the drug is abruptly stopped. But the pain of a terminally ill person and the need for continuing medication are not likely to stop, so there is no reason to be concerned about withdrawal symptoms.

Patients whose pain remains stable do not become tolerant to narcotics and demand higher and higher doses. An addict, on the other hand, who uses narcotics to get "high," often does become tolerant to a given dose and requires more and more of the drug to maintain the desired level of euphoria. However, if a patient's pain worsens, larger doses may be needed to control it and they should be given without hesitation. As the American Medical Association emphasized, "A dying person should never be allowed or encouraged to endure pain for any reason."

The greatest challenge for caregivers is to know when and how much pain medication to administer. Doctors who are knowledgeable about pain that accompanies terminal illness will often prescribe long-acting morphine, along with a shorter-acting form to be given between doses of the long-acting drug or if "breakthrough" pain occurs.

Most important for the caregiver is to provide pain medication around the clock on a regular basis and not wait until the patient's pain recurs. Pain specialists know that once pain begins to worsen, it is more difficult to control. As the medical association cautions, "Never wait until the person is experiencing pain before giving pain medication; doing so can cause him or her unnecessary suffering and distress."

Caregivers can adopt a technique widely used in hospitals to assess a patient's pain. Periodically ask the patient to describe his or her pain on a scale of 0 to 10, with 10 being the worst pain the patient has ever experienced. If the doses of medication prescribed are not providing sufficient relief, speak to the physician about increasing the amount.

Also, the medical association warns, "Pain control must continue without regard to a person's level of consciousness. A person who is in a coma cannot communicate, but he or she can still experience pain."

Other Sources of Comfort. Medication is not the only way to reduce the level of a patient's pain. Relaxation techniques like deep breathing, meditation, and guided imagery exercises can be useful adjuncts to drugs. For example, suggest that the patient close his or her eyes, relax all muscles, inhale slowly and deeply, and exhale slowly and completely, while concentrating on each breath.

Don't forget the magic of touch, as long as it does not distress the patient. You can provide comfort by holding the patient's hands, hugging, giving a back rub, foot washing, or giving a gentle massage. However, *the medical association warns against massaging the legs of a bedridden patient since it could dislodge a blood clot that travels to the lungs, causing a medical emergency.*

Getting the Help You Need

Let's get one thing straight from the beginning: you can't—and you shouldn't try to—do this job alone, not even if you are a trained nurse. There will be times when the services of others are needed, sometimes for mundane tasks like doing the grocery shopping or getting the car inspected, sometimes for matters directly related to patient care like bathing, changing the bedding, or administering certain treatments.

Often the help you need can be provided by another layperson—a willing and able family member or friend. You should never hesitate to ask for this kind of support, but you should know whom to ask and how to ask to maximize the chances of getting what you need done promptly and properly. Other times you may need the assistance of a health care professional who has the knowledge and experience required to best perform the needed tasks.

In February 2006 the Johnson & Johnson Consumer Products Company, in conjunction with the Office of the Surgeon General and leading aging and caregiving organizations, launched an online service to assist the growing legions of caregivers. Much of the advice that follows is derived from this site. You can access this service through the website www.strengthforcaring.com.

Delegate Responsibilities. Learning how best to enlist the help of others and divvy up responsibilities is the surest way to reduce your risk of burning out and compromising your own health in the service of your loved one. It's especially important to ask for help *before* you reach the breaking point. And you'll be more likely to get help from a person by saying "I could use some help" than by challenging the person with a blatant or subtle reprimand like "You're no help" or "You should help more."

In most families there are people who never seem to volunteer to help. But if you can identify how their special skills might be able to fill your needs, you are more likely to get what you need done. For example, if someone is skilled at using the Internet, ask that person to order your groceries online for home delivery. Someone else may have financial skills that can be a big help with paying bills and negotiating with medical institutions and insurers about charges and payments. Or you may have a handy relative or friend who can help with household repairs.

Another person may be able to do your laundry, help you move the patient so that the bedding can be changed, help to bathe and change the clothes of the patient, provide transportation to medical appointments, or simply pick up a prescription.

Or you may need someone to help out with other members of the family—a child or grandchild or the patient's spouse. And don't forget *your* needs for rejuvenation, rest, and refreshment. Perhaps you need a break to get to the hairdresser or get your nails done or go out to a concert, dinner, a grandchild's ballgame. Someone who can stay with the patient for just a few hours now and then can be a sanity saver for you.

Start by making a list of everything that has to get done on a daily or weekly basis. Then make a second list of everyone who might be able to help with one or another of these chores. Play on people's strengths and egos and respect their weaknesses. To a relative who's good at carpentry, you might say, "You're so good at building things. I really could use a ramp so I can get my dad out of the house more easily." But don't ask Aunt Rose, who's a nervous driver under the best of circumstances, to ferry you and your patient to medical appointments.

By matching each person's abilities to the tasks at hand, your chances of getting the help you need are greatly increased. And when someone says, "What can I do to help?" be sure to answer the question with one or more jobs you'd like done and words of appreciation, not "Thanks, but I'm managing." You'll get no points for being a martyr, and trying to do everything yourself can end up compromising your own health *and* your ability to continue to provide care for your loved one.

Don't forget about the young people in the neighborhood who may be more than willing to do various jobs to earn extra bucks— yard work, grocery shopping, dusting and vacuuming, or even "patient sitting" so you can get out for a hour or two.

Enlisting Professional Help. There are times and circumstances when a layperson is unavailable or unqualified to provide the help you need. That's when you have to call upon trained personnel to perform medical services or other tasks. Perhaps no one you know can build a ramp for your dad's wheelchair. Perhaps you need someone to provide medical care for your loved one during the night so you can get some sleep.

In virtually every community, there are professional resources available to help caregivers. The challenge is to find those to suit your needs. For nursing care, you may be able to call on a local visiting nurse association or a licensed home health care agency, or contact the local hospital's nursing department or social service department for recommendations. Your area's agency on aging and local churches, synagogues, or mosques can be referral sources for home health aides. Also, ask friends and neighbors or people you work with if they know or know of an individual who can be relied upon to provide the quality care you would give yourself if you could.

Perhaps what you need most is household help—someone who

can clean, shop, do laundry, and so forth, so that you have more time and energy for caregiving. Again, personal referrals are the safest bet. But lacking that, contact an employment agency. Be clear about your needs and ask for references (and follow up on all of them) for anyone the agency sends.

Whatever the referral source, interview the person to be sure you are compatible and both of you are clear about expectations. Prepare a written contract that specifies duties, salary, hours, time off, benefits, giving notice (for quitting or being fired), not smoking in the home, and anything else you deem important, so that there are no misunderstandings. After all, you don't want the person you hire to help you become an added stress. And if, after a few days or weeks, the person you chose does not seem to be working out, terminate the employment and start over.

Warning: The American Medical Association, among others, strongly suggests that when you hire an outsider to help with caregiving, you *take steps to minimize the risk of theft.* Keep valuables in a safe place, take an inventory of your loved one's valuable possessions, limit the aide's access to certain rooms of the house, and keep track of household expenses. Deposit all checks made payable to the patient yourself, directly into the patient's bank account. A home health aide should never have access to the patient's bank account or checkbook.

Caring for the Caregiver

A continually self-sacrificing caregiver may be no good to anyone, least of all to the patient he or she is trying to help. You *must* take good care of yourself if you are going to be able to do a good job for your loved one. Being good to yourself is not a selfish act. It is an essential part of the task at hand.

As Dr. Beth Erickson put it on the website www.strengthforcaring .com, "Taking care of YOU also amounts to caring for loved ones. If you aren't well, who will care for your loved one? The best way to help your loved one is to pay attention to your own health and needs. Only then can you pay attention to your loved one's needs. It serves no one if you are worn to a frazzle because of your devotion."

Many things that happen during the course of a terminal illness are out of your control. Your job is to recognize what you *can* control and focus on those measures. Of paramount importance is self-care. Caregivers who neglect their own well-being are at risk of developing a wide spectrum of health problems, including physical and mental exhaustion, clinical depression, heart attacks, and death.

Caregivers of terminally ill loved ones commonly harbor mistaken or distorted beliefs that can inhibit their ability to take good care of themselves. Among the ones I've encountered are these:

- As long as I'm with my loved one, nothing bad can happen.

- It's wrong for me to enjoy myself when my loved one is dying.

- I can't go out. What if my loved one dies while I'm gone?

If you find yourself thinking such thoughts, try to push them aside. They are counterproductive. Instead, follow the advice below offered by both health care professionals and laypeople who have served as caretakers for the terminally ill.

Schedule in regular downtime. Arrange to have someone—or several someones—fill in for you, perhaps for an hour every day or for several hours a couple of times a week. Get some exercise. Take a walk in the park. Meet a friend for lunch or tea. Participate in a book group or knitting club, play bridge, go to a movie—whatever suits your interests and can rekindle your spirit and energy. Relaxation is a psychic safety net that enables you to go back to caregiving refreshed and reenergized. A major report, "Caregiving in America," published in 2006 by the International Longevity

Center–USA, found that "finding time for oneself is the most frequently reported unmet need of family caregivers." Half of the more than one thousand caregivers surveyed said they had less time for family and friends and nearly half said they gave up vacations, hobbies, or social activities.

Eat regular, nutritious meals. Several people I know who cared for a loved one near the end of life lost weight and ended up looking old and haggard because they became so preoccupied with caregiving that they paid too little attention to their own meals. You should be eating three nutritious meals a day—a protein-rich food at every meal and lots of fruits and vegetables, with wholesome pick-me-ups between meals to sustain the energy you need for caregiving. If you're unable to prepare all such meals yourself, order in or ask family members or friends who've offered to help to bring you one good meal each day. Handy nutritious snacks include nuts, peanut butter, yogurt, and fresh fruit.

Find time to exercise. If you can't get out of the house to exercise, consider renting, borrowing, or buying indoor exercise equipment that you can use when the patient is asleep or not in immediate need of your services. Or get an exercise video and work out in front of the TV. Peggy, who was not able to get to her aerobics class while she cared for her dying relative, bought a video that enabled her to exercise for thirty or forty minutes a day without leaving the house. At first, she said, she felt guilty but then realized how much better she felt and better able to fulfill her caregiving tasks.

Get enough sleep. If you're up half the night caring for your loved one, try to nap during the day when the patient sleeps. If you are having trouble sleeping at night because you are anxious or depressed, talk to your doctor. A small dose of medication or a 3 mg tablet of melatonin (sold in health food stores and most pharmacies) may provide the relief you need.

Maintain your health care. If your health is neglected, you could become the next patient. Make sure you keep up with your own checkups, screenings, and medications. This is no time to put off routine physicals, mammograms, colonoscopies, or other such exams. Try to schedule your doctor appointments for a time when someone else can fill in for you as caregiver. Adopt a system that will help you remember to take your own medications and nutrient supplements. For example, you might set them out each week in a plastic Monday–Sunday pill planner, sold in most pharmacies, and take them at the same time each day.

Heed the signs of depression. Depression is a very common problem among family caregivers. Are you crying all the time, feeling overwhelmed or helpless, sleeping more or less than usual, lacking an appetite, or have you lost interest in activities you formerly enjoyed? Are you unduly irritable—"snappish"—or impatient, quick to fly off the handle or burst into tears when things don't go exactly as you had hoped or planned? Don't suppress your feelings—tears can bring relief. But don't wait until you suffer an emotional collapse to get help. Sometimes just talking to a good friend or empathetic health care provider about your feelings may be all you need to relieve your distress. Other times, professional counseling or antidepressant medication may be necessary. A study published in March 2000 in the *Annals of Internal Medicine* found that caregivers for terminally ill patients felt less depressed and better able to cope with their lives when they could talk to a doctor who simply listened to their problems and concerns about their loved ones.

Join a caregiver support group. If there is none in your area or you can't get out when the group meets, you may be able to participate in an online support group. Support groups are especially good for passing along tips that can make life easier for all who participate. You shouldn't have to reinvent the wheel. There's unlikely to be a challenge you face that others before you haven't already faced and resolved. Let them help you. For example, CancerCare, a national nonprofit organization that provides free professional support services for people affected, directly or indirectly, by cancer, offers face-to-face, telephone, and online support groups for caregivers of cancer patients. You can contact CancerCare by calling (800) 813-HOPE or by e-mail at info@cancercare.org.

Prepare yourself emotionally. This may well be the most challenging self-caring task. But as your loved one approaches the end of life, try to envision what your life will be like when your caregiving job is over. Will you return to work? Get involved with organizations that need volunteers? Pursue some long-postponed avocational interests—learn a new language, take art classes, become a master gardener? Having a plan for the future can ease your transition into life without the patient.

Prepare to reclaim your life. You should not feel guilty about this. After your loved one dies and legal and other necessities are out of the way, you deserve a vacation, perhaps a trip with a friend or a visit with relatives whose company you enjoy, or just some time alone in a beautiful place. Two weeks after her husband died of cancer, my friend Carole and I took a trip to Napa Valley and San Francisco, after which she returned home refreshed and better able to restart her life without her beloved mate of thirty-seven years.

How to Know and What to Do When the End Is Near

Family caregivers commonly fear that they will become terrified and not know what to do when their loved one is actively dying. It helps to know how to recognize when the body's systems are shutting down and death is near (see also chapter 7).

Symptoms commonly include rapid breathing, perhaps interspersed with periods of up to fifteen seconds of no breathing. The patient's arms and legs may become cold and look purplish, and as circulation slows, the underside of the body may be darker in color. The patient may spend more and more time sleeping, become difficult to arouse, refuse to eat or drink, and stop trying to communicate. You may notice a rattling sound (the infamous "death rattle") because secretions in the back of the patient's throat increase in volume and thicken.

When the end is very near, the patient's pulse gets weaker and breathing becomes shallower until both stop altogether. At the time of death, there is a loss of bladder and bowel control, the person is completely unresponsive, the jaw is relaxed and the mouth slightly open, and the eyes, which are slightly open, remain fixed on one spot.

The two most important roles for a caregiver at this time is to provide comforting touch and words during the dying process and to *refrain from calling 911*. Once emergency medical technicians are called in, they are obliged to do whatever they can to try to revive the patient. This only serves to prolong the agony of dying and usually results in the patient's dying in the hospital instead of at home, as the patient and/or caregiver wanted.

Wait twenty minutes after all signs of life seem to be gone before you call the physician or 911. This was the message given to my friend Linda when her ninety-four-year-old father was near death from congestive heart failure. The first time he seemed to stop breathing, she panicked and called 911, and the paramedics had no choice but to do everything in their power to keep him alive as they rushed him to the hospital. But they wisely told her that the next time this happens, she should wait twenty minutes before calling for medical assistance. A few days later, her father died peacefully at home.

Respect Wishes for Privacy or Company

Though most people say they don't want to be alone when they take their last breath, others want privacy. They do not want their survivors to live with the memory of witnessing their death, which is anything but a glamorous event. Fifty years later, I still have a clear picture in my mind of what my mother looked like the moment she died. And, to be honest, I wish I hadn't seen it.

My friend Helen was very upset when her longtime companion Bernie died the day she took time off for herself. She had sat at his bedside in a hospital hospice unit every day for weeks. But the very day the hospice nurse encouraged her to take a break was the day he died. Although there is no way to know this for sure, it is possible that he had clung to life as long as Helen was there, and he was finally able to "let go" when she left.

"It seems that some dying people actually choose the moment of their departure to coincide with their loved ones leaving the room," according to Susan R. Dolan, a registered nurse and former hospice volunteer. "On countless occasions I've witnessed family members, cramped and tired from lengthy bedside vigils, take a coffee break or seek a breath of fresh air and return to find that death had arrived," she wrote with her mother, Audrey R. Vizzard, in *From the Start Consider the Finish: A Guide to Excellent End-of-Life Care.*

However, for the vast majority of patients who would rather not die alone in a hospital, there is now a growing number of programs in hospitals and hospices around the country that arrange for trained volunteers to sit with patients who are actively dying, including those who are unconscious. One program, called No One Dies Alone, was introduced in 2001 by a nurse, Sandra Clarke, at Sacred Heart Medical Center in Eugene, Oregon. Volunteers— off-duty hospital employees or hospital volunteers—agree to be on call for one or more three-hour shifts each month. They may read, sing, pray, or talk to the patient, hold the patient's hand, or just sit quietly nearby.

Or, if the patient prefers to be alone, the volunteer may sit outside the room and just "be there"—a human presence as another life passes on to the Great Beyond.

FOR FURTHER READING

American Medical Association Guide to Home Caregiving. New York: John Wiley & Sons, 2001.

Flynn, Peggy. *The Caregiving Zone.* Lincoln, NE: iUniverse, 2006.

Ilardo, Joseph A., and Carole R. Rothman. *I'll Take Care of You: A Practical Guide for Family Caregivers.* Oakland, CA: New Harbinger, 1999.

Levine, Carole, ed. *Always On Call: When Illness Turns Families into Caregivers.* New York: United Hospital Fund of New York, 2000.

McLeod, Beth Witrogen. *Caregiving: The Spiritual Journey of Love, Loss, and Renewal.* New York: John Wiley & Sons, 1999.

Meyer, Maria M., with Paula Derr. *The Comfort of Home: A Complete Guide for Caregivers.* Portland, OR: CareTrust, 2007.

CHAPTER **9**

Hospice and Palliative Care: Don't Wait Until It's Too Late

Franklin Wyman was eighty-five years old when he was diagnosed with acute leukemia in December 2006. Rather than rush into treatment, he took time to review his options. He could choose aggressive treatment that might, or might not, buy him a year, or he could return to his suburban home where he and his wife could get whatever help they needed from Partners Hospice in Waltham, Massachusetts. Franklin chose home, where he could spend his days reading, surfing the Internet, and visiting with friends and family. "It's important to me to maintain my dignity until the very end and to be a good example for my family," he told Linda Keslar, a writer for *Protomag*.

A hospice nurse visited to check on him and make sure he had whatever medication he needed. A walker, wheelchair, and a portable oxygen generator were delivered for future use. Clinicians were at the ready to address any causes of discomfort. And a pastoral counselor and medical social worker were on hand to help him and his family with issues like depression, anxiety, and spirituality. At no time did Mr. Wyman doubt the wisdom of his choice.

An Underused Resource

Of the approximately 2.4 million deaths that occur among Americans each year, only 10 percent are sudden deaths, with no chance or need to make dying any easier for the patients or their loved ones. That leaves more than 2 million people who die of protracted illnesses, often with their last days or weeks on earth devastated by incapacitating pain, breathing difficulties, anxiety, depression, confusion, insomnia, nausea, vomiting, constipation, or other symptoms that can now be relieved by doctors who specialize in palliative medicine.

It is precisely such symptoms that hospice care was designed to treat. Symptoms that make it difficult or impossible for people near death to communicate effectively with loved ones, to right wrongs, to get their affairs in order, and to die in peace instead of torment. Symptoms that often leave families plagued with nightmarish memories of a death gone wrong.

Yet forty years after the first modern hospice was founded, about half of Americans are still dying without its many benefits. In 2005 more than 1.2 million Americans received hospice care. But many of them reaped the benefits of that service only during the last few days of life, cheating themselves and their families of the many benefits that hospice could have brought to their last weeks or months of life. After they die, their survivors nearly always say they wished they had accessed hospice care sooner.

As was aptly stated in a 2003 report, "Access to Hospice Care," compiled by the Hastings Center, "Death is an inevitable aspect of the human condition. Dying badly is not."

The report goes on to lament the fact that "too many Americans die unnecessarily bad deaths—deaths with inadequate palliative support, inadequate compassion, and inadequate human presence and witness. Deaths preceded by a dying marked by fear, anxiety, loneliness, and isolation. Deaths that efface dignity and deny individual self-control and choice.

"Although the acceptance and utilization of palliative and hospice care have grown, there are still over one million Americans who die each year without receiving the hospice or hospice-type services that would have benefited them and their families."

Dr. Gail Gazelle of Brigham and Women's Hospital in Boston says misunderstandings by both physicians and patients are largely responsible for the fact that hospice care is not nearly universal among those who die over a period of days, weeks, or months. Some think it is only for terminally ill cancer patients. Not true. Less than half of hospice patients have terminal cancer, Dr. Gazelle wrote in the *New England Journal of Medicine* in July 2007. "Nearly 40 percent of hospice admissions are for end-stage cardiac disease, end-stage dementia, debility, pulmonary disease, and stroke," she wrote.

Also, many mistakenly think hospice necessarily involves placing the dying person in a hospital-like facility. Not so. Hospice care is most often provided in a person's own home. Some people also mistakenly fear the expense. Again, not so. Medicare, the primary provider for 80 percent of hospice care, covers nearly every expense related to the terminal diagnosis for patients on Medicare, including all medication and equipment and all visits by hospice nurses and home health aides. Hospice services also include intensive emotional and spiritual counseling, twenty-four-hour crisis management, and bereavement support for at least one year after the patient dies. Most private insurers have adopted the coverage policies of Medicare, but you'd be wise to look into a non-Medicare patient's coverage before calling in hospice. However, since most hospice facilities are nonprofit organizations, the inability to pay for some or all of the care they provide may not be a barrier to their services.

The word *hospice* is rooted in the Latin concept of *hospitium,* or hospitality. Hospice is really not a modern concept. It originated in medieval times, when the term described a refuge where members of a religious order cared for sick and dying pilgrims. In 1967 a British physician, Dame Cicely Saunders, revived the term, establishing St. Christopher's Hospice in a London suburb that was devoted exclusively to the care of dying patients. Her disciples founded the first American hospice, the Branford Hospice, in 1971 in New Haven, Connecticut.

Today, hospice is considered the "gold standard" for end-of-life care. A recent study of 4,493 terminally ill patients found that, on average, those who chose hospice care lived a month longer than those who did not. Yet hospice remains sadly underutilized.

How Hospice Can Help

The goals of hospice care, as listed in the *Journal of the American Medical Association,* are to:

- Manage pain and any other symptoms that cause discomfort or distress.

- Create a comfortable environment for the patient.

- Allow the patient to be close to family and loved ones during the dying process.

- Give relief to the patient's caregivers.

- Offer counseling for the patient and those close to the patient.

Invariably, in study after study, families of patients who died while receiving hospice care have said that losing their loved one was far less painful than it might otherwise have been. Even grieving their loss was said to be easier.

Linda A. O'Brien, a geriatric nurse researcher and educator in Moorestown, New Jersey, described the humane care her mother received in a hospital-based hospice unit: "My mother experienced a massive heart attack and sustained severe heart muscle damage, although not enough damage to die immediately. It took her more than a week to make the journey, with increased breathlessness each day. She was moved to a beautiful hospice room from the intensive care unit. There she was lovingly cared for by family members, wonderful nurses, and pastoral care providers. My mother was kept pain-free and comfortable with a continuous morphine drip. She heard us, smiled, cried, and alternatively clung to us. We told stories of our family and our fondest memories of our childhood and growing up. We told her we loved her and that she was a wonderful mother. We wept, we hugged, and we laughed. My last memory of this incredibly important person to me is a slight knowing and noncommittal smile and one final sigh."

Probably no one has done more to get out the good word about hospice care than the strangest of bedfellows—"a man who would not die"—the humor columnist Art Buchwald. In the fall of 2006, just months after he became perhaps the only person to leave a Washington, D.C., hospice alive and well, his last book, *Too Soon to Say Goodbye*, was published describing in glowing terms what he had assumed would be comfort care for his last days on earth.

At age eighty, having lost half a leg to gangrene, having his kidneys shut down, and having been told he'd have to be on dialysis for the rest of his life, Mr. Buchwald told his doctor "enough already," he was ready to die. And so he entered a calm, clean, and caring hospice facility to await the Grim Reaper, which the doctor thought would pay him a visit within a few weeks.

But to everyone's surprise, especially his doctor's, Mr. Buchwald didn't die. Instead, his kidneys started working again—and continued working, allowing him to enjoy visits with his family and many friends and dignitaries and to write his book. Finally, after five months of having "a swell time—the best time of my life" in the hospice facility, Mr. Buchwald checked himself out and returned home to the ordinary life of a famous funny old man, living another six months until his kidneys failed once again.

With his book and columns, Mr. Buchwald said he hoped he's made *hospice* a household word. As he put it in the book, "Unless they've had some experience with it, the hospice is still a mystery to most people. Because hospice deals with death, people tend not to talk about it."

Yet he added, "The hospice gives a person the opportunity to die with dignity. It provides care, help, and as much comfort as possible." And not just for the person who is dying. "When the patient enters the hospice, an entire team sets to work to meet the family's needs—a doctor, a team of nurses, a case manager, a social worker, a chaplain, a nursing assistant, a bereavement coordinator, and of course, the volunteers."

Coincidentally, a few months after Mr. Buchwald left the Washington hospice, my brother-in-law, who was in the last stages of an incurable cancer, checked into the very same one. On a visit there, I witnessed firsthand the attention and caring to his pain, respiratory symptoms, personal hygiene, and spiritual needs provided by an ever-patient staff. Alas, my brother-in-law was not as lucky as Mr. Buchwald—his disease was unquestionably fatal—but clearly his distress was constantly kept to a minimum, allowing him unlimited access to family and friends to the degree he could tolerate.

As I mentioned earlier, hospice care is not only available in an outside facility. It can also be provided in the patient's home, as long as someone in the home is able and willing to serve as primary caregiver. In a letter to me at *The New York Times,* John E. Doherty of Oak Brook, Illinois, described the very peaceful end of his wife, Jeanne, whom he married in 1954. Jeanne was diagnosed with advanced liver cancer on March 3, 2006. Her oncologist immediately recommended hospice care, and Mr. Doherty wrote that after learning what hospice was all about, "We decided to try it.

> *The people that came into our home were the most knowledgeable, caring people I have run into in my lifetime. They knew their patient almost immediately, made her comfortable, treated her with respect and always deferred to her wishes.*
>
> *Jeanne died at home on March 29, 2006, her final days made tolerable by having the family nearby and hospice personnel always on call. I miss her very much, but I do know*

*that even though she was dying she always had a smile for us
and she and the hospice people made the whole episode easier
to accept.*

Many Wait Too Long to Enroll

Most patients who enter hospice receive its benefits for only a
short time. The average length of stay is less than three weeks.
One-third of patients enroll in the last week of life, and 10 percent
enroll in the last day of life. This is rarely enough time for hospice
personnel to establish a meaningful relationship with the patient
and the patient's family. It is often not enough time for personnel
to determine exactly what is needed to relieve the patient's pain
and other symptoms. It is just *not enough time.*

Why the delay? There are many reasons, starting with the fact
that Medicare has placed a six-month limit on the length of hospice care, and private insurers have followed Medicare's lead. This
limit requires the referring physician to "certify" that the patient is
highly unlikely to live six months longer. Physicians are notoriously
poor at prognosticating (see chapter 5), and with many chronic
diseases—like congestive heart failure or Parkinson's disease—it is
impossible to say just how much time a patient has left. Only when
patients are in the final stages of cancer or AIDS are doctors likely
to accurately assess their remaining life expectancy within a matter
of weeks.

Second, Medicare and most insurers require that patients entering hospice care give up any and all therapy that might prolong
their lives. Only treatments that ease their symptoms are covered
by Medicare. When patients or their families cling to the hope that
continued aggressive treatment—or a new therapy that may come
along—will abate the progress of the disease, they are understandably reluctant to abandon this possibility.

However, a few large hospices that can spread their costs among
hundreds of patients have expanded their coverage. They have

adopted an open-access policy to make the hospice program more available to patients who are willing to forgo disease-directed treatments but not those therapies that might keep them alive long enough, say, to attend a daughter's wedding or witness a grandchild's birth. In 2006 Capital Hospice, based in Washington, D.C., which cares for an average of more than eight hundred patients a day, paid for palliative chemotherapy, radiation, dialysis, blood transfusions, parenteral nutrition, antibiotics, and other costly intravenous medications.

Dr. Wendy Schlessel Harpham, who writes an award-winning column in *Oncology Times*, maintains that *hospice* and *hope* are not mutually exclusive. She wrote, "Hospice nurtures patients' hope as they approach the sunset of their survivorship. This hope takes a variety of forms: hope for being at home where they are more in control of their lives, for dignity and serenity, for meaningful interchange with loved ones, and for whatever other hopes grow large as their lives wind down."

Dr. David Casarett and colleagues in Philadelphia interviewed family members of one hundred patients who died in hospice. The interviews were conducted two months after the patients had died. Nearly all said there were aspects of hospice care they wished they had learned of sooner, particularly the availability of the hospice team and visiting nurse twenty-four hours a day, the coordination of care and services, and the spiritual and emotional support, which many had not realized they needed.

Dr. Casarett followed with a second study, recontacting family members one month after the patient's death. Families of patients with longer stays in hospice reported that they received more services, and that the services they received were more helpful. They identified *three months*—not three weeks, currently the average hospice stay—as the optimal length of hospice care. Of the families who said that enrollment was too late, 74 percent of patients had a length of stay of less than three weeks.

Most patients and their families wait for the doctor to say it is time to consider calling in hospice. But in addition to the general reluctance of physicians to predict a patient's remaining life expectancy, many doctors try, consciously or otherwise, to deny mortality. They are trained to fight disease with every weapon at their command and often view the death of a patient as a personal failure. Referral to hospice is a frank admission of that failure.

Many doctors also believe that referring a patient to hospice will be taken as a sign that the doctor has given up and will strip the patient of what little hope may remain for a better outcome. But, in fact, it is the rare patient in the terminal stages of illness who is unaware of the gravity of the situation. More often than not, a frank discussion with the patient about the unlikelihood of any future improvement comes as a great relief—the elephant in the room is finally acknowledged—and the patient can be freed of the toxic or painful effects of further treatment.

But doctors are not the only ones responsible for late enrollment in hospice. Patients and/or patients' families are also sometimes in denial about the futility of continued treatment of advanced disease, even in the most extreme cases. Common reactions from patients are "I am not that sick" or "I don't need hospice yet." And doctors are understandably reluctant to push a terminal prognosis on a patient or family that is not ready to accept it.

As a result, most hospice professionals can tell horror stories of receiving patients in the last days or even hours of life. As described in a report in *Patient Care* magazine, "When a patient comes into hospice very late in the course of illness, there is simply not enough time to realize the benefits hospice can confer. Finding the right combination of palliative measures takes time; so does relieving the patient's anxieties and fears and assisting the family in adjusting to their impending loss."

Drs. K. Mitchell Russell and Susan B. LeGrand of the Center for Palliative Medicine at the Cleveland Clinic put it this way in June 2006 in the *Cleveland Clinic Journal of Medicine:*

"Hospice care is optimal when relationships between the hospice team and the patient and family have time to develop. Experienced hospice workers help prepare patients and families for what they can expect throughout the stages of illness and dying, what to do when common symptoms arise, and how to react when unforeseen events occur. When patients are already too ill or time is too short, adequate preparation is left unrealized."

And while it is true that hope for a remission or cure of the patient's illness is necessarily abandoned when hospice is called in, hope can be refocused on different goals, like "spending quality time with loved ones and finding closure to strained relationships or unfinished business," Drs. Russell and LeGrand said. "Hope should not interfere with the planning and providing of realistic care for present needs."

For patients who are reluctant to abandon the idea that they might get better, the doctor or family members might respond, "Let's hope for the best and prepare for the worst."

Before a decision about hospice is made, it is important that patients know they can leave hospice at any time if their condition improves and they want additional life-sustaining therapy. This would not compromise their ability to return to hospice later if the therapy proves ineffective, intolerable, or inconsistent with their goals.

Hospice Provides Palliative Care

Palliative care is synonymous with comfort care. It focuses on relieving such symptoms as pain, anxiety, nausea, and breathing difficulty. It also includes emotional, social, and spiritual support for patients and their families.

In theory, every patient (and patient's family), whether soon to die or on the road to recovery, should receive palliative care. Unlike hospice care, which is a subdivision of palliative care, palliative care is not conditional on either a patient's limited life expectancy nor a need to relinquish possibly curative or life-prolonging therapy.

These are the palliative care services you should expect from hospice:

- **Pain management.** Pain and the distress it causes can nearly always be relieved and often entirely eliminated in patients receiving hospice care. Hospice health professionals strive to identify the sources of pain and provide relief with drugs or other methods (see Palliative sedation below). Too often, outside of hospice care, physicians are reluctant to administer adequate doses of pain medication to dying patients for fear of causing addiction. This is ridiculous on its face, since it matters not a whit if someone who is dying becomes addicted to opioids.

- **Symptom management.** In addition to treating pain, hospice aims to relieve such symptoms as nausea and vomiting, weakness, bowel and bladder problems, mental confusion, fatigue, and difficulty breathing. In many cases, a common remedy for pain relief—morphine administered by mouth or continuous drip—also alleviates breathing problems and the anxiety that accompanies them.

- **Emotional and spiritual support.** This kind of help, often provided by social workers and pastoral counselors in hospice, is vital for both patients and their families when dealing with the stresses of critical illness and impending death.

- **Support services.** When patients are receiving home hospice care, families must be told about the patient's problems and be advised about when and how to give medication and recognize symptoms that require immediate medical attention. Some hospices help with transportation, shopping, and preparing meals. And some provide respite care—time off for the primary caregiver. Help with financial problems and creating a support network of other family members, friends, neighbors, or clergy may also be provided.

- **Palliative sedation.** Sometimes dying patients—especially those dying of cancer—experience distressing symptoms, like intolerable pain, difficulty breathing, or uncontrollable shaking, that cannot be adequately relieved by standard therapies. Such symptoms destroy the possibility of a peaceful death and are extremely distressing not only for the patient but also for the family. In such cases, the only option is to administer medication that induces unconsciousness. This should be done only when other means of symptom relief have proved ineffective or have caused intolerable side effects. It is done to relieve symptoms, not to shorten the patient's life, though that is a likely consequence. It is also done when the patient is so close to dying that any effect on the length of survival will be minimal. Doctors who use palliative sedation operate under the doctrine of double effect. According to this doctrine, intentionally causing death is wrong. But without incurring any legal risk, physicians may order high doses of opioids and sedatives as long as the intent is to relieve suffering and not to cause the patient's death.

Sources of Hospice Care

There are many ways today in which hospice care can be accessed:

- Especially in large metropolitan areas, there may be one or more free-standing hospice facilities, often affiliated with a nearby hospital.

- Most larger hospitals now have hospice units within their walls and can easily move patients from intensive care units or medical beds into hospice beds.

- A growing number of nursing homes now also have hospice units or an affiliation with a hospice organization that provides access to twenty-four-hour hospice personnel.

- Assisted living facilities also sometimes maintain affiliations with hospice providers. Consider checking on this before moving a frail or ailing elderly person into such a facility.

- Hospice care can be provided in a private home, as long as there is someone available at home who is able and willing to serve as the primary caregiver. Hospice personnel visit one or more times a day, as needed, sometimes supplemented by a visiting nurse service. *Note:* it is important for patients receiving hospice care at home to have a "do not resuscitate" notice posted on their refrigerator or some other prominent place in the home.

To avoid having to make a decision during a time of acute emotional stress or dire physical need, it is a good idea to make inquiries about hospice care well before it is needed. If home hospice care is not an option, try to find a service near enough so that loved ones can visit the patient as often as they might want.

To locate hospice services in a particular area, you might start by contacting the National Hospice and Palliative Care Organization at (703) 837-1500, or log on to the organization's website—www.nhpco.org—and click on Find a Provider. The organization recommends that when contacting a hospice facility or provider, you ask the following questions:

- What services are provided? Specifically, you might want to know if costly treatments to relieve symptoms, like blood or platelet transfusions or radiation therapy, are available. Also inquire about the availability of pastoral or spiritual services for both the patient and the patient's family.

- What kind of support is available to the family/caregiver? Does the hospice provide respite care for a caregiver who needs a break? How does the hospice program help family members cope with the patient's death?

- What roles do the attending physician and hospice play? Patients should not have to terminate their relationship with the physician who had been in charge of their care prior to entering hospice. You may also want to know how many patients are assigned to each staff member.

- What does the hospice volunteer do? Can a volunteer run errands for the patient or family, or visit with the patient when family members or friends cannot be there?

- How does hospice arrange to keep the patient comfortable? Does the staff regularly discuss pain and symptom control with patients and their families?

- How are services provided after hours?

- Can hospice be brought into a nursing home or long-term care facility or the patient's home?

- Are all hospice expenses covered by Medicare or the patient's private insurance?

The Hospice and Palliative Care Organization has also established an online program, Caring Connections, that provides free information and resources for coordinating end-of-life care. The program is accessed through www.caringinfo.org. Another helpful Internet source is www.hospicenet.org.

A HOSPICE DOCTOR FINDS JOY

Dr. Michael J. Brescia, executive medical director of Calvary Hospital, a hospice network in New York City, got "hooked" on hospice as a young physician just getting started when a friend asked him to fill in for him on a New Year's weekend in 1962.

Forty-six years later he is still there. Here, excerpted from a letter to supporters, is how he described the potential transformation that can takes place in a well-run hospice.

So often when I first enter the room of a new patient brought to Calvary from another hospital, my heart breaks.

A dear woman has been badly neglected. Her hair is a mess. She is pale and thin because she is often so nauseous she can't eat. Pain distorts her face so that she has to force a smile.

Her daughter and her son sit at her side, tense and vigilant to make sure we don't add to their beloved mother's suffering. The first thing I do is to thank them for coming to us and giving me the opportunity to serve them. I truly believe it is my honor to be with them and to serve them at this crucial time in a person's life and a family's life. I know there is so much I can do to relieve their suffering.

And there is so much suffering to be relieved. There is the physical suffering of the patient, of course. It still angers and frustrates me that too many doctors and nurses turn away from patients once the possibility of cure is lost. But beyond the physical suffering, the fact of abandonment causes enormous emotional suffering. It makes you a non-person. And that is the ultimate suffering.

I tell every new doctor who comes to Calvary, "You must learn to heal the family, as well as the patient." Young doctors need mentors and instruction in how to relieve suffering. Sadly, they rarely get that in medical school. It's my dream that some day, all doctors will think of themselves as comforters as well as healers.

FOR FURTHER READING

Buchwald, Art. *Too Soon to Say Goodbye.* New York: Random House, 2006.

Dolan, Susan R., and Audrey R. Vizzard. *From the Start Consider the Finish: A Guide to Excellent End-of-Life Care.* Parker, CO: Outskirts Press, 2007.

Fins, Joseph J. *A Palliative Ethic of Care: Clinical Wisdom at Life's End.* Sudbury, MA: Jones & Bartlett, 2006.

"I see it! I see it! That bright white light! Quick! Get me my straw hat, my cane, and my tap shoes!"

CHAPTER 10

Spiritual Care: Lighten and Enlighten an End-of-Life Journey

When Jan Jeffrey received a life-threatening diagnosis of a cancer that would wipe out her blood's ability to clot and her immune system, she knew she was, as she put it, "at the bottom of a pit." But out of the depths, she said, "I called to thee O Lord. I realized I had two choices: to live each day to its max, or go into a deep depression. So I chose the more positive route."

Jan began an e-mail saga of her journey through cancer and what she had learned about life along the way. The most important lesson, perhaps, was not to postpone living. She said, "I have no regrets. Bill and I lived each day. We didn't wait until we retired. We hiked in the Alps, in the Rockies. We did all these wonderful things."

Of her extensive e-mail correspondence, she said, "It was the best support I had. It was so therapeutic to share my experiences and get responses back, ultimately from about two hundred people. I reconnected with a lot of people—high school friends and others I've known through the years. This was probably more therapeutic than all the chemotherapy I received during these last two years.

"If I've learned anything from my experience, it's to be open about it. It seems like *everyone's* so frightened of death."

Jan, in effect, constructed her own spiritual course to carry her through two and a half years of illness to the end, which she faced with great equanimity. But Jan was an unusual take-charge person, a characteristic that enabled her to muster all the emotional and spiritual support she needed to remain positive to her dying day. Most people need help to identify and give voice to their spiritual needs and to find ways to fulfill them. Failing to do so can make the dying experience far more traumatic than it might otherwise be.

As Karen E. Steinhauser, PhD, a palliative care specialist in Durham, North Carolina, and her coauthors stated in the *Archives of Internal Medicine* in 2006, "Dying patients confront complex spiritual concerns that influence the course of their illness, treatments chosen, relationships with loved ones, and overall quality of life." Yet these concerns are widely ignored by the physicians and nurses who care for patients struggling with life-threatening disease.

While professionals—clergymen, social workers, and sometimes doctors and nurses—may be called upon to assist dying patients through their spiritual journey, family members and friends are generally more available and can be as effective, or even more effective, in this role. In this chapter you will learn just how important attention to spirituality can be at life's end and how you, as well as trained professionals, can participate.

Spirituality Versus Religiosity

People who are deeply religious often turn to a higher power to provide the comfort they need to pass from life to death with minimal emotional trauma. My mother-in-law, for example, who believed in an afterlife and felt her fate was in God's hands, had no qualms about dying and needed little or no hand-holding when her time came. At age eighty-four she had lived a full life, given much to many, and left several marvelous legacies for her community and family to cherish. In her last hours, with her minister at her bedside, she was able to say good-bye to three generations of relatives and friends who loved and admired her.

If only dying was always that simple! More often than not, even among people with strong religious beliefs, spiritual issues arise that health care professionals may not recognize or may think they are not capable of addressing or have no responsibility to address. But failing to take these issues into account and confront and resolve them when possible often compromises treatment plans and can seriously complicate the dying process.

First, I should clarify the distinction between religiosity and spirituality. A religion is a set of texts, practices, and beliefs about the transcendent that are shared by a particular community. Religiosity is defined by the strength of one's beliefs or by the frequency of one's religious practices. Deeply religious people often do not fear death; some even welcome it because they believe it will take them to a better place.

Spirituality is about a person's relationship with the transcendent questions that confront one as a human being and how a person relates to these questions. Spirituality *can* be about a relationship with a higher power, but it can also be about nature, art, music, family, or community—the beliefs and values that give a person's life meaning and purpose. Spirituality involves such matters as a person's relationships with family members or friends; the meaning of the person's illness, suffering, and death; the value of the person's life and what of value might persist after the person dies.

Spiritual care, then, helps people who are dying feel whole, fulfilled, and in harmony with their world and the people in it. Those who are dying need to know that they are valued. Regardless of a person's religious persuasion, attention to spirituality fulfills a deep, basic human need.

In their very helpful little book, *Parting: A Handbook for Spiritual Care Near the End of Life,* Jennifer Sutton Holder and Jann Aldredge-Clanton point out that attending to spiritual needs often brings relief from pain or improves the person's ability to cope with pain. They tell the story of Manuel, who, as he lay dying with unmanageable pain, expressed deep anguish over the many years during which he had been alienated from his son Tony. A sister succeeded in locating Tony, who immediately tape-recorded a message to his father, telling him he loved him and he wanted bygones to be bygones. Manuel listened again and again to the tape, his pain lessening with each repetition.

Prepare Yourself Spiritually

Erin Tierney Kramp was hovering between life and death, secluded in a "bubble" room with an abdominal infection and no immune system to combat it, when she began what she called a spiritual journey. She reestablished a deep relationship with God, who taught her that "it did not matter *what* I did in my life, whether I swept floors, became a surgeon, created companies, or gave all my money to charity. What mattered was not what I did, but *how I did it.* Did I allow God's love to flow through me as I lived every day? Was I compassionate, and did I touch the souls of the people around me?"

In the incredible book she coauthored, *Living with the End in Mind* (which, I am sad to say, is out of print, which is why I quote it extensively below), she described her approach to spirituality. "I did not evaluate my life based on my present circumstances. Instead, I envisioned my life coming to an end, reviewing my life with God, and then worked backward. My spirit led the way. I realized I could reach out to people, one soul at a time. If all I did was to improve someone's day or lighten a person's load, I would be living according to my purpose."

Her husband, Doug, also reestablished his connection to God during the rocky course of his wife's ultimately fatal illness. This reconnection with God gave him "an immediate sense of relief" and helped him face the enormous challenges ahead. "Looking back on the last four years, Doug says there was no way he could have handled it all without his relationship with God. Despite everything he has been through, his life has flourished. Both of us are convinced we could not have weathered the last few years so well without God's hand holding us up.

"Only through our spiritual selves did Doug and I achieve a sense of inner peace and well-being. As we integrated the spiritual with the physical, mental, and emotional, we achieved a balance and happiness we had never felt before. We have come to believe that our internal joy at the time of death rests primarily on our spiritual well-being."

The Kramps' advice? They point out that "preparing yourself spiritually does not necessarily mean choosing a religion." It means "taking time to define your beliefs, meditate and pray, and reflect on your purpose in the world." It means choosing "your spiritual tenets in the context of the inevitability of your death." It means taking "time to think about your spiritual beliefs in the context of eternity." Among their many recommendations as to how to incorporate spirituality into your life are these:

- Spend time with people who "exude spiritual strength," people who can "reinforce your faith and dedication to your highest priorities, and can allow you to explore meaningful spiritual issues that may otherwise go ignored."

- Resolve issues that have created a wedge between you and others in your life. "Contact people whom you have hurt in some way or about whom you feel remorse. Ask for their forgiveness. Bring issues that have come between you out in the open."

- Read inspiring books or listen to inspiring books on tape. Whether or not you agree with their messages, they can help you think about and question your own beliefs and give you "an opportunity to deepen your spirituality and avoid the stagnation that can come from complacence."

- Rejoice in your trials. This may sound like a tall order when facing a life-threatening illness or certain death. Yet Erin wrote that "I am thankful for the last four years. Without my illness, I would not have experienced so much emotional and spiritual growth. I would have continued to live my easy life, coasting along, and would have missed out on all there was to learn by facing up to the challenge."

• Live your life in light of your sense of purpose. "As you discover your purpose in the world, allow your convictions to govern your actions every day." She suggested that "each morning, whether you are healthy or ill, consider that you have another day to live your life" and "think about how you can integrate into your daily life what's important to you. You might find your mind calming down while you actually enjoy and accomplish more each day."

• If you are living with a life-threatening illness, "create an environment that is conducive to spirituality." Erin spent a lot of time in her bedroom while battling her illness. She kept spiritual readings and a tape player with scripture on tape nearby, and when she awoke at night feeling weak and anxious, she turned to their "positive affirmations" to help calm her. Others may find themselves calmed by photographs, plants, music, poetry—whatever helps them stay in touch with their spiritual selves.

The Kramps are at heart a religious family that became reunited with their faith in God when faced with a life-threatening crisis. But humanists—those with no religious affiliation or inclination but who view this life as all there is and a moral life as desirable in itself—can also face spiritual crises when approaching the end of life. As Julian Baggini and Madeleine Pym wrote in 2005 in the medical journal the *Lancet*, "As death approaches, people of all beliefs often feel the need to unburden themselves of past secrets or achieve some form of closure in unresolved difficulties. Dying can be as fearful for humanists as for anyone else. Humanists' needs are not fewer than, just different from, those of religious believers."

What Family and Friends Can Do

"Parting," as Romeo and Juliet knew so well, "is such sweet sorrow." Ideally, this would also be true for everyone approaching the end of life. Of course, we live in a real, not an ideal, world. But even in our real world, it can be possible—and it is certainly desirable—for as many people as possible to be at spiritual peace at the end of their lives.

In their aptly titled book, *Parting*, Ms. Holder, a geriatrics chaplain, and Ms. Aldredge-Clanton, chaplain coordinator for oncology at Baylor University Medical Center in Houston, provide guidance for lay companions who hope to ease the spiritual passage for someone who is dying. These are among the many approaches they have found helpful:

Presence. Your mere presence lets those who are dying know they are not alone. Your promise should be "I will come back; I will not abandon you" and you must be sure to fulfill it.

Listening. People who are dying often face questions about the meaning of life. Your job is not necessarily to provide answers or solutions but to listen, to let them speak freely and openly without advice or contradiction.

Acceptance. Do not deny that death is near. Rather, affirm that the person's life and accomplishments have meaning and offer assurance of value and love.

Candor. Let it be known that no topic is verboten—you're willing to talk about anything, even things no one else wants to hear or should hear. You may not be able to help the person resolve feelings of guilt or resentment, but just letting the person give voice to them can be healing in and of itself.

Humor. Dying need not be a deadly serious affair. The more humor that can be introduced into the process, the less dreadful it is likely to seem. Don't be surprised if humor is introduced by the patient; go along with it for as long as you and the patient are enjoying it.

Patience. Mood swings are common among the dying and can sometimes try the patience of the calmest of spiritual caregivers. One day you may find the patient praying for a quick end to this life. The next day, when you may be grieving in anticipation of your loss, you may find the patient laughing and cracking jokes with a visitor. If the patient doesn't feel like talking, don't be afraid to be silent; your presence speaks loudly enough.

Advocacy. Find out how the dying person wants to be cared for and do whatever you can to make that happen. Help the person achieve maximum physical comfort, since pain and other debilitating symptoms can block the path to spiritual peace.

Courage. Don't be afraid to be vulnerable and face hard questions like "Why me? Did I do something wrong?" Your job is to validate, not contradict, the feelings of the dying person, regardless of what they are—anger, fear, pain, guilt, joy, or peace.

Hope. Stay focused on whatever form of hope is achievable—a visit from a grandchild, a more comfortable day, a chance to sit outside and see the flowers or listen to the birds.

Creativity. Try to come up with pleasant surprises, such as a musician or musical group the patient is likely to enjoy, memorable decorations for the patient's room—whatever meshes with the person's interests and pleasures during healthier times.

Sensitivity. Choose wisely when deciding to engage in spiritual conversations. Take the person's mood, discomfort level, and interests into consideration. Spiritual content can be drawn from any of a wealth of topics—old times, trips taken, antics of children, recipes gone awry. When visiting my brother-in-law Gordon in a Washington, D.C., hospice, my husband regaled him with memories from their childhood, including some naughty adventures, which conveyed the message to Gordon that he would not be forgotten.

You may find it challenging at times to engage the patient in conversations that go beyond the superficial—What did you eat today? Are you comfortable? Shall I open the curtain?—and instead delve into deeper spiritual issues. You might try to broach the spiritual by asking such questions as: What is most important to you now? What do you hope for? Is there anything you are afraid of? Are there things you are worried about that we might discuss? What might be a source of comfort for you—music, scriptures, hymns, art, inspirational writing, pleasant memories?

When the patient you are trying to help resists opening up, try to think of what might enable you to bridge the gap between conversations that are superficial and those that are enriching and deeply meaningful.

Ms. Holder and Ms. Aldredge-Clanton described a woman named Susan whose father was dying in hospice. But Susan couldn't seem to move the conversation beyond the daily "numbers game"—medical readings like blood pressure, oxygen level, and pulse rate. Then she hit upon an idea. She made a list of "Your Ten Best Gifts" from father to daughter and at an appropriate time read them aloud to her father. The two of them cried together. Thereafter, their conversations "went to deeper, richer places of the soul," and Susan's list continues to provide her with happy memories of her father long after he died.

What Doctors Can Do

In a survey of hospitalized patients published in 1994 in the *Journal of Family Practice,* 77 percent said their doctors should consider their spiritual needs, 37 percent wanted their doctor to discuss religious beliefs with them, 48 percent wanted their doctors to pray with them, and 68 percent said their doctors had never discussed religious beliefs with them.

Dr. Christina Puchalski, a geriatrician who has designed a "spiritual assessment" for physicians and others to use when interviewing dying patients, notes that while medicine has become increasingly technical and time-pressured in recent decades, the nontechnical aspects of medicine have been sorely neglected. Few doctors are trained to discuss nonphysical reasons for a patient's suffering, and few take the time to find out what gives a person's life meaning and purpose—the time to see the *person* beneath the *patient*. It is time, she says, to reestablish the "compassionate, caregiving roots of the doctor–patient relationship."

One of Dr. Puchalski's patients told her, "I'm a naturalist, and looking at trees makes me feel really centered and with purpose." The woman added that if she were dying, she would want to be in a hospice with a window next to some trees, because that's what gives her life meaning and purpose. As the doctor pointed out, this is not the kind of information that would emerge from a typical medical assessment, or even from a psychosocial interview that asks how a patient is coping with illness.

Even a physician who lacks special skills in dealing with spiritual issues can help by paying attention to "patients' ultimate concerns, by being present with them and demonstrating that they are worthy of time and attention, and by listening to what the dying have to tell about life and its meaning," wrote Dr. Daniel P. Sulmasy, medical ethicist at St. Vincent's Hospital and New York Medical College.

A deeply religious person is not immune to having spiritual issues, some of which may be related to the person's religious beliefs. Some people, for example, have an unsophisticated relationship with God; they think childlike thoughts—"If I pray, God will cure me"—and when that doesn't happen they feel abandoned and despairing. Or a patient may say, "I really believe in

God, but I'm wondering if he's there for me right now. I'm feeling very abandoned by him." Dr. Puchalski said she might talk to such a patient herself or defer to a chaplain who can help the patient sort out this issue and come to some kind of resolution. "There's no magic fix. You can't give a pill for that," she said. Nor can you say, "Oh sure, God's there for you. Don't worry about it."

"Negative religious coping is associated with guilt, anxiety, fear, and denial," Dr. Sulmasy wrote in the *Journal of the American Medical Association.* It "warrants referral to pastoral care or the patient's own clergy," since negative religious beliefs "can sometimes result in unwarranted suffering and distorted decision-making at the end of life." He noted that the prayers of patients and families for miracles can lead them "either to reject medical recommendations or to demand medical interventions that the treating team believes are inappropriate."

In failing to listen carefully to a patient's hidden message, the doctor can misinterpret the patient's treatment decisions. For example, Dr. Sulmasy said, "Patients demanding futile care in the expectation of a miracle may really be expressing a sense of being out of control, interpreting discontinuation of a particular treatment as a sign of abandonment, or possibly experiencing guilt, denial, or even pathological ambivalence." Other patients might believe that agreeing with the doctor's decision to stop treatment "amounts to giving up on God before God has given up on them," the doctor said.

To be sure, medicine—or at least medical education—is changing, which offers the prospect of a more empathetic medical profession in the future. More than sixty medical schools in the United States now include some teaching about spirituality and medicine, and most of them are required courses, Dr. Puchalski reported. In addition, the Association of American Medical Colleges and the National Institute for Healthcare Research cosponsor an annual conference called Spirituality, Culture, and End-of-Life Care to foster more attention to spiritual issues among practicing physicians.

FOR FURTHER READING

Holder, Jennifer Sutton, and Jane Aldredge-Clanton. *Parting: A Handbook for Spiritual Care Near the End of Life.* Chapel Hill: University of North Carolina Press, 2004.

Kessler, David. *The Needs of the Dying.* New York: Quill, 2000 (originally published as *The Rights of the Dying.* New York: HarperCollins, 1997).

Kramp, Erin Tierney, and Douglas H. Kramp, with Emily P. McKhann. *Living with the End in Mind.* New York: Three Rivers Press, 1998.

Shepard, Martin. *Dying: A Guide for Helping and Coping.* Sag Harbor, NY: Permanent Press, 2000.

CHAPTER 11

When a Child Is Dying: Surviving the Nightmare

This is by far the most difficult chapter I've had to research and write. As a mother of two and grandmother of four, I can only imagine what it must be like to have a child who dies suddenly or develops an incurable illness. I find it hard to imagine even though I lived through the experience vicariously with several close friends who lost much-loved children—a three-year-old who drowned, a nine-year-old who succumbed to leukemia, a thirty-one-year-old who died of colon cancer. Just thinking about these beautiful lives snuffed painfully short brings tears to my eyes.

But the fact is, sometimes children do experience life-threatening illnesses and injuries. Sometimes children die. And somehow the experience has to be borne by the parents and grandparents who nurtured and loved them, by the siblings who may have alternately worshipped them and wished them gone, by the friends who shared their joys and sorrows.

In the *New England Journal of Medicine* in April 2004, a team of specialists who care for critically ill children wrote, "The success of medicine in improving survival rates among children with cancer, congenital heart disease, and prematurity has had the unintended consequence of offering false hope to parents that death can always be averted." The authors recognized that "for an adult, particularly one who is elderly or suffering from a long, debilitating illness, death is often an acceptable, and even a desired, outcome; in contrast, a child's death remains emotionally difficult, unnatural, and unexpected for families and health care providers alike."

About fifty-five thousand children die each year in the United States, just over half of them in the first year of life, often the result of premature birth or congenital diseases or defects. Beyond infancy, the most common causes of childhood deaths—both sudden and protracted—are unintentional injuries, genetic and prenatal disorders, cancer, and intentional injuries. All told, about 30 percent of childhood deaths are due to injury and 8 percent are the result of a prolonged illness. For example, while incredible progress has been made in curing childhood cancers, still one child in four who develops a malignancy dies of it sooner or later.

The loss of any young life is tragic indeed, a disruption of the natural order of things. The effects on families are often tragic as well. As was stated in the *Journal of Palliative Medicine* in 2005, "The death of a child alters the life and health of others immediately and for the rest of their lives." Experts say that parents typically never "get over" the loss of a child, but rather learn to adjust and to integrate the loss into their lives. Still, the death of a child remains one of the most stressful life events imaginable.

One-fourth to one-third of parents who lose a child report that their marriage suffers strains that sometimes prove irreparable. More than a third of surviving siblings have been described by themselves, their parents, and/or their teachers as having adjustment problems that interfere with their health and ability to form friendships. And the parents face a higher than normal risk of an earlier death from both natural and unnatural causes.

While no one with any sense would say that proper treatment by health professionals can erase the pain of losing a child, the *New England Journal of Medicine* authors wrote, "How a child dies (especially if the parents believe that their child suffered) directly influences parents' abilities to continue their lives and role functions during and after a child's death [and affects] siblings' abilities to make and maintain friendships."

Therefore, while the primary goal of medicine is to save the lives of children with life-threatening injuries or illnesses, health professionals also have a responsibility to make a dying child's last months, weeks, days, and hours as comfortable as possible *and* to also pay attention to the needs and feelings of family members who must live through the experience and beyond it.

Children Need and Deserve Comfort Care

A child is not simply a small adult. Children and their families have needs that differ from those of adults who are facing the end of life. Currently, far fewer children than adults receive the kind of comfort care that can ease both their ability to withstand the agonies of therapy and their ability to achieve a physically—and perhaps even emotionally—painless end to their lives.

In 2000 the American Academy of Pediatrics published guidelines for caring for children with life-threatening and terminal conditions. The goal, the academy said, should be "to add life to the child's years, not simply years to the child's life."

Palliative care—that is, constant attention to alleviating pain and other distressing symptoms—should be incorporated into treatments that are aimed at cure for children (and, I might add, for adults as well), not just something instituted when all attempts at treatment have failed.

"Playing by adult rules simply does not well serve children with a life-threatening or terminal condition," said Dr. Marcia Levetown, palliative care specialist at the University of Texas Medical Branch in Galveston. "Palliative care is not a substitute for curative or life-prolonging therapies. It's needed from the time of diagnosis, and it should not be implemented only when we've exhausted all other options." Ann Armstrong-Dailey, who founded the Children's Hospice International in Alexandria, Virginia, and others who have heard from parents recognize that "the real time of crisis is the time of diagnosis of a life-threatening condition."

And when cure is illusive, comfort care—the kind that adults receive through hospice services—is essential to a peaceful end of life. But because of insurance limitations and the lack of appropriate facilities for children, fewer than 5 percent of all dying children in America now receive the benefit of hospice care. When reimbursement for these services exists, it is typically less than $100 a day, which is woefully inadequate. And because so few children are admitted to hospice care, those who administer that care rarely develop and maintain enough expertise in helping dying children and their families to do it right.

Also, predicting how long a child will survive—a current requirement of being referred for hospice care (see chapter 9)—is more challenging than predicting survival time for adults. According to Ms. Armstrong-Dailey, the kinds of conditions that claim children's lives differ from the common killers of adults. This makes it difficult for physicians to determine *whether* or *when* a sick child might be dying. Furthermore, children and their families need the kind of support hospice care offers much earlier in the course of illness than adults do, so even if it were possible to predict a child had less than six months to live, that would not be early enough.

Joan Stephenson, PhD, writing in the *Journal of the American Medical Association*, noted that "children who die—along with many others who ultimately triumph over life-threatening conditions—often suffer needlessly because of lack of palliative and hospice care."

In a groundbreaking report in 2003, *When Children Die: Improving Palliative and End-of-Life Care for Children and Their Families*, the Institute of Medicine of the National Academy of Sciences recommended that hospice rules be revised, at least with regard to children suffering from life-threatening illness. One reason is that it is understandably extremely difficult for parents to call a halt to therapy aimed at treating their child's disease. In addition to a six-month life expectancy, current rules require that patients receiving hospice care abandon disease-oriented treatments.

Dr. Joanne Wolfe of the Dana-Farber Cancer Institute in Boston and coauthors found that parents lagged well behind physicians in recognizing that children with cancer had "no realistic chance for cure." In a study published in November 2000 in the *Journal of the American Medical Association*, the researchers surveyed 103 parents of children being treated for cancer and forty-two pediatric oncologists caring for those children. The doctors recognized the futility of continued cancer treatment a full three months before the parents acknowledged it. But when both the physician and parents recognized sooner that the child could not be cured, "elements of palliative care were more likely to be integrated into the child's care. Specifically, hospice was introduced earlier, and parents were more satisfied with the quality of home care during the end-of-life care period," the authors concluded.

Parents Can Help . . . and Need Help

All this can and must change, and families facing the crisis of a child with a fatal injury or illness can help make it happen, not only for their own sake but also for the sake of sick children and their families well into the future. The pediatrics academy guidelines insist that children and their families should be eligible for palliative and respite care regardless of the predicted length of their survival, and that this kind of care—and adequate reimbursement for it—should be provided simultaneously with life-prolonging therapies.

A first step might be for parents—and physicians—to recognize the fact that despite the improved survival rates among children with cancer, congenital heart disease, and the effects of premature birth, the death of a child cannot always be averted. As the pediatric palliative care specialists wrote in the *New England Journal of Medicine*, "Families, and some physicians, may view death more as a therapeutic misadventure than as a natural process resulting from disease. Recognition that death is inevitable often lags behind the reality of the medical condition, leading to a treatment approach that is inappropriately aggressive."

In other words, parents and doctors often don't know when to stop tormenting a dying child with yet further attempts to avert the inevitable. And, studies have shown, parental recognition that a child will not survive typically lags well behind that of the child's physicians, although there are doctors, too, who remain proponents of aggressive therapies and who mistakenly consider palliative care a sign of quitting because they are unable to admit they cannot "fix" a child.

Sometimes it is up to parents to stand back, face the reality of the situation, assess how much suffering a child can and should withstand, and say to the child's doctor, "Wait a minute. What are we doing here? Are we going beyond what is reasonable and possible? Have we lost sight of the big picture? Is there likely to be a good outcome at the end of all this?"

Sometimes it is up to parents to recognize that "doing everything" is not doing anyone any good, and especially not their child. Sometimes it is up to the parents to say, "Enough already. We can't stand to see how much pain and suffering our child is going through. Let's just make our child as comfortable as possible and give us time together to share the rest of our child's life as best as we can."

And sometimes children make the decision to give up what to them is a futile battle for survival. Hilary Bowen, the nine-year-old I knew and loved who died of leukemia, told her parents that if she was unable to live the life she once knew and enjoyed, she didn't want to live any longer. She was tired of being sick, of being subjected to yet another round of therapy, and despite it, getting sick over and over again. She realized, well ahead of her parents and even her doctors, that there was nothing more to be gained by continued attempts at life-prolonging therapy. And though it broke their hearts, her parents eventually realized they had no choice but to let her go.

Parents are responsible for all medical decisions involving children under eighteen. While such children may tell their parents just what they do and do not want in the way of therapeutic or resuscitative attempts, these requests are not legally binding, even if they are recorded on a notarized living will. If the child is a minor, the parents' word prevails even if it is counter to what the child wants or doesn't want. But when such disagreements arise, parents might be wise to step back and ask themselves if perhaps the child's choice is the correct one.

Problems also arise when parents request continued therapy that their child's doctors consider futile, such as providing tube feeding for a child whose brain has been irreparably damaged and is now in a persistent vegetative state (see chapter 6) or continued respiratory support for a child who has been diagnosed as brain dead. Thus far, in cases considered by physicians to be medically futile, the courts have sided with the parents. But rather than face an emotionally and financially draining court battle, parents might consider the treatment goal stated by Dr. Chris Feudtner of the Children's Hospital of Philadelphia. He maintains that both doctors and parents have to "make sure that all of our choices are really consistent with our deepest desires for what's best for the kids given what they're up against."

Caring appropriately for critically ill and dying children also requires appropriate care for their parents. Most parents need what caregiver organizations call respite care—a chance to remove themselves briefly from the emotionally and physically draining situation they are facing and get away from it all, even if that only involves going to a movie or having coffee with friends. If the sick child is at home, someone—if not a home health aide, then a friend or family member—should be available to stay with the child for brief periods so that the parents can get away to recharge their batteries.

Parents also often need family members and friends to step in and help with ordinary life tasks like grocery shopping, cooking meals, paying bills, caring for and entertaining the other children in the family. Having the sick child's siblings over for meals or a sleepover, taking them along on a vacation, or simply helping them with their homework can go a long way toward alleviating parental concerns and guilt about neglecting their healthy children.

What Parents Want from Doctors

When children face a life-threatening illness or injury, the lives of their parents are thrown into complete disarray, emotionally and physically. Too often, their needs are not met, not even halfway, which can compromise the care they can give both to the sick child and their other, healthy, children *and* the attention they can pay to their own well-being.

Elaine C. Meyer and colleagues at Children's Hospital Boston and the Harvard Medical School surveyed fifty-six parents (thirty-six mothers and twenty fathers) whose children—from newborn to eighteen years of age—had died after life-sustaining treatment was discontinued. The goal was to identify parents' priorities when their children were undergoing end-of-life care. Their results were published in March 2006 in the journal *Pediatrics*.

Keep us informed. First and foremost, parents said they want honest and complete information: "Answer all questions. Give all information—parents can handle it. What we cannot handle is not knowing what is going on. If something is wrong, tell us." "While you don't know the exact outcome for any particular child, more often than not this is the course of the next few hours, days, weeks, months . . . this would give us a better perspective to face and make better decisions down the road rather than responding to the limited situation/crisis immediately in front of us."

A previous study revealed that only 14 percent of parents were adequately informed about their child's deteriorating physical condition as death approached. In the Boston study, when parents were well informed, their children were more likely to receive timely palliative care and referral to hospice care.

Access to staff. Parents want ready access to the hospital staff, not just to obtain information about their child but also to gain reassurance, trust, and emotional peace of mind. Parents felt staff members were too often in a hurry and reluctant to meet with them. The inability to stay in contact with the attending physicians or nurses caring for their children resulted in considerable stress for parents. Often, the doctor would visit the child when the parents were not there, which gave some parents the not-so-far-fetched idea that the doctor was deliberately avoiding them.

One parent suggested that hospital physicians establish "office hours at the bedside." Even communication with the staff through e-mail can be helpful, some parents said. The study's authors wrote, "Unfortunately, some parents must work hard to get information: to ask the right questions, track down the right people, and be at the bedside at the right time," all of which "can add to the emotional and logistic burden of parents who are already under considerable stress."

Coordinate care and communication. When there were "too many cooks" with differing opinions and when communication and care were not coordinated, parents often became distrustful of the care their child was receiving and developed a nagging, anxiety-provoking sense of "not knowing what is going on." Some parents preferred to have a single physician serve as spokesperson for the medical team while others suggested that parents meet periodically with the medical staff to discuss the varying points of view about how their child should be treated—whether it was time to stop life-prolonging therapy or keep going.

Compassion and support. Parents need to know that those caring for their child recognize what they are going through and show that they really care, "not that it's just a job." As one parent put it, "Personal touch becomes so important to people who are functioning at a low level. The staff becomes the only link between you and the unknown." Parents greatly appreciated it when staff members were honest and did not provide false hope, when they shared the parents' grief and listened to what parents had to say because, as one said, "in the long run, the parents do know what is best for their child."

Parents also want the opportunity to be physically close and to care for their child, especially during the final days and hours of the child's life. They do not want to be rushed or intruded upon during these special moments—the time in which they "say good-bye" to their child—before or after the child has died.

A MOTHER RECALLS HER BABY'S LAST DAY

In 1981 Karen Roush, a registered nurse and now clinical editor of the *American Journal of Nursing*, gave birth fourteen weeks early to Vincent Cass. In his first three weeks, Vincent overcame several small problems common to premature infants but then developed a life-threatening condition called necrotizing enterocolitis that perforated his colon. Despite surgery and a blood transfusion, Vincent died. Twenty-five years later, in an essay in the journal, Ms. Roush recalled that fateful day, excerpted as follows:

I thought you would live. When you went into surgery, the doctor told us that your chances of making it through were nil. But you did. And so I thought you would live. Even when your hands and feet started turning blue, when the blue started creeping up your arms and legs. I watched your heart rate on the monitor slowing and your blood pressure dropping, and still I thought you would live. It's like that, you know, when something unimaginable is happening, like watching your baby die.

I wanted to hold you those last moments of your life, I

didn't want you to die in a stranger's hands and be brought back to me cold and still. I rocked you. I held you against my chest, pressing your face against mine. Sometimes when I'm missing you I'll hold my arms like I did then, remembering how it felt.

The nurse crouched next to us, her arm tight around my shoulders, physically holding me together. I lowered you to my lap, and she touched your face and hair. "He was such a beautiful baby," she said. I've always been thankful for those words. You were beautiful.

I don't know how long I rocked you before handing you to your father. The doctor . . . was crying and saying how sorry he was. How unexpected it was, what a good baby you were. I remember agreeing, calmly, saying I know, we never expected it either. I didn't cry. I was in shock.

I wish I had understood what it meant, leaving you that last time. The finality of it. I would have rocked you longer. I would have gotten a lock of your hair. When the nurse explained that after we left they would bathe you and dress you in one of your gowns, I would have asked to do it, if only I had thought it was a possibility. I would have taken care of you. I wouldn't have missed those last loving acts of a mother.

—Reprinted with permission from the
American Journal of Nursing,
September 2006.

Needs of a Dying Child

Parents and medical personnel can best meet the needs and answer the questions of a terminally ill child if they take a moment to step into the child's mind. Adults know that death is a permanent affair, at least with regard to life on earth. But children do not necessarily share that understanding. Depending on the age and maturity of the child, the concept of death has different meanings, and sometimes no meaning at all.

Age 0 to 2. Infants and toddlers possess no concept of death. Their needs at the end of life are for love and attention from familiar persons, maximum physical comfort, consistency, and having their favorite toys.

Age 2 to 6. At this age, magical thinking comes into play. Young children typically regard death as temporary and reversible, like sleep, and may believe that death can be caused by thoughts, such as punishment for misbehavior. They need maximum contact with parents and correction of any misconceptions or feelings of guilt that their illness is a punishment or that they somehow brought it upon themselves. Child psychologists suggest the use of precise language—using the words *death* and *dying*—when speaking to children under six.

Age 6 to 12. Older children develop an adult concept of death as permanent and irreversible. They need to be told the truth; most children readily see through lies and euphemisms, which only prevent honest, forthright, and emotionally meaningful communication. If children request detailed information about their disease or prognosis, it should be given. Their efforts to achieve control and mastery of their lives should be supported, for example, by allowing them to participate in decisions regarding their care and what may happen if and when they die. They need to be reassured that no matter what happens, they will not be abandoned or forgotten and will always be loved. And they need to maintain contact with their friends and siblings for as long as they are able.

Teenagers. Adolescents tend to be more metaphysical, ready to explore the spiritual meaning of death and examine the meaning, purpose, hope, and value of life. Every effort should be made to re-inforce the child's self-esteem, independence, and need for privacy. Terminally ill teenagers should be allowed to participate in deci-sions, have ready access to their friends, and feel free to express strong feelings—even rant and rave against the unfairness of it all. Truthfulness is critical—they always know when you are lying. No good can come from telling children who say they know they are dying that this is not so or they shouldn't talk like that, which only cuts off meaningful communication when the child needs it most.

AT any age, children who are dying should be allowed, if not en-couraged, to grieve. Like Hilary, they may grieve for their declin-ing physical abilities, their lost opportunity to interact normally with their friends, and their inability to participate in age-appropriate activities, including school and play. Many children who are dying worry about the emotional and physical well-being of their families. How will their parents and siblings cope with the loss when they die? Who will take their place in the family? It is important for parents to remember that however hard it is to lose a child, a dying child is losing everyone and everything that is pre-cious to him or her, along with dozens of years of life unlived. A child's anticipatory grief can be as intense and complex as a par-ent's grief, if not more so (see chapter 15).

Easing the End of a Child's Life

Many children suffer unduly because parents—and sometimes physicians—are reluctant to withdraw treatments like feeding tubes that are sustaining the life, such as it is, of a dying child. Some peo-ple assume incorrectly that once a life-prolonging measure is in use, it cannot legally be withdrawn. But this is not the case when the pa-tient is near death with no chance for recovery. As Mildred Z. Solomon of Harvard Medical School and other experts on the ethics of pediatric end-of-life care stated in the journal *Pediatrics* in October 2005: "When allowing death is justifiable, parents and health care professionals should know that there is no sanction against withdrawing treatments already underway. If the view is that any intervention already being offered cannot be withdrawn, then many children may suffer needlessly and opportunities for comfort care and for interactions with parents and siblings may be diminished."

It is perfectly natural for parents to regard feeding a child as a loving, nurturing act. But as with an adult, a child approaching the end of life cannot make good use of food, which can sometimes cause more harm than good. "In fact, medically supplied nutrition may prolong the dying process and, near the end of life, can cause congestions, excessive bodily secretions, and considerable discomfort," Dr. Solomon and coauthors stated. "In certain instances, a child's interests may best be served by forgoing enteral and parenteral nutrition and hydration"—that is, not giving either food or liquids.

Pain management often presents another dilemma for parents and physicians. In the Solomon study of 781 clinicians, approximately half of attending physicians and more than 40 percent of medical residents and nurses agreed with this statement: "When clinicians give inadequate pain medication, they do so most often out of fear of hastening the child's death." However, the authors noted, "such fear is misplaced on clinical, ethical, and legal grounds." In fact, they added, one study "showed that patients who receive effective pain relief may actually live longer than patients whose pain remains untreated."

In other words, neither parents nor physicians should hesitate to provide however much pain medication dying children may need to make their last days on earth as comfortable as possible. Indeed, failure to adequately control a child's pain is a leading cause of intense parental distress and a factor that often contributes to extreme and prolonged grief reactions after the child dies.

When a Child Dies Suddenly

As difficult as it can be to have a child whither away and die from an incurable illness, at least parents have a chance to gradually come to grips with the inevitable outcome and say their good-byes. However, the sudden death of a child—either from illness or injury—can be emotionally catastrophic, leaving parents struggling with overwhelming feelings and searching for explanations as to how such a tragedy could have happened.

Often, parental feelings are intensified by guilt: Why did I leave those pills around where the baby could find them? Why did I leave the baby in the tub and go out to answer the phone? Why didn't I walk my son to school? Why did I have that drink before I picked up my son at his friend's house? Why did I say he could play football in school? Why did I let her go swimming with her friends when I knew there would be no lifeguard there? Why didn't I insist that he always wear a helmet when he went biking . . . skateboarding . . . ice skating . . . skiing? Why didn't I realize how sick she was instead of waiting so long to get her to the emergency room? Why did I leave someone else in charge of my child?

Physicians at Children's Hospital Boston described the case of a healthy eighteen-month-old toddler who was struck by a car when she chased a dog out onto the street. Her parents were at work at the time, and her grandfather, who had been taking care of her, went into shock and developed heart palpitations when the accident happened. You can well imagine the level of guilt experienced by both the grandfather and the child's parents when they realized that efforts to control the swelling of the child's brain failed and she was declared brain dead. The parents quickly made the decision to donate the toddler's organs so that other children might live, a decision that slightly assuaged their indescribable anguish over losing their daughter (see chapter 16).

When a child dies suddenly, the family typically has had no prior relationship with the health care professionals involved. Too often in such situations, the parents' distress is magnified by what they perceive as "uncaring" or "detached" or "unemotional" interactions with emergency room personnel. On the other hand, parents often express gratitude for what they regard as acts of kindness, demonstrations of affection and caring for their child, and emotional expressions about the tragic situation. For example, the social worker who was called in to help as soon as the toddler was brought to the emergency room revealed to the child's mother that she, too, had lost a child and so had some idea what the mother was going through. The two of them cried together, which the mother found comforting.

But what many parents don't realize is that doctors, nurses, and other health professionals are usually taught that they should not disclose anything personal or share feelings with patients or their families, which can leave health professionals wondering just how to behave in the face of such tragedies. The Boston authors suggest that medical personnel need to loosen up—that they should "not fear displaying their empathy and own emotions, for this is the very substance that can convey one's humanity."

Furthermore, when faced with the death of a child, members of the medical staff also need to release often profound feelings of uncertainty, powerlessness, and hopelessness as well as genuine grief, feelings that can become especially intense when they have labored for hours or days to try to save the child.

Continuing Care After a Child Dies

Care of the child—or of the family—does not stop after the child has died. In fact, when a fatally injured child has been declared brain dead, which is the legal definition of death in all fifty states, parents may demand that treatment with life-supporting measures be continued for a time. Although there are no legal grounds on which to base such treatment, continuing with it for a while can give families time to absorb the devastating news and help them come to grips with the tragic reality. Experts say that the process of grieving may remain blocked when parents are in conflict with health care providers as to when treatment should be terminated.

After a child dies, family members often want to spend time alone with their child—time to hold and rock the child, climb into bed with the child, or bath and dress the child. These acts have proved to be highly beneficial to grieving families and should not only be allowed but should also be actively encouraged by the medical staff.

Also helpful to families is to obtain such keepsakes as a lock of the child's hair or an imprint or mold of the child's hands and/or feet. Parents who have been questioned after their child's death say that these mementos help to ease their grieving, according to physicians who work in pediatric emergency rooms.

Family members also may benefit greatly from meetings with nonmedical personnel—a chaplain, social worker, child-life therapist, or psychologist, whose services should be extended not only to parents but also to grandparents, siblings, friends, and classmates of the dead child. If such services are not automatically offered, parents and teachers would be wise to request them, since they can help people work through their grief and avoid complicated grief reactions (see chapter 15).

FOR FURTHER READING

Finkbeiner, Ann R. *After the Death of a Child: Living with Loss Through the Years.* Baltimore, MD: Johns Hopkins University Press, 1998.

Sirois, Maria. *Every Day Counts: Lessons in Love, Faith, and Resilience from Children Facing Illness.* New York: Walker & Company, 2006.

CHAPTER 12

What to Say: Conversations at the End of Life

A friend—a young mother of two school-age children the age of my own—was dying of breast cancer. I postponed visiting her until her final weeks of life *because I didn't know what to say*. And, when I finally did see her, I said all the wrong things. I talked about my life, what I was working on, what my children were doing, what was happening in the neighborhood. Not once, in the course of an hour's visit, did I ask her about herself—her thoughts, feelings, fears, wishes.

I found out later that after I left, my friend cried her heart out. She cried because, as she told her husband, I was so alive and she was dying and would miss out on all the things I'd talked about.

In the decades since her untimely death, I've learned a lot about how to talk with someone whose days on earth are numbered in single or double digits.

As Virginia Lynn Fry wrote in *Patient Care* magazine some years ago, "The great majority of us will not die sudden, unwarned, traumatic deaths. But, rather, we will live with slow, chronic, managed conditions that finally end our lives. This means we have time. Time to end our lives with meaning, connection, and a sense of emotional and spiritual healing."

But this kind of closure and comfort is not possible if we cannot communicate in a meaningful way with one another, if we cannot acknowledge what is soon to happen and open the door to discussions that can help a dying person know that his or her life has meaning, even in its final days and beyond.

Silence Is Not Golden

In 1958, when my mother was afflicted with an incurable cancer, most people didn't talk about death. They didn't even talk about cancer. Although she was being treated in a cancer hospital, the word *cancer* was never mentioned. We repeatedly assured her that she would get well, though we—and she—clearly knew she wouldn't. Twice in the course of her declining months she tried to end her life, first by slitting her wrists and, when that failed, by drinking rubbing alcohol. But, alas, neither occasion was used to open a discussion of what she was thinking and feeling, a discussion that might have relieved her desperation and made her remaining time on earth less awful.

My father and I (though not my twelve-year-old brother) knew she was dying, but we denied her the opportunity to make sense of the life she had lived and pass along her boundless wisdom as a lasting legacy. I never even got the recipes for the dishes she cooked so well. We denied her—and ourselves—the opportunity to say good-bye, to tell her how much we loved and admired her and how very much we would miss her. And we especially denied my brother the opportunity to come to terms with what was about to change his life irrevocably.

At that time, my father and I were under the misguided impression that denying the reality of the situation in my mother's presence was synonymous with emotional strength. I was only sixteen years old at the time, but I remember clearly how angry I was with my mother's younger brother, who cried when he visited her in the hospital. How dare he cry in her presence, I thought, when what she needed most of all was hope for a recovery. It took me years to forgive him, years to finally learn that what she really had needed most was for all of us to cry with her, to cry for the years of life she was going to miss and for the years we all would miss being with her as a loving wife and mother. In fact, I was so determined to be "strong" during her last months that even after her death it took me a full year before *I* could cry and truly mourn her loss.

Richard P. McQuellon, PhD, director of the psychosocial oncology and cancer patient support programs at Wake Forest University Baptist Medical Center, sent me a most helpful article, "Turning Toward Death Together: Conversation in Mortal Time," which he'd written with Michael A. Cowan, PhD, of Loyola University and published in the *American Journal of Hospice and Palliative Care.*

"Strength," these experts wrote, "does not lie in stoic, unemotional encounter, but rather in full exposure to one's own emotional responses, including intense angst." They urged that those in contact with someone who is dying should help the person "wrest life-enhancing meaning and value from a situation in which many can find only despair. They do so primarily by their willingness to engage in authentic conversation with the one who is dying. Authentic conversation has the power not only to enhance how people cope practically with dying, but to illuminate and enrich the very meaning of life for patients and caregivers alike as they enter the sacred moment of mortal time together."

In his book, *"I Don't Know What to Say": How to Help and Support Someone Who Is Dying,* Dr. Robert Buchman, an oncologist at the University of Toronto, pointed out that "one of the biggest problems faced by terminally ill patients is that people won't talk to them, and the feelings of isolation add a great deal to their burden."

Contrary to what many people seem to think, talking about dying does not create new fears and anxieties among those who are terminally ill. Rather, those people who are dying and have no one to talk to typically have the highest levels of anxiety and depression. And shame, as well, because they are ashamed of the fears and anxieties they cannot express. There is much that friends and relatives can do to make dying a less lonely and frightening experience.

Create a Conducive Atmosphere

Drs. McQuellon and Cowan cautioned against what they called "polite civility—collusion in denying the severity of the patient's condition." Rather, this is the time for empathy—for attempting to walk in the patient's shoes. How is this accomplished? First and foremost, by *being a good listener* and creating an atmosphere that is conducive to conversation. Chaplain Mary E. Johnson of the Mayo Clinic says "let the person know that you're willing to listen, to hear his or her concerns."

Your behavior, the tone of your voice, even your facial expression, help to convey the impression that you are ready and willing to engage in a meaningful conversation.

- Start by taking off your coat, if you're wearing one. Then sit down at eye level with the patient, as closely as you would sit if the person were healthy.

- Next, move or remove any obstacles between the two of you that might create distance or prevent eye contact, including items on the bed tray. Eye contact is critical if the patient is to feel comfortable talking about feelings, wishes, fears, and anxieties, so be sure to look at the person when either of you is talking.

- Don't hesitate to make physical contact. If touching or kissing was appropriate when the person was healthy, it is appropriate—indeed, desirable—now as well. A sincere hug, kiss, pat on the arm, or squeeze of the hand can be worth a thousand words.

Don't launch into a monologue about what you are doing or what is happening to mutual friends or relatives, which could convey the impression that you are not interested in the patient's concerns. Focus on the patient. Try to determine, first, whether the patient wants to talk and, second, what the patient wants to talk about. You might start by asking, "Do you feel like talking?" For openers, it's okay to ask, "How are you feeling today?" or "What can I get for you?" or "What can I do to make you more comfortable?"

While you should let the patient take the lead in talking about sensitive topics and deep concerns, you can encourage such a conversation by asking "Are there things you'd like to say or things that you're worried about?" Listen not only to what is said but *how* it is said, as well as what the patient means but does not say. When sensitive topics are raised, you can encourage continuing conversation by saying something like "Yes, I understand" or "Tell me more" or simply reflecting back what you heard.

But you should not say "I know how you feel" since you can't possibly know unless you, too, are dying. Most important is not to contradict a patient who says something like "I know I'm going to die soon." And don't try to change the subject when the *d* word is raised. A statement about approaching death is your opportunity to ask the patient about lingering concerns or words of wisdom or any other thoughts that the patient wants to convey or pass along for posterity.

Gird Your Loins for Strong Feelings

Be prepared for anger. That is one of the emotional stages dying patients are likely to go through, and some never go beyond it. If you are a close relative, the anger may be directed at you because you're the one who's there and the patient knows you will not abandon him or her. But it's important to realize that the anger really is not meant for you personally, so try hard not to respond in an argumentative fashion.

For example, the patient might say with contempt to a healthy spouse, "I feel dreadful and you're no help." Rather than rise to the bait with a response like, "This is no picnic for me either" or "I'm doing my best" (to which the patient might reply, "Well, your best is not good enough!"), it's better to ask "How bad do you feel?" or "What's bothering you the most?" or "Is there something else I can get for you?" Or, if you're really in tiptop emotional control, you could address the anger directly by saying, "I know you're angry. You have a right to be angry. I'd be angry, too, if I were in your shoes. Let's talk about it."

Be prepared, too, for denial. According to Chaplain Johnson, "Denial is an important coping mechanism—a form of terror management. We deny because the reality is too frightening. Denial is a form of natural protection that allows us to let reality in bit by bit. It allows us to continue living as we contemplate death."

Some terminally ill patients remain in denial until their dying day. They may ask repeatedly, "I'm getting better, aren't I?" or "When can I get out of here?" Or they may make statements like "I'll be back in the saddle before you know it." You won't gain anything by either agreeing with or denying such optimistic statements. Far better to respond with a vague statement like "Let's hope so" or try to redirect the patient's thinking by asking, "What have the doctors told you?"

Or you might try a hope-for-the-best-but-prepare-for-the-worst-statement like "What if you don't get better? Shouldn't we make some plans just in case?"

This would allow the patient to remain in denial but also may provide an opportunity to make the kinds of preparations, for example, writing a will or living will or assigning a health care proxy or simply determining where the person would want to be when death comes, that can reduce the emotional and physical anguish often associated with the end of life.

Rather than "acceptance" of an imminent death, this approach might be considered an "accommodation—learning to live as fully as possible, while accommodating to the presence of this circumstance in your life," Chaplain Johnson said. "Do you have to accept that you have a life-threatening illness? Do you have to accept that you're going to die before you thought you would? No, you don't."

For some, fear is behind their denial. They may fear being in pain or losing control of bodily functions, mental ability, and personal autonomy. They may fear being abandoned or becoming a burden to those they love. Invite such people to talk about their fears; even if you have no ability to erase them, just speaking about them is often a relief. And, you never know, you just may be able to offer realistic reassurance.

On the other hand, some patients are filled with despair and have lost all hope. You might find things to say that offer short-term hope, like "Your grandson is coming to visit next week" or "Let's talk about the things you want people to remember about you."

But be sure not to make promises that cannot be kept, for example, "Surely you'll feel better tomorrow" or "You'll be able to go home in a few days" (unless, of course, that is what the doctor has said). You can, however, reassure the patient that everything possible will be done to keep her or him as comfortable as possible, including relieving her or his pain, no matter how bad things get. And you might reassure her or him that you'll always be there, if that's a promise you know you can keep.

What Is—and Is Not—Okay to Say

Don't be afraid to say that you don't know what to say. Just being there and staying close can say a lot. Don't worry about lulls in the conversation. It's okay to be quiet. Silence when used properly can be golden. Sitting quietly and holding the patient's hand conveys caring and empathy, often more so than any words.

One of my biggest mistakes when visiting someone who is seriously ill is to compare that person's medical experience with that of someone else. I might talk about my own hospital experiences, or about someone whose health or circumstances are more dire, or about someone with a similar disease who recovered or who is managing to live a full life despite the disease.

While my intent may be to cheer the patient up or convey hope, the effect is likely to be just the opposite. I have to remind myself that each person is unique and faces unique challenges. Talking about other people's misery redirects the conversation away from the patient. Being told that someone else with a similar disease managed to beat it can make the person who is losing the battle feel even worse. Or it can be a source of false hope that simply delays the patient's ability to face the inevitable and take care of matters that need to be dealt with before death occurs.

But it's okay, even desirable, to talk about the past—about happy or funny times and events you shared with the person. Sharing memories lets the person know he or she will not be forgotten. It's okay, even desirable, to laugh together. When my brother-in-law Gordon was dying of an asbestos-related cancer a few years ago, my husband and I visited him in his hospice room. My husband, who has a fabulous memory for events in the distant past, regaled him with stories of their childhood. And while it was difficult for Gordon to laugh, he did his best. It was obvious to us both how much he enjoyed the visit and the knowledge that he and the events of his life would not be forgotten. Too often, these memories are saved for the funeral or memorial service, when the person they concern is no longer around to hear them.

Encourage the person to talk about his or her life, the particular joys, the childhood adventures and misadventures, the best-laid plans that went humorously awry, and, as Chaplain Johnson suggests, "the marvelous stories that get told around the campfire."

It's okay, even desirable, to talk about mutual interests—sports, theater, current events, politics. Such conversations give patients the opportunity to escape briefly from the reality of their situation. Rarely do patients want to spend all their time thinking about their disease and how they feel.

Or, if you've exhausted subjects to talk about and your relationship with the patient is a close one, remember that touching is a very powerful form of communication. You might offer to massage the patient's hands and feet or rub lotion into his or her exposed skin. Or simply stroke the patient's head or hold his or her hand.

What is *not* okay is to give medical advice unless the patient asks you for it and you are qualified to give it. Telling the patient about other people you may know or heard of or have read about who were supposedly saved by a particular doctor or alternative remedy is not helpful. If there really were miracles out there, they'd be used at every major medical center. No one is suppressing news of a cure for cancer or heart disease or multiple sclerosis in order to perpetuate his job or organization. Remember, the heads of all medical organizations have loved ones who have died, or will die, of the same diseases. If there were cures out there, surely they would have used them to save their loved ones.

It is also not okay to overstay your welcome. Be sensitive to the patient's tolerance. When the patient's attention seems to be drifting, or pain or discomfort is getting worse, or eyes are beginning to close, it's time to leave. Many patients nearing the end of life are on a schedule of pain medication and are likely to be very groggy and need to sleep for an hour or so after the drug (usually morphine) is administered. It is often helpful to call in advance of your visit to find out the best times for you to come—when the patient is likely to be awake and most comfortable and not overwhelmed by other visitors.

Doctors, Too, Must Know What to Say

You've no doubt heard any number of stories about doctors, and perhaps nurses, too, who do not know how to talk to a dying patient, who say the wrong things, if they say anything at all, or refuse to acknowledge what some people call the elephant in the room. Before lambasting the physician for insensitivity, please remember that rarely are doctors taught how to behave around a person who is dying. Their training is nearly always entirely focused on preserving lives, not easing deaths.

As Dr. Pauline W. Chen, author of *Final Exam: A Surgeon's Reflections on Mortality*, put it in an article in *The New York Times*, "Patient deaths, for many doctors, represent a kind of failure, and so without really thinking, we look the other way."

A two-year, multimillion-dollar effort to improve communication between patients and doctors on end-of-life care resulted in great disappointment. The effort, which involved frequent reports to physicians on patients' expected survival and employed specially trained nurses to talk with patients, families, physicians, and hospital staff about prognoses, pain control, and advance care planning, did nothing to improve communication between physicians and dying patients. As the researchers concluded, the doctors "did not wish to directly confront problems or face choices."

This study, the Study to Understand Prognoses and Preferences for Outcomes and Risks of Treatment, or SUPPORT, was a wake-up call for the medical profession. Spurred by its findings, specialized curriculums in end-of-life care were created, and medical licensing boards began to include this expertise in their competency requirements. (For more on the SUPPORT trial, see pages 179–81.)

Serious efforts are now under way at some medical schools to improve the ability of future physicians to communicate in a meaningful way with dying patients. For health professionals already on the firing line, several leading medical journals have been publishing continuing education articles to help practicing physicians do a better job of treating and communicating with dying patients. Since 2000 the *Journal of the American Medical Association* has published an excellent, bimonthly series of reports under the rubric "Perspectives on Care at the Close of Life." The reports are available free online at www.jama.com, so even if doctors are not subscribers or don't have time to read the issues when they are published, the articles can be printed out and read at a more convenient time. Similar educational series about dealing with dying patients have appeared in the *American Journal of Nursing*, and anyone interested can access them free at www.ajn.com.

Often, the medical team caring for a dying patient has had only a brief relationship with that person and thus may have to earn the trust of the patient and the patient's family before meaningful conversation can take place. If you encounter a physician who seems insensitive or averse to this task, a relative or friend might be able to provide the guidance the physician needs, perhaps by making a copy of the box that follows and handing it, with appropriate humility, to the physician in question.

When it is unlikely that continued treatment will enable a severely ill patient to recover, the physician's goal should be to help the patient prepare for the worst while hoping for the best. Dr. Anthony L. Black of the Veterans Administration Puget Sound Health Care System in Seattle and coauthors, writing in March 2003 in the *Annals of Internal Medicine,* suggested that, in giving equal time to hope and preparation, the doctor might say, "I will do everything I can to optimize your chances. I am hoping for the best. I think that, at the same time, we need to prepare for the worst in case the treatment is not effective. Preparing for the worst does not mean I'm giving up on you; it helps me arrange the best medical care for you, no matter what happens."

If the patient reacts to such a statement with fear, sadness, anxiety, or anger, this can open the door to discussions as to what is behind these feelings and help the patient deal with them constructively: "Address fears, clarify priorities, and strengthen relationships with loved ones, all components of a good death," the doctors noted.

IMPROVING DOCTOR–PATIENT COMMUNICATION

Dr. James A. Tulsky of the Center for Palliative Care at Duke University Medical Center created the following tips on how doctors can establish trust with hospitalized patients, as printed in the July 20, 2005, issue of the *Journal of the American Medical Association*. He pointed out that "taking care of patients in the hospital often requires physicians to develop relationships quickly and does not allow much time to engender trust through experience."

- *Encourage patients and families to talk.*
  "Tell me what you understand about your illness."
  "We've just met and there is so much going on with you right now. To help me get to know you better, can you tell me about your life outside of the hospital?"
  "I'm sure that this illness has been a lot to absorb quickly. How are you coping with this?"

- *Do not contradict or put down other health care providers, yet recognize patient concerns.*
  "I hear you saying that you didn't feel heard by the other doctors. I'd like to make sure that you have a chance to voice all of your concerns."
  "It sounds like Dr. Jones left you feeling very hopeful for a cure. I'm sure he really cares about you, and it would have been wonderful if things would have gone as well as he wished."

- *Acknowledge errors.*
  "You're absolutely right. Four days was too long to have to wait for the CT scan. Any excuses we have won't make you feel better."

- *Be humble.*
  "I really appreciate what you've shared with me about the side effects of the medication. It's clear that the approach I had suggested is not going to work for you."

- *Demonstrate respect.*
  "I am so impressed by how involved you've been with your father throughout this illness. I can tell how much you love him."

- *Do not force decisions.*
  "We've just had a very difficult conversation, and you and your family have a lot to think about. Let's meet again tomorrow and see how you're feeling about things then."

What Patients and Families Want and Need

Especially when dealing with a potentially fatal illness, physicians tend to present information accompanied by a bucketful of uncertainty. They toss out statistical probabilities about good and bad effects of various treatment choices. Patients, or their families, who usually have little or no medical knowledge, are then forced to make decisions about treatments they know little about. Yet surveys have shown consistently that most patients want to get as much information as possible, and they want their doctors, who have far more expertise, to help guide their treatment decisions.

Patients also want doctors to pay attention to their feelings, especially after they have just received bad news like "Your cancer has spread to your liver" or "I'm afraid this latest treatment is not working as I'd hoped." This kind of information can be so emotionally overwhelming that patients are unable to hear or understand much about what is subsequently said with regard to the illness or revised treatment plan (see chapter 5). They often need time to let the facts of their situation sink in—time perhaps to cry or discuss the matter with loved ones—before they can make rational decisions about how to proceed.

A common complaint of patients and their families is that doctors and nurses often impede discussions of emotionally laden issues by changing the subject or ignoring the patient's concerns. Even in a hospice setting, where the feelings of patients are supposed to be paramount, one study showed that only 40 percent of patient concerns were disclosed. As a result, physicians and nurses may remain largely in the dark about the degree of patients' distress or what they are most worried about.

Discussions with doctors that focus solely on symptoms and treatments often fail to address the most pressing concerns of dying patients: a fear of loss of dignity, abandonment, and isolation. Doctors and nurses can foster more illuminating and meaningful conversations by asking open-ended questions or making empathetic statements that address emotional concerns. For example, Dr. Tulsky suggested a doctor might say, "Are you feeling scared?" or "This must be terribly hard" or "I can't imagine what you're going through, but I'm impressed with how you've been able to cope."

Finally, it is the job of health care professionals to foster hope—not false optimism but genuine hope within the context of what the future is likely to hold. Too often, Dr. Tulsky noted, physicians are afraid that the facts will destroy hope, and so they give patients overly optimistic prognoses or no such information at all. When patients with a terminal illness are not fully aware of their prognosis, they tend to overestimate how much time they have left, which can rob them of the opportunity to use their remaining time to fulfill dreams, strengthen relationships, put their affairs in order, and come to terms with their fate. Studies have shown that failing to provide appropriate information about prognosis and the availability of palliative care can cause unnecessary pain and suffering for dying patients (see chapter 9).

On the other hand, there are patients who, despite being told that there are no other treatments available to reverse their advanced disease, cling to the hope for a miracle and perhaps insist on trying highly experimental or alternative therapies. While it's not the job of doctors to refute patients' hope for a miracle, it is their job to encourage patients to prepare for the worst while hoping for the best or, to put it another way, to prepare for the possibility that the treatment will fail.

COMMUNICATING WITH HOPE

Dr. Tulsky emphasized that "talking about treatment choices at the end of life does not necessarily rob patients of hope. Redirecting the patient's goal toward realistic hopes and being present with compassion can serve as a powerful act in helping patients make decisions while maintaining a hopeful outlook." He suggested the following approaches:

- *Hope for the best but prepare for the worst.*
  "Have you thought about what might happen if things don't go as you wish? Sometimes having a plan that prepares you for the worst makes it easier to focus on what you hope for most."

- *Reframe hope.*
  "I know you are hoping that your disease will be cured. Are there other things that you want to focus on?"
  "I wish, too, that this disease would just stay in remission. If we cannot make that happen, what other shorter-term goals might we work toward?"

- *Focus on the positive.*
  "We've been talking about some treatments that are really not going to be effective and that we don't rec-

ommend you use. But there are a lot of things we can still do to help you—let's focus on those."

"What sorts of things are left undone for you? Let's talk about how we might be able to make these happen."

Finally, when a patient dies, the doctor's communication responsibilities do not end. Yet many people I know who have lost loved ones say that the doctors in charge barely took the time to say "I'm sorry for your loss," let alone bother to acknowledge admirable qualities of the deceased or perhaps explain why further treatment would not have helped.

Those physicians who feel they cannot face the family could at least write a meaningful note of condolence, like the one James Johnson received after his wife, Laura, died at the Mayo Clinic following a two-month battle against a rapidly progressive lung disease. Dr. Philippe R. Bauer, a critical care pulmonologist who was most responsible for Laura's care, wrote the following to Mr. Johnson:

Laura gave a great lesson to all of us. Not only was she a strong person, but she was able to build around her an outstanding circle of amazing and astonishing family members.

It was a great privilege for me to participate in her care. I wish I had known her better and under different circumstances. However, I learned from her, and would like to convey my sincere condolences to all of you.

Sally Rosen's mother received an even more remarkable letter from Dr. Richard Amerling, nephrologist at Beth Israel Medical Center in New York, who had cared for her courageous daughter for several years before her death. The letter was addressed postumously to Sally, who died at age forty-three of complications from a genetic syndrome.

Dr. Amerling wrote,

I wanted you to know what a rare privilege it has been to know you and to be involved with your care. I knew from the first it would be most challenging. I knew your time on earth was to be short, and the day would come, all too soon, when you would leave us. It made our moments together ever more precious.

One of the enduring rewards of being a physician is learning lessons from patients. In this regard you were certainly my greatest teacher. Though it hurt to bear witness to your suffering, your visits always brought sunlight. Your ability to deal with adversity with courage and humor remains a source of inspiration. By carrying forth your struggle with grace, bravery, and dignity, overcoming adversity and triumphing even in death, you taught us all how to live.

That, I think, is how all doctors should behave after a patient dies. Don't you agree?

FOR FURTHER READING

Buckman, Robert. *"I Don't Know What to Say": How to Help and Support Someone Who Is Dying.* New York: Vintage Books, 1992.

Callahan, Maggie, and Patricia Kelley. *Final Gifts: Understanding the Special Awareness, Needs, and Communications of the Dying.* New York: Poseidon Press, 1992.

Halpern, Susan P. *The Etiquette of Illness: What to Say When You Can't Find the Words.* New York: Bloomsbury, 2004.

Keeley, Maureen P., and Julie M. Yingling. *Final Conversations: Helping the Living and the Dying Talk to Each Other.* Acton, MA: VanderWyk & Burnham, 2007.

CHAPTER 13

Doctors Who Disappear: What Can Be Done About It

R obert Green was angry, actually furious, and he let the doctor know it. Only now it was too late to help his beloved wife, Hinda, who had died weeks earlier of lung cancer. Mr. Green wrote to her oncologist:

> Hinda was treated successfully by you for almost seven years. During that time, she developed a relationship of confidence with you which, given her many unhappy past experiences with doctors, was both encouraging and surprising.
>
> And yet, at the end, to her (and my) profound disappointment, you failed her. When you realized that you could do no more to reverse her progressive disease and that death had become inevitable, you abandoned her. The empathy you had displayed was replaced by what she experienced as indifference.
>
> Your coldness during her final weeks made it more difficult for us because she felt that she had lost the medical anchor you had provided and no longer had a doctor she could trust to explain what was happening to her as her body withered and her vulnerability grew. Much precious time was wasted trying to turn her mind from your dismissal of her that she experienced as a professional and personal betrayal. Which I believe it was.
>
> What she wanted you to do was simple: she wanted you to

*speak to her with courage; she wanted you to show a bit of
concern, which would have meant as much to her then as all
the chemotherapy you prescribed when there was still hope;
she wanted you to help her die more peacefully—as you had
promised that you would but did not. It would have been a
consolation to her and to the family and friends who loved her.*

Mr. Green continued with a plea, both to Hinda's physician and
to *all* doctors who treat patients they will ultimately lose:

*Would it have cost you so much to have picked up the tele-
phone to speak with her after almost seven years of treatment? Would it have been so intolerable to you to have looked
into her eyes and told her that you wished her well and
wanted a chance to say good-bye? Were you truly unable to
offer even a shred of comfort, a word of condolence to her
family? Had she really become no more than another statistic,
a failure you preferred to brush aside?*

    *I am asking you to help ensure that oncologists like yourself
who work with many patients they are bound to lose not
abandon them emotionally as you did. I am asking that you
suggest that your hospital consider setting up a training program for doctors like yourself so that other patients can be
spared the pain of the rejection Hinda experienced. Because it
is my conviction that doctors treating terminally ill patients
have a moral obligation to stand with them from start to finish
even when, at the end, those patients must be transferred to
hospice care.*

An All-Too-Common Experience

I'm sure the anguish expressed by Mr. Green and the emotional
pain experienced by Hinda have been—and will be—shared by
countless dying patients when the doctors who have piloted their
treatment abandon them when therapeutic medicine can no

longer help. This is the time when caring words, a gentle touch, an "I'm sorry" or "I will miss you" are what is needed to ease their passage to the Great Beyond.

Other families may not be as eloquent or as forthright as Mr. Green, but their pain—and the pain experienced by their dying loved ones—is no less.

Dr. Diane Meier, director of the palliative care service at Mount Sinai Medical Center in New York, calls this "a common and devastating problem" that she has seen happen "hundreds of times."

"It compounds the losses a thousandfold," Dr. Meier said. "Patients wonder what they did to offend their doctor, why they are no longer worthy of attention. And, of course, the patients do not realize that since they 'failed' therapy, the doctors feel they 'failed' the patients.

"When patients are so sick, the doctor–patient relationship is deeply personal and vulnerable and unequal. Doctors need to know the cost of their behavior for their patients, whose interests they are sworn to put first."

She explained further that the "profound hurt" dying patients experience when they are abandoned by their doctors "distracts them from the important family and existential work they should be attending to while they are dying."

But it doesn't—it shouldn't—have to be this way. Doctors can learn to be human beings first and doctors second, or, if that is too much to expect, at least to remain compassionate human beings while they serve primarily as physicians. Patients and families can help to facilitate this lesson, as Mr. Green tried to do. But to accomplish this noble goal, it may help to understand why so many doctors act like Hinda's in the first place.

Why This Happens

Humanity undone. In his book *How We Die*, Dr. Sherwin B. Nuland suggests that "of all professions, medicine is one of the most likely to attract people with high personal anxieties about dying. We become doctors because our ability to cure gives us power over the death of which we are so afraid."

But even when students enter medical school with more realistic attitudes, with a recognition that death is as much a part of life as birth, their education usually works against them. In her book *Final Exam: A Surgeon's Reflections on Mortality,* Dr. Pauline W. Chen points out that "even those medical students chosen for their humanitarian qualities . . . may have their generous impulses profoundly suppressed by their medical education," which emphasizes treatments, drugs, procedures all aimed at cure, or, if that is not possible, long-term control of a chronic disease, but teaches little or nothing about what to do when these methods fail.

As Dr. Chen noted, many of the attending physicians assigned to teach medical students and new doctors "have not only their own difficulties in dealing with death but also little insight into how these attitudes affect the care they give terminal patients. Even our textbooks . . . provide us with little or no help with the dying. Thus without guidance or advice, few of us ever adequately learn how to care for patients at the end of life." She added, "The attitudes we physicians have toward death become reinforced each and every time we learn from our attendings and then go on to teach others."

A failed attempt. This does not mean, of course, that no one has tried to change the way doctors care for people who are dying. Millions of dollars were spent on a four-year study begun in 1989 and conducted at five university hospitals. The study is known by the acronym SUPPORT—Study to Understand Prognoses and Preferences for Outcomes and Risks of Treatment, an admittedly confusing title. The study's goal was, first, to assess the quality of care provided by the medical profession to patients with life-threatening diagnoses and, second, to actively intervene to improve the quality of care received by terminal patients.

As expected, the assessment revealed a profound lack of awareness of the needs of the terminally ill. Many of these patients experienced prolonged deaths while being treated with costly, invasive, life-sustaining technology, and spent their last days in an intensive care unit, all but cut off from the family and friends they knew and loved.

In effect, the study revealed that dying in a hospital is neither comfortable nor supportive and often causes, rather than reduces, suffering for patients.

A majority of the physicians caring for these very sick patients had no idea what the patients may have wanted in the way of resuscitation if their hearts or respiratory systems failed. Furthermore, pain suffered by these patients was often inadequately relieved. Family members reported that half of the hospitalized patients who remained conscious at the end of life experienced moderate or severe pain at least half the time, causing emotional as well as physical distress.

Even more disturbing, however, was the outcome of two years of active intervention by specially trained nurses who served as liaisons between patients and their families and the patients' physicians and hospital staff. The nurses provided information to doctors about what patients wanted with regard to resuscitation and other life-prolonging treatments. They facilitated conversations between patients and doctors, and they provided emotional support to patients and their families. Reports on the patients' expected length of survival and interviews with patients and their families were included in the patients' charts.

The goal was to enhance communication between patients and physicians and inform doctors of the patients' life expectancy and what patients wanted in the way of aggressive treatments at the end of life.

But after two years, the study revealed no noticeable improvement in how doctors cared for terminally ill patients. During the last six months of life, the terminally ill still underwent aggressive treatments, many of them in intensive care units. A large percentage of patients still complained of inadequate treatment for their pain. And many physicians still had no idea what their patients may have wanted with regard to cardiopulmonary resuscitation and artificial life support.

Furthermore, having an advance directive—a living will—had no effect on whether or not the doctors used resuscitative efforts at the end of life. The doctors simply could not let patients go, even if that's what patients had said they wanted and those wishes had been explicitly communicated to their doctors.

"Despite the researchers' efforts, the doctors did not change," Dr. Chen wrote in her analysis of the study findings. "Dying patients continued to be a profound source of unease that physicians avoided or ignored."

What can explain such a dismal and disappointing result? Dr. Chen listed several possible reasons: "One may be that physicians cannot bear to undermine a patient's optimism and will continue aggressive therapy in order to maintain a glimmer of hope.

"Another reason may be the increased specialization of our medical system; since dying patients are often under the care of a myriad of specialists, no single physician is ultimately responsible for facilitating end-of-life choices. These terminal patients and the difficult associated discussions end up being punted to and fro between doctors until the topic either is forgotten or becomes irrelevant."

Sometimes, of course, the circumstances of a patient's hospitalization are a factor. Whether as a result of an accident or illness, a patient may be brought to the emergency room and placed on life-sustaining machines before any doctor had an opportunity to determine that the patient is terminally ill or fatally injured. Then the challenge becomes one of stopping—rather than never starting—life-supporting treatments, which both doctors and families may find it hard to do.

A physician's religious beliefs can also throw a monkey wrench into the dying experience. In a study conducted at four Israeli hospitals, "very religious physicians were much less likely to ever stop life-sustaining treatment provided to a suffering terminally ill patient." They were also much less likely to approve of providing adequate pain relief for a terminally ill patient if the medication might hasten the patient's death.

Do finances play a role? Dr. Chen thinks they may, since prolonged treatment is financially remunerative for the doctor and since some doctors are afraid of being sued if they discontinue aggressive treatment or administer adequate pain medication that inadvertently hastens the patient's death. And, if you'll permit a note of cynicism, of course insurance doesn't reimburse hospitals for the care of dead patients.

Dr. Chen also suggested that patients who are in denial about their prospects for recovery play a role in blocking appropriate terminal care. "As many as 10 percent of patients hospitalized with advanced cancer are in severe denial, while an additional 18 percent exhibit moderate levels of denial," she wrote.

Honesty on hold. Is it always denial at work, or may it sometimes be a failure of doctors to convey the truth to patients? As Sharon R. Kaufman noted in . . . *And a Time to Die,* "According to a study of terminally ill cancer patients, many choose to undergo aggressive therapies that are not beneficial and increase suffering because they do not understand the prognosis for their condition." Patients in this study routinely overestimated their chances of living another six months and thus requested continued treatments for their disease that only added to the distress of their dying (see chapter 5).

When doctors focus only on hope for a good outcome, patients remain unaware of their limited life expectancy and may unrealistically devote their time and energy to treatments that are unlikely to work. Yet most doctors are reluctant to disabuse patients of overly optimistic beliefs about their survival chances. Knowing that they have been less than honest with their patients, these doctors find it difficult to confront the limitations of modern medicine and may withdraw when it becomes clear that the patient is dying.

Yes, telling patients that death is nearer than they think will destroy hope for a prolonged survival. But it opens the door for much more: the end-of-life opportunities to finish important business, help loved ones plan for a future without them, and say heartfelt good-byes to family and friends—all opportunities that are denied those who die suddenly, say, from a heart attack or in an accident, or in this case who die without knowing how near the end would be.

Fear of feelings. Of course, physicians do have feelings, and like ordinary folks, they may try to run from feelings that are too painful.

- Doctors have an especially difficult time when dying patients in their care are close to them in age, or the age of their family members, and may retreat rather than face the anguish associated with the patients' impending death.

- Some doctors find themselves getting too attached to patients and feel a need to distance themselves when the end is near to assuage the pain of losing patients who have become friends.

- Even when the doctor–patient relationship has been short, doctors can mourn the loss. A study of doctors' emotional reactions to the recent death of a patient found the following, which may account in part for the avoidance behavior of Hinda's physician: "Doctors are moved by the deaths of strangers for whom they care, and they are often powerfully affected by the deaths of patients with whom they have forged close relationships."

The study also found that attending physicians who teach interns and residents "do not often discuss these strong emotional responses," and that "a conspiracy of silence toward emotions can potentially cause trainees to develop maladaptive coping patterns." And so the cycle of not dealing with death goes on . . . and on . . . and on.

Contrary to popular belief, doctors don't become immune to the effects of "losing" a patient. A study by medical and nursing professionals at the University of Pittsburgh was conducted among 188 doctors, medical residents, and interns who cared for sixty-eight patients who died in the hospital. It revealed that most of these health professionals experienced at least a moderate impact from a patient's death, and the longer a doctor had cared for a patient, the stronger was the doctor's emotional reaction. The researchers recommended that medical teams, and especially younger doctors, would benefit from a staff debriefing following a patient's death.

The son of an elderly man nearing the end of his life told an interviewer for the *Journal of the American Medical Association*, "I think it is important that doctors care about the patients and exhibit some sense of caring, rather than just going through the perfunctory medical functions. There's a kind of loneliness when you're trying to deal with [the dying of a loved one]. I'm sure that doctors can't get too emotionally involved; there has to be some detachment, but still, a friendly attitude and warmth is a good thing."

Dr. Dan Shapiro, a psychologist at the University of Arizona Medical Center in Tucson, spends much of his professional time helping medical students and young physicians learn to be more understanding, compassionate, and communicative with their patients. Unfortunately, he says, while all medical schools profess to have some end-of-life training built into the curriculum, "it varies widely in scope and depth." A quarter to a third of schools have formal programs in which students work with dying patients, and, Dr. Shapiro said, "These do make a difference in how well prepared the students feel."

The psychologist, who himself had been a deathly ill cancer patient as a young college student, said he understands why so many doctors become hardened and callous and turn away from patients who are dying. "It's really painful for them. When doctors are faced with a patient who is not going to make it, they feel incompetent, impotent, insecure, and a great sense of loss, especially if they have cared for the patient for a while and grown attached to the person."

However, when the doctor does it right, the rewards are great.

Dr. Marc Adelman, director of the intensive care unit at Saint Michael's Medical Center in Newark, New Jersey, believes that every single patient, once determined to be terminal, deserves as dignified and compassionate a death as possible. The rewards he routinely receives for remaining a caring presence until the end of a patient's life are reflected in this letter: "Our family cannot thank you enough for your commitment, support and care of our mother. You have been a constant source of solace and understanding for us during one of the most difficult times in our lives. We will never forget your dedication and compassion. You symbolize the very best of your profession and we feel blessed and privileged to have had you as our doctor."

What Patients and Families Can Do

Dr. Meier, a specialist in palliative care, believes that families can help doctors do a better job with dying patients. She recognizes that most doctors "have no script" for dealing with patients who are dying so "they go offstage." Many doctors are unable to face the inevitability of their own death, and when their patients are dying "they feel as if they have failed because they've been taught that they have no role to play, nothing to contribute, unless they can cure."

Furthermore, Dr. Meier noted, "Physicians, like everyone else, are often tongue-tied when confronted with the inevitability of death."

She suggests that family members should try to appeal to the doctor's human side by saying something like this: "My wife is very attached to you and wants to see you before she dies" or "My husband is feeling hurt because he hasn't seen you these last weeks and time is running out."

Patients, too, can help to keep their doctors from disappearing when the end is near by acknowledging how the doctor feels but also letting the doctors know the importance of their continuing involvement. Here is the gist of what one woman said to her doctor when she realized her advanced cancer was no longer responding to treatment: "I know you hoped to cure me and now you feel badly that you couldn't. And I know you did your very best to contain my illness these last months. I'm very grateful to you for that and the time it gave me. But I also want you to know that, now that we've run out of treatment options, it's very important to me that you stick with me until the end."

Problems with physician abandonment often arise when a terminally ill patient is referred to hospice or when a palliative care team is called in to provide comfort care. The referring physicians, whom patients believe to be the ones still in charge, seem to think their job is done and now others must "hold the patient's hand" (metaphorically speaking) through the remaining days, weeks, or months of life.

However, experts in palliative care say that referring physicians should not jump ship without first negotiating a change in command with the patients and family members involved. When a patient is transferred to hospice or palliative care, the patient or a family member may have to speak up and let the primary physician know that his or her continuing contact with the patient is both expected and necessary.

Dr. Adelman explained that referring doctors may not realize how important their continued involvement is to patients who are near the end of life. They may think that the patients have been turned over to other health care professionals and are now in good hands. So if patients want the referring doctor to stay close, they just may have to say so.

"In any relationship, you must ask for what you need," Dr. Adelman said. When a patient is nearing the end of life, he suggested that the patient [or the patient's family, on behalf of the patient] should say to the doctor: "I really need you now. I need your comfort and your wisdom. Please don't abandon me." Dr. Adelman believes that "most—although not all—doctors would respond positively to a plea like that."

Dr. Shapiro agrees that patients and/or families can say things to help doctors stay involved and emotionally responsive to people who are dying. For example, his own mother, who was battling advanced lung cancer at the time, told her oncologist, "I want to stay connected. The worst thing that can happen is that you'll tell me something and I'll cry. But then I'll stop crying and we'll go on from there." Dr. Shapiro said it may also help to tell the doctor that "I'm not saying I need you to fix anything. But I do need you to be with me throughout."

Mickey Martinez, who held off the Grim Reaper for three years despite an initial diagnosis of metastatic colon cancer, had the kind of oncologist we would all wish for if we had an incurable cancer. The doctor, who practices at one of the nation's leading cancer treatment centers, told Mickey not to worry because he was going to be with him for the long haul. And he was, much to the relief of Mickey and his devoted family.

At the very same center a few years earlier, however, Mickey's friend and neighbor, Frank Crewdson, was treated by an oncologist who simply disappeared when it became obvious that Frank was not responding to the treatment he prescribed. And instead of telling Frank himself that he was sorry the treatment wasn't working but that he'd see to it that Frank would be kept as comfortable as possible, he sent in one of his young associates who told this desperately ill patient, "There's nothing else we can do for you," in effect, giving him a death sentence with no safety net and nothing to hope for.

Training Compassionate Doctors

Dr. Shapiro maintains, "We're still in the dark ages when it comes to helping doctors cope with the tragedies they witness over and over again in the course of their careers." As you saw from the SUPPORT study, it is very hard to change the way doctors react and behave once they are fully trained and entrenched in practice patterns. The best chance for breeding a more empathetic brand of physician, most experts believe, is to start at the very beginning— with the selection of medical students not just for their high grades and medical board scores but also, as Dr. Adelman put it, "for their hearts, their integrity." Medical schools simply do not pay enough attention to personal qualities, the kinds of human beings they train to become doctors, he maintains.

That said, there is still hope for improvement once students are in medical school. A concerted effort to improve future doctors' approach to patients at the end of life was made at the University of Iowa's Roy J. and Lucille A. Carver College of Medicine in Iowa City. In a lecture-based course on end-of-life care, second-year medical students engaged in four activities to promote self-reflection about death and dying:

1. Visualizing their own deaths

2. Documenting their prior experiences with death

3. Writing essays in reaction to the content of the course

4. Participating in small group sessions led by physicians

The object of these activities was to help students become aware of their own attitudes toward death and how they would care for patients at the end of life. Prior experience with simply lecturing students on this subject showed that knowledge alone was not enough to influence their behavior. The researchers believed that an exploration of students' attitudes through self-reflection might help them deal more effectively with these highly emotionally charged issues.

For example, in the documentation activity, students were asked to identify their first experiences and feelings surrounding death, since attitudes toward death are often based on these early expo-sures. And in the group sessions, the physician-leader talked about his or her own positive and negative experiences in providing care to dying patients and prompted the students to discuss their own concerns about how they would care for patients near death.

Many of the students expressed concern about how far they should go in expressing strong emotions to patients, families, and colleagues. They worried about losing their composure and about coping with the personal pain and grief that may result from caring for a dying patient. As one student wrote: "How can we, as physicians, be both caring and yet slightly removed in order to not let the death of a beloved patient kill us, especially if working in a field that brings with it many of these types of situations (i.e., oncology)."

Another wrote: "I'm scared about feeling helpless when the point comes that there isn't anything else to do except be supportive and treat symptoms. I anticipate feeling somewhat guilty at those times, even if it is no fault of my own. It will definitely take lots of experience before you learn the right balance of involvement/support and detachment."

But as Dr. Adelman described his own feelings when dealing with dying patients, "Even though I may suffer a lot in the process—and it can be quite painful to go through all those emotions—developing a closeness with patients and their families and bringing them through critical care and end-of-life issues—are among the most satisfying experiences I have in medicine. If you go into medicine only caring about cures and successes, your satisfaction will be very limited."

Students were also concerned about "saying the right thing" to both patients and families. As one student wrote about talking to a mourning family, "I hate death and that's probably why I'll never become really comfortable with the idea, but I will try."

Still, all was not lost. After watching a film in which a patient describes her feeling of not being listened to by some of her health care providers, one student wrote: "Although we cannot save everyone, we can make their dying process one of dignity. Although the person is terminal, they are still a person. We as physicians must take into consideration what the patient's wishes are. We need to stop and ask ourselves, 'Are we performing a procedure that will benefit the patient in the long run, or are we doing it for our comfort because we feel that we must do something?' As physicians, we have to realize that our way is not always the right way and most importantly listen."

This is the kind of physician I want caring for me when my time comes. It is the kind of physician every patient and every patient's family deserves to have when the end is near.

FOR FURTHER READING

Chen, Pauline W. *Final Exam: A Surgeon's Reflections on Mortality*. New York: Alfred A. Knopf, 2007.

Nuland, Sherwin B. *How We Die: Reflections on Life's Final Chapter*. New York: Vintage Books, 1995.

Tolstoy, Leo. *The Death of Ivan Ilyich*. New York: Bantam Books, 1981.

CHAPTER 14

Assisted Dying: What to Consider When Illness Is Unbearable

D r. Jack Kevorkian, the Michigan physician popularly known as "Doctor Death" for openly helping terminally ill and severely incapacitated patients end their lives, brought into public dialogue a subject that has plagued those who have cared for dying patients for decades. Every year countless doctors and nurses, family caregivers and friends are asked to help the patients they serve hasten an end to their misery. As of 2007 only one state—Oregon—had made it legal for physicians to assist the dying by providing lethal doses of medication, and only under certain well-defined circumstances (see the Oregon Death with Dignity Act on pages 204–5). But the passage of Oregon's Death with Dignity Act in 1994 and its implementation in 1997 sparked scores of professional articles and research studies on physician-assisted dying and galvanized public opinion on the subject.

Many Americans—70 percent in a Harris poll conducted in April 2005—said they believed "the law should allow doctors to comply with the wishes of a dying patient in severe distress who asks to have his or her life ended," and 67 percent said they would favor a law like Oregon's in their state. In another national poll in March 2008, 66.3 percent favored such a law.

The practice legalized in Oregon, as well as in the Netherlands, Belgium, Switzerland, and the Northern Territory of Australia, has

"Before we try assisted suicide, Mrs. Rose, let's give the aspirin a chance."

been dubbed physician-assisted suicide. But, according to a sixty-eight-year-old Oregon woman who was diagnosed with advanced breast cancer in 2000, "I think of this as 'doctor-aided dying' or 'compassionate aid in dying.' This has nothing to do with suicide in the traditional sense."

Clarifying the Terms

The Oregon law (despite the theoretical public endorsements given in polls, comparable laws were soundly defeated in seven states) specifically permits only that under certain well-defined circumstances a physician can provide patients with a means to end their lives, hence the term *physician-assisted suicide,* or PAS. In most cases this means providing a terminally ill but mentally sound patient who is not clinically depressed with a dose of medication that will result in death if the patient chooses to take it.

This is legally and medically different from Dr. Kevorkian's practice of euthanasia, in which the physician injects the patient with a drug that causes death. Since euthanasia (some call it mercy killing, others medically assisted murder) is illegal in all fifty states, Dr. Kevorkian's flouting of the law landed him in jail. PAS is also different from providing a terminally ill patient who is near death and suffering intolerably with enough medication to relieve the patient's symptoms even though the drug may hasten that patient's death.

Though both lay and professional interest in the use and legality of PAS and euthanasia mushroomed in the 1970s and has since been a hot topic in both research and casual conversation, it is hardly a new concern for both patients and physicians. In 1923 Sigmund Freud, the world's first and foremost psychoanalyst, was diagnosed with oral cancer and subsequently endured more than thirty surgeries and primitive radiation therapy. He remained productive during his remaining sixteen years of life, but when his pain was no longer bearable, he reminded his doctor of an earlier promise to assist him in dying.

When the doctor, Max Schur, said he had not forgotten, Freud "sighed with relief, held my hand for a moment longer, and said 'I thank you.'" Following several injections of morphine, Freud "lapsed into a coma and did not wake up again," Dr. Schur reported.

Drs. Jack D. McCue of San Francisco and Lewis M. Cohen of Springfield, Massachusetts, believe that "knowing that he could ask his physician to intervene when life became unbearable might have allowed him to continue his productive professional life during those unsettled years, while undergoing multiple disfiguring surgical procedures and nearly unendurable pain." The doctors described Freud's death as a "good" one: "Freud's end was purposeful, brief, relatively devoid of suffering, consistent with ego ideals, and allowed for resolution and reconciliation."

But since Freud's day, many treatments have become available that can ease the symptoms of most terminally ill patients. Today we have hospice care, which focuses on relieving the symptoms of dying patients and is available in most parts of the country. And palliative care services, dedicated to providing comfort care for suffering patients (dying or otherwise) and their families, are gradually becoming more prominent in hospitals nationwide (see chapter 9).

None of which guarantees, however, that all patients with terminal illnesses can avail themselves of either palliative or hospice care or that these services, when available, can always relieve their agony. Studies of dying patients who seek a hastened death have shown that their reasons often go beyond physical ones like intractable pain or emotional ones like feeling hopeless. Often the reasons are existential: recognition that their lives have lost all meaning; concern that they have become an undue burden to their loved ones; desire to avoid a protracted death, or distress about the time and money being "wasted" in prolonging their lives, which are destined to end soon anyway.

For example, in December 2007 Mrs. Gloria C. Phares of Weldon, Missouri, described her consternation with her ongoing existence in a letter to me at *The New York Times* after reading an article I wrote about elderly suicide.

"I was healthy until 90 and then boom! Atrial fibrillation; deaf, can't enjoy music or hear a voice unless 10 inches from my ear; fell, fractured my thigh and am now a cripple; had a slight stroke the day after my beloved husband died after 61 years of marriage. I've lived a happy life but from here on out it's all downhill. Is there any point in my living any longer? I'm not living—just existing. I very much want to die but our society doesn't let me. Oh for a pill to ease myself out and end my pain, pain, pain."

Twenty-two years earlier Betty Rollin, journalist and author, published the story of her mother's determination to take control of her own death after a clearly losing battle with ovarian cancer. In her very personal, moving, and beautifully written book, *Last Wish*, Ms. Rollin, desperate to help the mother she adored, described her search for an effective means of granting her dying mother's wish to determine the time of her last breaths. Finally, with a fatal dose of pills at her disposal and a plan of action in place, Ms. Rollin's mother, Ida, tells her daughter and son-in-law, "I am a most happy woman. And this is my wish. I want you to remember . . . ," and then she is gone.

Dr. Timothy E. Quill of the University of Rochester School of Medicine believes his personal experience makes clear the occasional need for an assisted death. As he wrote in May 2004 in the *New England Journal of Medicine:* "I recently helped my father to die. He was an engineer, independent, always on the go and in charge. He began to deteriorate rapidly from an ill-defined dementing illness, and his confusion and intermittent agitation did not respond to the standard treatments that were tried. He had made his wishes clear about avoiding any prolongation of his dying, but now he had lost the capacity to make decisions for himself.

"Furthermore, we did not know whether his remaining life span was measured in months or years. He was unable to sleep or relax at night, despite trials of neuroleptics, antidepressants, and antianxiety agents. My mother was exhausted, but neither of them wanted their home to be invaded by strangers. How were we to honor his wishes and values and help him to find dignity and peace in the last phase of his life? . . .

"Symptom-directed measures recommended by multiple consultants were ineffective. His agitation was also worsening as he became more unable to walk. We elected to try low-dose phenobarbital [which kept him mildly sedated and comfortable]. He subsequently appeared more peaceful than he had in months. He awakened periodically to exchange a few words, but he almost completely stopped eating and drinking. He died peacefully five days later."

Dr. Quill has no regrets about easing his father's passage to the Great Beyond. "Because my father had been very clear about his wishes while he was still mentally competent, and because our family understood how the system works and had the relevant knowledge and resources, we were able to use our fragmented health care system to provide him with comprehensive and humane end-of-life care."

However, he added, *"Most families are not so fortunate."* Knowing there are last-resort options "is very important to those who fear being trapped in a life filled with suffering without the prospect of a timely escape. Those who know that escape is possible often feel free to expend their energy on other more important matters, and most will not need that escape if they receive adequate palliative care. A few, however, like my father . . . will end up in conditions of unacceptable suffering."

It is for these few, then, that PAS or euthanasia has become a preeminent concern. As the Oregon experience to date has clearly demonstrated, only a tiny fraction of patients in the terminal stages of illness are likely to avail themselves of an option like PAS. In Oregon, only 1 percent of patients have asked their doctors for prescriptions that could hasten their death, and only 0.1 percent have received approval or followed through.

Those who do hasten their deaths are generally self-reliant, accomplished individuals who value self-control and find it humiliating to have to be cared for by others. People like this cannot bear the thought of spending their last days in a morphine haze, soiling their bedsheets, and being turned over by nurses. "It's not that their pain can't be controlled," Katrina Hedberg of the Oregon Department of Human Services told AARP in 2003. "It's that to control it they give up what makes their life meaningful."

Weighing the Options

Most physicians surveyed have said either that they are not in favor of legalizing PAS, or if it were legalized, they would be unwilling to participate in the practice. Their reasons range from religious objections to a negation of their chosen role as healers.

Dr. Diane Meier, for example, was an early advocate of PAS, and in 1992 she was among the first to publish guidelines for performing it. She believed that patients knew best what was best for them, and that the medical profession's failure to accede to a dying patient's request to hasten death was the epitome of arrogance.

But within a decade, Dr. Meier, a geriatrician who now heads the palliative care program at Mount Sinai Medical Center in New York, did a complete about-face. It all began with an eighty-seven-year-old patient who lived alone and was beset by a host of medical problems: arthritis, loss of hearing and eyesight, diabetes, and high blood pressure. Barely able to walk, constantly irritable, and unable to live the life she once knew, she repeatedly asked Dr. Meier for a pill to end it all.

Instead, Dr. Meier talked at length to the woman, who revealed a litany of problems involving her poor relationship with her grown children. Instead of writing a prescription, the doctor made a few phone calls, urging the children to set aside their resentments and visit their mother, which they did. When the old wounds were healed, the woman said she was ready to die, which she did five days later without any medical assistance.

In Dr. Meier's experience, when a patient asks to die, "nine times out of ten it's an expression of despair" and an attempt to communicate that despair to her doctor. But unlike Dr. Meier, most doctors are either too busy or not trained to deal with such feelings. She has found, however, that when palliative care is fully and properly administered—when patients' physical symptoms, emotional anguish, and family problems are well attended to—nearly all rescind their requests for a hastened demise.

A common problem involves the failure to identify and treat depression in terminally ill patients, in part because most physicians are not trained in psychiatry and in part because they *expect* people with devastating progressive and incurable disease to be depressed. Doctors may also miss other, often subtle, psychiatric symptoms that could underly a patient's wish for a hastened death, including anxiety, delirium, and mild dementia. The Oregon law does not require a psychiatric consultation when a patient requests PAS unless the referring doctor believes the patient's ability to make rational decisions is compromised.

Although the Oregon law requires that a patient seeking PAS be mentally alert, Dr. Meier says that the judgment of dying patients is most often clouded by "intermittent confusion, anxiety, and depression." Dr. Meier and others have found that when underlying depression is recognized and adequately treated, the desire for an assisted death nearly always disappears.

Dr. Meier fears that legalizing PAS could lead to a patient's premature death and missed opportunities to identify and relieve suffering and to complete critical life tasks. Other concerns of those who oppose PAS include a risk of subtle or overt coercion by caregivers who want it all to end, family members who seek an inheritance, or health care providers who want to be free of a time-consuming patient who is not going to get well. Dr. Meier says it is impossible, as the Oregon law requires, for a doctor to certify that a patient's request for PAS is not coerced.

Some doctors may empathize with a patient's desire for a hastened death because they identify with the patient's suffering and feelings of helplessness and because they feel impotent at not being able to fix these problems. As Dr. Meier put it, "Physicians are often particularly intolerant of lack of power and control and particularly unwilling to accept the fact that there are some things that cannot be fixed or made better." Yet there are no provisions in any PAS laws for examining the unconscious motives of the doctor.

It can be, as some say, "a slippery slope" to legalize the ability of doctors to kill patients or, as is legal in Oregon, to provide them with the means to kill themselves.

Another concern involves the frequency with which patients change their minds about seeking a hastened death, a factor somewhat built into the Oregon law, which requires a fifteen-day waiting period between the request for PAS and a prescription for the drugs to carry it out. In Oregon, nearly half the patients who received palliative care after requesting PAS subsequently withdrew their request.

Dr. Ezekiel J. Emanuel, a bioethicist at the National Institutes of Health, and coauthors Dr. Linda L. Emanuel and Diane L. Fairclough, studied the attitudes of terminally ill patients toward PAS and euthanasia. Of 988 patients, 60.2 percent hypothetically supported the practices, but only 10.6 percent seriously considered requesting either option for themselves. Those who would consider a hastened death were more likely to be depressed, to have major caregiving needs, and to be experiencing unrelieved pain. However, two to six months later, when the patients were reinterviewed, half of those who had been considering a physician-assisted death had changed their minds.

On the other hand, Dr. Emanuel and colleagues also found that almost an equal number of patients who were not initially interested in an assisted death had begun considering this option two to six months later. Ultimately, of the 256 patients who had died by the end of the study, only one had died by euthanasia or PAS, one had unsuccessfully attempted suicide, and one repeatedly asked for her life to be ended but was refused by her family and physicians.

Proponents of PAS argue that aiding the death of a patient who is terminally ill or suffering severely from an incurable debilitating illness is a compassionate act and that refusing to provide assistance in dying merely prolongs the person's suffering. Refusing to help such patients die, proponents maintain, is tantamount to abandoning them in their time of greatest need and inflicts irreparable, unacceptable harm.

In Belgium, where euthanasia is legal, many patients with advanced AIDS do not request a hastened death even if they become severely ill. But doctors there say that knowing euthanasia could be available to them on request enables them to cope better with their uncertain future and improves the quality of their lives.

I cannot help thinking that both opponents' and proponents' arguments have merit. In 1958 when my mother's idea of life was de-

"Grandma's going to Florida."

stroyed by the unrelenting progression of ovarian cancer, she twice tried to end her life, first by cutting her wrists at home and then by drinking rubbing alcohol in the hospital. Though she was "rescued" in both instances, no attempt was made to deal with the physical and emotional anguish that prompted her desperate moves. Perhaps, if palliative care had been an option way back then, or if a psychiatric consultation had been ordered, it could have relieved her feelings of desperation. At the same time, having witnessed her physical deterioration and existential suffering firsthand, I believe that even with the best possible physical and emotional support, had I been in her shoes, I, too, would have chosen the option of a hastened demise.

In another instance, a beloved high school teacher of mine, then in his nineties and residing in an assisted living facility, pointed to several housemates who were seriously demented and told me, "I don't want to end up like that. My memory is going, and I want to know that someone will help me die before my mind is gone." I empathized strongly with his desire—I wouldn't want to live, either, if I were demented, no matter how strong my body—but as a distant friend I was in no position to help him directly. Instead, I suggested he discuss his wishes with his physician and his children. Happily, he died a few years later of natural causes, his mind and memory still very much intact.

As you can see, one doesn't have to be terminally ill to wish for a hastened death. Sally D. of San Francisco, at age sixty, said that three years earlier she "was an active hiker, horseback rider, employee, wife, and a happy woman" until she suffered a series of surgical screw-ups that left her "a virtual invalid" unable to eat solid food, her innards torn apart, and her body in "constant intractable pain" despite powerful painkillers. Her remaining option: a pelvic neurectomy, an operation that would stop the pain but leave her paralyzed from the waist down. "So, after three years and hundreds of various treatments, I'm ready to *stop*. Over these last three years, I've discovered the underground network of 'assisted dying' help, the complete disregard of mainstream western medicine doctors, and the amazing strength, the deep grief, and the loneliness of people who are facing terrible illness and want to end their suffering."

Although the American Nursing Association has taken a stand against medically assisted deaths for the terminally ill, clearly some nurses are tortured by their inability to act. Fifteen years had passed since Karen Roush, a registered nurse and editor at the *American Journal of Nursing,* watched helplessly as her best friend Steven lay dying of AIDS. He didn't seem afraid of death or pain but he was terrified of losing his mind. He asked for her help if things got too bad. He said, "Don't let me end up like my grandfather," whom he had watched die incontinent and demented. As Ms. Roush recalled her tortured feelings at the time, "I had promised to take care of you. Now I sit by and do nothing while you lie diapered, delirious, suffering. It would have been so easy to accomplish what you had asked."

Opting for a Patient-Controlled Death

Are there viable alternatives to having a doctor help a patient die? In the United States there is a volunteer-run organization, Final Exit Network, that helps members with incurable conditions that cause intolerable suffering find a peaceful way out of this life. The organization does not limit its services to people who are terminally ill. It serves members suffering from cancer; neurological diseases like ALS, Alzheimer's, Parkinson's, and Huntington's; motor neuron diseases like multiple sclerosis and muscular dystrophy; respiratory diseases like emphysema; and degenerative ailments like congestive heart failure, stroke, and AIDS. However, it only helps those whose family, friends, or caregivers know about the plan and are not strongly opposed. Those accepted must be "cognitively functional, physically strong enough to perform the required tasks, and able to procure the items required." The network can be reached on the Web at www.finalexitnetwork.org; by mail at PO Box 965005, Marietta, GA 30066; or by phone at (800) 524-EXIT (3948).

Some patients choose their own method to hasten death that requires no outside assistance. According to Dr. Linda Ganzini, psychiatrist and palliative care specialist at Oregon Health and Science University School of Medicine, when a patient voluntarily refuses food and fluids, the result is nearly always a peaceful death within two to three weeks. Dr. Ganzini questioned all 429 nurses working in hospice programs in Oregon. Of the 307 responses she received, 102 nurses said that in the previous four years they had cared for a patient who deliberately hastened death by voluntarily refusing food and fluids. The reasons given: the patients were ready to die, they saw continued existence as pointless, and they considered their quality of life poor. Within fifteen days, 85 percent of the patients had died. On a scale of 0 (for a very bad death) to 9 (for a very good death), the nurses gave the quality of the deaths among these patients a median score of 8.

Dr. Peter Reagan, a family physician in Portland, Oregon, recalls an elderly patient who had been debilitated for years by severe arthritic pain and who sought, but did not qualify for, a physician-assisted death. Disappointed, she opted instead to stop consuming all food and fluids. Dr. Reagan was surprised to see his long-suffering patient become self-confident and seemingly happy. Her family gathered and visited for a week. Then, with no request for any other care, her body failed rapidly and she died in peace.

Another published case involved a forty-three-year-old Utah woman with rapidly progressing amyotrophic lateral sclerosis— ALS or, as it is commonly called, Lou Gehrig's disease. The disease causes a loss of control of all bodily functions, although the mind remains fully alert. Within four months of the Utah woman's diagnosis, she was unable to bathe or dress herself. No medicine was able to relieve her nightly pain. Knowing she had the option to end her life by voluntarily refusing to eat and drink gave her peace and relieved the pressure on her husband of having to help her commit suicide if her situation became intolerable. In her final months, friends helped her prepare two decades' worth of birthday gifts and notes for her six-year-old daughter. That done, she began her fast. After two days, she no longer felt hungry and required only a moistening mouth spray and pain medication. On the thirteenth day of her fast, she began a morphine infusion through a pump, lapsed into unconsciousness, and died three days later.

For patients unable to speak for themselves, their designated health care agents can request withdrawal of food and fluid, suggests Dr. Stanley A. Terman, a psychiatrist and medical director of Caring Advocates and Peaceful Transitions.

"Palliative and hospice care has focused on control of symptoms, spiritual concerns, and the family's needs," Dr. Ganzini explained. "But our data suggest that there is a group of patients for whom the most important goal is remaining in control and not being dependent on other people. We need to do a better job of recognizing these people and helping them plan for the end of life."

Or, as Dr. Meier has put it, "Our society should not be reduced to offering patients a choice between inadequate care and suicide."

Among the 171 patients who died with a physician's assistance in

Oregon from 1998 to 2003, the most common patient concerns were fears about losing independence (87 percent), an inability to participate in enjoyable life activities (83 percent), loss of dignity (82 percent), and fear of losing control over bodily functions (58 percent). Less frequent were concerns about being a burden (36 percent), inadequate pain control (22 percent), and costs of medical treatment (2 percent).

THE OREGON DEATH WITH DIGNITY ACT

As of this writing Oregon was the only jurisdiction in the United States to have legalized PAS. After surviving several legal challenges, the act became law in 1997. These are its terms.

All patients requesting assisted suicide must:

• *Be eighteen or older and reside in Oregon*

• *Be capable of making and communicating health care decisions*

• *Have a terminal diagnosis with a life expectancy of six months or less*

• *Make two oral and at least one written request for a prescription for lethal medication to his or her physician. Oral requests must be separated by at least fifteen days, and written requests must be signed by the patient in the presence of two witnesses.*

In addition, the physician who prescribes the medication and a consulting physician must:

• *Confirm the diagnosis and prognosis*

• *Establish the patient's capacity to make health care decisions*

> • *Order a psychiatric referral if either physician believes the patient is impaired by a psychological disorder, such as depression*
>
> The prescribing physician must also discuss alternatives to assisted suicide with the patient, including hospice and palliative care, and must request (but cannot require) that the patient notify next of kin of the request for assisted suicide.

Considerations if You or a Loved One Seeks a Hastened Death

Long before the advent of the Oregon law some physicians have been willing to provide dying patients with a means to end their lives. In Oregon, before PAS was legalized, 7 percent of 2,761 physicians surveyed reported that they had written a prescription knowing that their patients intended to use it to take their own lives. In a national survey published in 2000, 10.8 percent of 3,288 oncologists (doctors who treat cancer) reported having performed PAS during their careers. And in San Francisco, 53 percent of 228 physicians who cared for patients with AIDS said they had granted a dying patient's request for PAS.

So, you may find that your doctor or your loved one's doctor is willing to participate in PAS. Or, if the doctor is unwilling, he or she may be willing to refer you to another doctor who is. Should you then jump at the chance for a hastened death? Not, the experts say, before carefully considering several critical factors:

- Why does the patient want help in dying? The reasons should be fully explored and dealt with. If, for example, the patient fears intolerable pain, assurance can be given that severe pain can nearly always be controlled. However, if the patient's pain or other symptoms prove uncontrollable, a request for terminal sedation or PAS might be honored.

- Does the patient fully understand the request? Depression, anxiety, or confusion can cloud a patient's mind. All potential psychological impediments to clear judgment should be explored and treated before acceding to a request for PAS.

- Is someone other than the patient behind the request? If a caregiver has repeatedly spoken of the impossible burden of caring for the patient, subtle coercion may be the reason for the request for PAS. Or perhaps there is a relative or friend awaiting a substantial inheritance.

- Is the request consistent with the patient's religious or spiritual beliefs? A patient whose religion is strongly "pro-life" or who believes that suicide is immoral may be very conflicted in seeking PAS.

- Has the patient considered other options? Hospice care for those expected to die within six months or palliative care for those who may or may not die soon is widely available and, more often than not, can prompt patients to lose interest in PAS. Voluntary refusal of food and fluids is a viable alternative that is free of the legal burdens of PAS. Or if the dying process becomes too much to bear, sedation could be administered to ease the symptoms and, at the same time, legally hasten death.

- Has the patient's request been discussed with family members or significant others? Concern about the effects of PAS can rightly focus on those who will be left behind as well as the person who is dying. Also, patients who request PAS because they believe they are too much of a burden on family or friends might rescind the request if they can be reassured that this is not so.

More information is available from the End-of-Life Consultation Program, an adjunct of what used to be called the Hemlock Society but is now known as Compassion & Choices. With the aid of the consultation program, a forty-one-year-old woman with an extremely aggressive form of multiple sclerosis was helped to die. She saw herself as no longer viable and was pronounced terminally ill by two doctors and mentally sound by a psychiatrist before the program stepped in to help. The organization does not reveal details of how death is hastened for fear of providing too much information for other people at risk of suicide.

Compassion & Choices counsels patients about hospice care and other alternatives to a hastened death. And many patients so counseled do change their minds. The organization is there for those whose desire for a hastened death remains immutable. Those interested can contact Compassion & Choices at PO Box 101810, Denver, CO 80250-1810, or by calling toll-free (800) 247-7421.

IF YOU ARE A PHYSICIAN

In an ongoing series in the *Journal of the American Medical Association*, Perspectives on Care at the Close of Life, supported by a grant from the Robert Wood Johnson Foundation, Drs. Paul B. Bascom and Susan W. Tolle of Oregon Health and Science University suggested a series of questions for doctors to ask when a patient requests PAS. They are categorized by areas of exploration potentially relevant to the patient's request. Many of the same questions can be used by friends or family members to explore a patient's desire for a hastened death.

AREA	QUESTIONS
Expectations, fears	*How do you expect your death to go?*
	What concerns you most about dying?

	What are your greatest fears?
	What's the worst thing that could happen to you as you die?
	Have other people close to you died?
	How did their deaths go?
Options for care	What do you understand about your options for end-of-life care?
	How specifically would you like me to assist you?
Patient goals	What are your goals for whatever time you have remaining to live?
	What is the most important thing for you right now?
	If you were to die now, what would be left undone?
Family, caregivers	What does your family think about this decision?
	How has your illness affected your family?
	How will your family react if you proceed with PAS?
Relief of suffering	Are you suffering right now?
	What is your principal source of suffering?
	What kind of suffering concerns you most?

	What is your most troublesome symptom right now?
Patient values	*What is your quality of life right now?*
	What gives your life meaning right now?
	How bad would your quality of life have to be for your life to have no meaning?
Rule out depression	*Are you depressed?*
	What things in life still give you pleasure?
	Have you had a good life?
	Do you have any regrets?

FOR FURTHER READING

Humphrey, Derek. *Final Exit: The Practicalities of Self-Deliverance and Assisted Suicide for the Dying.* New York: Delta Trade Paperback, 2002.

Rollin, Betty. *Last Wish.* New York: PublicAffairs, 1998.

Terman, Stanley A. *The Best Way to Say Goodbye: A Legal Peaceful Choice at the End of Life.* Carlsbad, CA: Life Transitions Publications, 2007.

Warnock, Mary, and Elisabeth MacDonald. *Easeful Death: Is There a Case for Assisted Dying?* New York: Oxford University Press, 2008.

CHAPTER 15

Grief: It's Not a Disease

J ust as we were born to love, laugh, and be happy, we were born to cry and grieve. Grief is a normal part of being human, and when you lose someone you love—or you are about to lose everyone you love—it is natural to feel sad, disoriented, and overcome with grief.

"I don't want to lose you," C. S. Lewis (played by Anthony Hopkins) said in the movie *Shadowlands* to the recently found love of his life, Helen Joy Gresham (played by Debra Winger), who was dying of bone cancer. She replied, "The pain then is part of the happiness now." Some days after her death, Mr. Lewis wept with her young son, Douglas, over their mutual loss. When he regained his composure, he said to Douglas, who wanted to know why she had to die, "The pain now is part of the happiness then. That's the deal."

As Dr. Robert Hansson, a psychologist at the University of Tulsa who studies grief, put it, "Feeling grief is the burden we face because we're capable of becoming attached and loving people. It's a natural process—it hurts, but most people can work through it and go on."

In *The Courage to Grieve,* a book that two of my friends who had lost their husbands—one suddenly and the other after a three-year illness—found extremely helpful, Judy Tatelbaum says, "That we can grieve and recover often seems an amazing feat, yet human resilience is amazing. Grief is a wound that needs attention in order to heal. Unfortunately, our misconceptions about grief keep us from developing the courage we need to face grief. Many of us fear that, if allowed in, grief will bowl us over indefinitely. The truth is that grief experienced does dissolve. The only grief that does not end is grief that has not been fully faced."

No "Right Way" to Grieve

People who have been through the process, and experts who study it, have found that there is no one "right way" to mourn the death of someone you love. As Amitai Etzioni, professor of sociology at George Washington University, wrote following the death of his thirty-eight-year-old son, who left behind a two-year-old son and pregnant wife, "There is no set form for grief, and no 'right' way to express it."

You've no doubt heard a lot about the "normal" stages of grief—the same ones that a dying person is supposed to pass through (but rarely does—see chapter 2): denial, anger, bargaining, depression, and finally acceptance. According to this theory, once acceptance is reached a bereaved person can remember the deceased without emotional suffering and can view the future positively.

But there is little scientific support for this or any other theory of grief that describes it as occurring in orderly stages. Two researchers who reviewed the scientific literature concluded that not all individuals go through the same grief process. Everyone does not experience intense distress that gives way to recovery. Some, in fact, do not show distress at all, while others remain highly distressed for far longer than would be expected.

People who are terminally ill face it in ways unique to their individual personalities and their usual way of coping with life stresses. Likewise, mourners choose different routes, and some may never come to accept their loss.

Dr. Etzioni, whose wife had died in a car accident twenty-one years earlier, was warned not to "wallow too long" in anger when his son died. But, he said, "I was, and am, angry. To make parents bury their children is wrong; to have both my wife and son taken from me, for forever and a day, is cruel beyond words."

He also noted that many therapists may caution the bereaved against keeping so busy that they avoid "healthy" grieving. Dr. Etzioni chose instead to follow the advice of an Israeli relative who is a psychiatrist, who told him, "We are not to ask why, but what."

To Dr. Etzioni, "The 'what' is that which survivors in grief are bound to do for one another. My family, close friends, and I keep busy, calling each other and giving long answers to simple question like 'How did your day go today?' " They take turns playing with his little grandson, and friends spend nights with his son's widow and plan to be there to hold her hand when the baby is born.

George Bonnano, psychologist at Columbia University Teachers College, and Camille B. Wortman, psychologist at the State University of New York at Stony Brook, conducted a very revealing study of 766 married couples. At least one partner of each couple was over age sixty-five. The couples were followed for up to eight years, and when a spouse died the researchers assessed the bereavement experiences of the widow or widower over time. This is what they found:

- 46 percent of the survivors were "resilient." They experienced transitory distress, but scored low in depression both before the death and at six and eighteen months after their spouse died.

- 11 percent followed a common grief course, with rather severe depression at six months that was largely gone by eighteen months.

- 16 percent, who were not initially depressed, nonetheless were devastated after their spouses died and experienced prolonged depression.

- 8 percent had been chronically depressed beforehand, and the depression deepened following their spouse's death.

- But 10 percent who had been depressed prior to the death of their spouse did very well afterward, perhaps because they had been in a bad marriage or were relieved to be free of the burdens of caring for an ill spouse.

- And the final 9 percent did not fit into any category.

"Clearly, the five stages of grief don't necessarily fit," Dr. Robert A. Neimeyer, professor of psychology at the University of Memphis and editor of the scientific journal *Death Studies*, said of these findings. "There is no one pathway through grief."

This was well demonstrated by the 233 individuals who participated in the Yale Bereavement Study, which reassessed their feelings over the course of two years following their loss. Each had had a family member or loved one who died from natural causes (not an accident or other traumatic event). Natural causes account for 94 percent of all deaths in the United States.

The researchers, who published their findings in the February 21, 2007, issue of the *Journal of the American Medical Association*, found that at every six-month interval following the death, acceptance—not anger or denial—was the leading symptom of grief, and it increased with time. Second in importance was yearning, which was significantly more common than depression and which diminished gradually with time. Third was depression, followed closely by disbelief, both of which also diminished with time. Anger was the least common reaction among those whose loved ones had died naturally.

However, the researchers noted, reactions among the bereaved tend to differ when a death occurs unexpectedly. Those who survive a family member's traumatic death are much less likely to experience "acceptance" within a year or two of their loss and more likely to experience disbelief and anger and have great difficulty making sense of their loss.

Several studies have documented that grief following an unanticipated death differs from that when a death is expected. Unanticipated loss can overwhelm a person's ability to adapt, leaving them unable to grasp the full implications of the loss. Following an unexpected death, acceptance can be long in coming. The loss may seem inexplicable—it just does not make sense, and neither does the world—which explains in part the prolonged agony of those who lost loved ones on September 11, 2001.

The reaction to a death also varies according to how close a relationship the deceased had to the survivors. Joan Didion, in her cathartic book, *The Year of Magical Thinking*, written a year after the sudden death of her husband John Gregory Dunne in December 2003, put it this way: "Grief, when it comes, is nothing we expect. It was not what I felt when my parents died: my father died a few days short of his 85th birthday and my mother a month short of her 91st, both after some years of increasing debility. What I felt in each instance was sadness, loneliness, regret for a time gone by, for things unsaid, for my inability to share or even in any real way to acknowledge, at the end, the pain and helplessness and physical humiliation they each endured.

"My father was dead, my mother was dead . . . but I would still get up in the morning and send out the laundry. I would still plan a menu for Easter lunch. I would still remember to renew my passport.

"Grief is different. Grief has no distance. Grief comes in waves, paroxysms, sudden apprehensions that weaken the knees and blind the eyes and obliterate the dailiness of life."

Ms. Didion and her husband had a very close and loving relationship. They both worked at home and always reviewed each other's writings, offering constructive criticisms and corrections. There was almost no place Ms. Didion could go, nothing she could do, that failed to remind her of her overwhelming loss. She spent the year "bringing him back" many times a day—asking herself, "What would John think about this?" "What would John do if he were here?"

Some would say Ms. Didion experienced what therapists now call complicated grief, which should be treated professionally. But I suspect most people would recognize that the depths of her prolonged pain reflected the depth of her relationship with her late husband and realize that eventually Ms. Didion's anguish will abate on its own and she will succeed in reorganizing her life so that it is satisfying and even joy-filled despite her profound loss.

Sandy Cross reported the following to the East End Hospice in Westhampton Beach, New York, where her father had spent his last days: "This past Thanksgiving marked the second anniversary of my father's death. The first year without Daddy was so different from this second year without him. That first year was filled with a pain of emptiness. Hollow, aching emptiness. Tears—so many for so long.

"The second year is easier—all the 'firsts' have come and gone. First Christmas, first Father's Day, first birthday . . . During the second year, I found much of the emptiness replaced with a love from my father that slowly began to fill my heart, pushing out the emptiness, little by little. I feel like the luckiest daughter in the world to have had such a caring, loving father."

Anticipatory Grief

Both those who are dying and the people who love them often grieve in anticipation of their losses. A terminal diagnosis changes the nature of a person's existence, taking away a sense of control over one's life and overthrowing all plans for the present and hopes for the future. People who know they will die soon can experience many of the feelings common to those who have lost loved ones: shock, anger, denial, helplessness, sorrow, and depression. After all, people who are dying will lose everyone and everything they have ever loved.

They may begin counting the days to the end, and greet each dawn with the realization that the end is a day closer. Life may seem surreal. They are often unable to fit back into the pattern of life they lived prior to their diagnosis, and they may withdraw socially and detach themselves prematurely from people and the world. This premature separation from life can be exacerbated by friends and acquaintances who avoid people who are dying out of shock, dismay, and not knowing what to say (see chapter 12).

Likewise, those who will survive the loss of a loved one may feel intense grief in advance of their loss. "Symptoms" of anticipatory grief may include any of the following:

- Thinking of past good times and the value of their relationship

- Becoming preoccupied with how long their loved one will live

- Rehearsing the actual death in their minds

- Thinking about what life will be like without their loved one

- Reviewing regrets and feelings of guilt

- Alternating between acceptance and denial

- Feeling sad and depressed and perhaps "detaching" themselves from their loved one to avoid the pain of grief

- Experiencing a "roller coaster" of emotions about the illness and their relationship with their loved one

Anticipatory grief is not necessarily a bad thing. It can help people complete unfinished business and facilitate communication between loved ones. It can give people the opportunity to plan and prepare for the end and to say their good-byes in special ways. By anticipating their loss, survivors may be able to make better sense of it as a predictable event.

Studies have shown that anticipatory grief does not mollify or shorten the grief experience following a death. It can, however, result in emotional numbness at the time of the death, causing survivors to question their love for the deceased because they seem to lack feelings. Survivors who have worked through intense feelings of grief before a death may indeed appear emotionless at the time of death and may be seen by others as callous or uncaring. This could have the unfortunate consequence of reducing the support the bereaved receive from others, or it can result in prolonged family conflicts over a presumed lack of feelings for the deceased.

Some people try to hide anticipatory grief, thinking they must remain "strong" for the person who is dying or the children. They may try to put on a brave face for other family members and friends. Lorraine Kember, author of *Lean on Me: Cancer Through a Carer's Eyes* about her experience caring for her dying husband, said that counseling helped her unleash her hidden feelings and "stop acting as if everything was okay, when nothing was okay." In counseling, she said she "could take off my brave face and let my defenses down."

If counseling is not an option, Ms. Kember suggests that people keep a personal diary, recording their feelings every day. As she recalled, "My diary was without a doubt my strongest coping tool. I wrote in it daily, often in the form of poetry, pouring my anger, my fear, and my heartache onto the pages. Periodically, I would read back through it, and through this I came to know myself very well. Later I could see my strength coming through."

Common Symptoms of Grief

How people experience grief is influenced by their cultural and religious backgrounds, as well as by practical issues like financial security and the need to care for young children. And the intensity of grief among survivors is influenced by who has died. Those who lose a child typically suffer far more severely and far longer than those who lose a spouse, no matter how loving or intertwined a relationship the couple may have had.

In addition, the expression of grief may differ depending on whether the death was sudden and unexpected or followed a protracted illness. In the latter situation, survivors often experience "anticipatory grief"—knowing what lies ahead, they have already worked through much of the process of mourning in advance of the death, and they may be greatly relieved that their loved one's suffering is finally over.

With a sudden death, there is no opportunity to prepare for life without the deceased. There can be no anticipatory grief. In fact, what often happens is an initial state of shock such that survivors seem not to be grieving at all. They go numbly through the motions of funerals and burials and only days or weeks later are struck by the reality of their loss and can begin to work through their grief.

It is perfectly normal for people who have lost loved ones to feel sad and lonely; to cry, sometimes unexpectedly; to feel guilty about things they think they should have said or done before their loved one died; to have trouble sleeping and eating, and to retreat from social events, especially those that remind them of the deceased. It may be helpful to reassure the bereaved that their feelings of devastation and diminished functioning will pass, even if they may find it hard to believe at the time.

James Johnson, who had been married to Laura for nearly forty-three years, found himself "living in a fog" in the weeks following her death from a rapidly progressive lung disease. His sister-in-law, whose husband Bruce (Laura's twin brother), had died after a long illness several years earlier, said something James found both informative and reassuring. "Expect the fog to last maybe three months," she told him, "and then gradually start to lift."

The bereaved may also find comfort in knowing that feelings of guilt are a normal part of grieving. It is perfectly normal for the survivor to wonder "Did I do the right thing?" "Could I have done more?" "Was I there enough?" "Did I say the right things?" Chaplain Mary E. Johnson of the Mayo Clinic said that "feeling guilt in the wake of a loss allows us to take an inventory of ourselves. Most of the time we'll come to some peace and the guilt will fade." If it doesn't, it may be helpful to talk to someone who will listen to you as you work through this aspect of grieving.

Gradually, in normal grieving, these early symptoms subside over a period of weeks or months and the bereaved return to a normal life, albeit a somewhat different "normal" than before their loved ones died. It is also completely normal to have some of the same symptoms return on special occasions—birthdays, holidays, anniversaries of the death, and happy events like the birth of a grandchild—that the deceased will necessarily miss.

Though it may be hard to imagine in the immediate aftermath of a death, most people adjust with time, and many emerge with new strength as time goes on and they master new challenges on their own.

What Many Find Helpful

While there is clearly no one way to handle grief, there are "helpful hints" that others say eased their way through the experience of losing someone they loved. Most important, however, is to accept the indisputable fact that death is a natural part of living. People live, and sooner or later they die. We all do. As my husband so often reminds me, "None of us gets through this life alive."

- Admit the reality of the loss. Although initially denial is normal, especially when the death occurred suddenly, continuing to deny that the person is gone can become an emotional and physical problem.

- Show your emotions. If you feel like crying, shouting, ranting, or whatever—it's healthy to vent those feelings, at least at the outset.

- Don't blame yourself for what you may think you could have done to prevent what happened. Such "if only" thoughts are natural, but rarely is a person's death someone else's fault.

- Don't rush your grieving. Everyone needs time to heal—some longer than others. Allow yourself the time you feel you need.

- Know that feelings of grief do ease as time passes, even though you never forget the person or your loss.

- Allow other people to help you, and if they don't offer, don't hesitate to ask for the help you need.

- Talk about your feelings. Sharing the burden with others helps to ease the anguish you feel.

- Don't try to smother your grief with alcohol or drugs. You have to experience grief if you want to cope successfully with your loss.

- Adopt and maintain a routine pattern for eating, waking, and going to sleep.

- If you have trouble sleeping at first, your physician may prescribe a sleep aid. But know that many of these drugs are addictive; use them only for a short time—no longer than two weeks.

- If you feel you are coping poorly with your loss, or if agonizing grief persists beyond three months, consider seeking professional counseling,

Expect birthdays, anniversaries, and holidays to be especially difficult times, especially in the first few years after your loss. Consider finding ways to celebrate that would honor your loved one and provide you with happy memories. One way might be to set up a small table or cabinet with photographs, quotations, and special memories or mementos of your loved one. Raise a toast to your loved one's memory. Light a special candle. Make something—a blanket, quilt, scarf, collage—that reminds you of the person you lost. Plant something special in the yard or in a pot to remind you of your loved one.

When Grief Is "Complicated"

I'm sure that you have often heard it said about someone who has lost a loved one that "He (or she) is bearing up so well under the circumstances." This may reflect one of two possible scenarios. In one, you may be seeing only the person's public demeanor, not the anguish, depression, loneliness, and so on that the person experiences when alone. In the other, the person may have consciously or subconsciously suppressed the mourning process. The unresolved pain of the person's loss may eventually rear its head in less obvious ways, say, as protracted depression or heart disease or perhaps even cancer.

When a brilliant cousin of mine committed suicide at age twenty, we were shocked by the fact that his mother, who had devoted her life to the boy's well-being, showed no evidence of mourning, either publicly or privately. Her optimistic personality remained intact and she went about her life as if nothing had happened. But almost a year to the day after her son's death, she was diagnosed with a colon cancer that was very large but miraculously had not spread. Coincidence? Maybe. But maybe not.

People die of broken hearts in novels and plays, and also in real life. Edward Bloustein was president of Rutgers University when his wife, Ruth Ellen, whom he still adored after thirty-seven years of marriage, died during treatment for breast cancer. Dr. Bloustein, who described his feelings the night after she died as "unbearable emptiness," was never able to overcome the pain of his loss and the depression that accompanied it. Thirteen months later, at age sixty-four, he died of a heart attack.

Bereavement has been repeatedly linked to an excess risk of death, particularly in the early weeks and months after the loss of a loved one. In addition to grief-induced deaths from "natural" causes, there is also an increased risk of suicide, especially among men over sixty who lose their wives.

A long-term study conducted in Denmark among 21,062 parents who had lost a child and 293,745 who had not, revealed a nearly fourfold increase in deaths from unnatural causes in mothers and a smaller increase in such deaths in fathers within three years of the child's death. There was also an increase in deaths from natural causes among mothers, but not fathers, whose children had died ten to eighteen years earlier.

Complicated grief reactions, which therapists now call prolonged grief disorders, occur among an estimated 10 to 20 percent of bereaved persons. Since there are approximately 2.5 millions deaths a year in the United States, and each death leaves an average of five people bereaved, more than a million people a year develop complicated grief.

Typically, grief shares symptoms with two other well-known emotional problems: depression and post-traumatic stress disorder. Like people who are depressed, the bereaved often experience sadness, guilt, and a loss of interest in life's pleasures. They may lack energy, have trouble sleeping, and lose their appetite for food and pleasure. And, unique to the bereaved, they may experience intrusive thoughts about the person they lost and attempt to avoid reminders of their loss. Such symptoms may persist for weeks following the death of a loved one.

But when sadness and other symptoms persist for months—often six months or more—grief is considered unduly prolonged. Those with prolonged grief are likely to experience a sense of disbelief about the death, anger and bitterness over the death, recurrent pangs of painful emotions accompanied by intense yearning and longing for the deceased, and preoccupation with thoughts of the deceased.

In complicated or prolonged grief, the bereaved may be plagued by images of the person dying, guilt over how they had interacted with the deceased, sadness because they missed the person, continued longing for contact with the person, preoccupation with positive thoughts about the person, unexpected and often pervasive painful reminders of their loss, and deliberate avoidance of situations and people that remind them of their loss.

Children who have lost a parent are at risk of complicated grief reactions that may go unrecognized. Symptoms vary according to the age of the child. Preschoolers may develop an intense attachment to the surviving parent and severe separation anxiety that persists more than six months after the death. They may regress behaviorally, for example, by "losing" toilet training.

During the early school years, children experiencing complicated grief may refuse to go to school, develop phobias or physical symptoms that have no physical basis, talk about killing themselves to be with the parent who died, or become emotionally or behaviorally hard to control.

Preteens may avoid interacting with their peers, experience academic decline, do poorly in sports or other activities outside of school, become increasingly moody or angry, and display more negative behaviors.

In early adolescence, complicated grieving may be marked by refusal to go to school, persistent depression or lack of enjoyment, a new use of drugs or alcohol, adoption of an unsavory group of friends, precocious sexual behavior, and persistent complaints of physical symptoms that have no cause.

In late adolescence, complicated grief reactions are more like those of an adult but may also include dramatic mood swings, withdrawal from peers or group activities previously enjoyed, poor academic performance, and high-risk behaviors like drug and alcohol abuse, sex, and antisocial activities.

When grief becomes complicated and the bereaved have difficulty returning to a meaningful existence and enjoying former pleasures, professional treatment often—but not always—can be helpful. Treatment of complicated grief is important because unresolved grief can have serious, even fatal, health consequences, including high blood pressure, stroke, heart attack, substance abuse, and suicide.

One well-designed study of nearly one hundred people diagnosed with complicated grief reactions found that a cognitive-behavioral approach was more effective than traditional talk therapy in helping the bereaved come to grips with their loss and get on with their lives. Part of the more effective therapy involved having the bereaved "revisit" the death—retell the story of the death, listen to a recording of the story, and have an imagined conversation with the deceased. In addition, the bereaved do exercises in which they gradually confront situations they had been avoiding because they were reminders of the loss. Little by little, those situations become less painful.

When the bereaved are seriously depressed, they may be treated with antidepressant medication to help lift their mood enough to make them more amenable to grief therapy. While it was painfully clear to those who knew him that Dr. Bloustein experienced an unrelenting depression after his wife died, he never sought treatment, a failing that his family still frets about nearly twenty years later.

Can a Support Group Help?

George and Bess Spillman of Ann Arbor, Michigan, had been married for thirty-seven years when he died of osteosarcoma, a cancer of the bone. Bess was overcome with what she called "a veil of sadness." She would find herself crying without warning in the middle of the day or as she drove down the road.

"I wanted to be able to smile and laugh and think of all the wonderful things about my husband," she said. "I didn't want to dwell on those last days. I wanted especially to remember the fact that all his hopes and dreams came true for him."

With the help of a hospital-based support group, Bess was able to unearth the happy memories she had suppressed about her husband while she was focused on his last days. It was a difficult process but a cathartic one that helped her feel as if she was on the right track to handling her grief.

But, and this is an important but, the common assumption that most, or even many, people benefit from a bereavement group or bereavement counseling is now being seriously questioned by experts on death and dying.

According to findings published by the Center for the Advancement of Health, "A growing body of evidence indicates that interventions with adults who are not experiencing complicated grief cannot be regarded as beneficial in terms of diminishing grief-related symptoms."

The center's "Report on Bereavement and Grief Research" found very little evidence for the effectiveness of interventions like crisis teams that visit family members within hours of a loss, self-help groups that attempt to foster friendships through shared bereavement experiences, efforts to educate bereaved persons about how to work through grief, and a host of other therapeutic approaches long believed to help the bereaved.

In fact, the studies indicate, grief counseling sometimes makes matters worse for the bereaved, whether the death was sudden and traumatic or occurred after a long illness. The makeup of bereavement groups, which may influence their effectiveness, can be very distorted: one man among half a dozen women, one young person among many older ones, several people who were recently bereaved in a group that includes a person still suffering intensely a year or more after the loss.

Furthermore, bereavement counseling is typically offered when it is least needed—in the immediate aftermath of a death. A more appropriate time, experts say, would be six to eighteen months later, if the person is still suffering intensely.

Most bereavement groups focus on emotional issues, which, as you might guess, is most helpful to women. But men usually grieve differently; they are more likely to benefit from a cognitive approach that focuses on their thinking processes.

For people experiencing uncomplicated grief, far more useful than therapy is the empathy and emotional and physical support provided by friends, relatives, and caring neighbors and colleagues who help out during the first weeks and months after a death. To help relieve the weight of bereavement, consider offering meals, helping with household chores, organizing an enjoyable outing, providing a shoulder to cry on, and at work, temporarily taking over some responsibilities.

Also important is not to force bereaved individuals who naturally avoid emotions to confront their grief and "let it all hang out." Dr. Bonanno of Columbia University has reported that even three years later, such people show no traumatic consequences as a result of suppressing their grief.

A group experience, however, can be very helpful to children who have lost a parent or sibling. Camp Good Grief, a free week-long bereavement camp for children run by East End Hospice, is designed to give children the special tools they need to cope with their loss. Trained professionals and volunteers engage the children in a variety of activities—art, music, structured play, and group therapy. The children learn that they are not alone and that their grief is a normal reaction.

Preserving Memories

Fourteen years after the premature death of Arthur Ashe—tennis champion, humanitarian, educator, and first African American man to win a major tennis title—his widow, Jeanne Moutoussamy-Ashe, unveiled an interactive website, www.arthurashe.org, to commemorate his spirit. It almost brings this incredible man back to life. In it we hear his words and perspectives on topics ranging from education, protest, and AIDS to, of course, tennis.

Ms. Moutoussamy-Ashe told *The New York Times*, "I want to bring him to life on those computers so he's not just bricks and mortar. I can see children playing interactive games with him. It'll be a safe place for them to come, for them to understand the important aspects of his legacy about education and learning."

Professionals who deal daily with the bereaved had traditionally focused on helping them resolve their grief, forget the loss, and move on. Today there is a different perspective.

"We are less wedded to seeking closure, to the idea of saying 'good-bye' to the one who died," Dr. Neimeyer of Memphis said. "We now recognize the importance of finding healthy ways to sustain a relationship with a deceased loved one, to maintain continuing healthy bonds, for example, by carrying forth their projects.

"Closure is for bank accounts, not for love accounts. Love is potentially boundless. The fact that we love one person doesn't mean we have to withdraw love from another." In other words, survivors can be open to loving someone else while preserving their love for the deceased.

Experts now talk, not of recovering from grief but of "reconstitution"—"a decrease in the frequency and intensity of grief and a gradual return to previous levels of functioning" is how three experts put it in the *Journal of the American Medical Association.*

Robert S., whose mother died of cancer just after he turned thirteen, preserves his mother's memory in the way he conducts his life. Three years later, in an interview published in the journal, he said: "The biggest thing for me is how much I've pushed myself, whether it has been in sports or academics, because I knew how hard she tried to stay alive, and to stay healthy. I feel like I'd be shortchanging her, or shortchanging myself, if I didn't apply myself as hard. In that sense she taught me, inadvertently, about work ethic. I'm able to translate what she did, and use it as drive and motivation in my own life."

My own mother died just before my seventeenth birthday, seven weeks before I graduated valedictorian from high school. Her death was no surprise to me—she'd been ill with an unstoppable cancer for nearly a year, and I visited her almost daily in the hospital during her last months. In the aftermath of her death, I was stoical. I remember thinking that I had to be strong for my poor father and my thirteen-year-old brother, who had been clueless about his mother's inevitable demise. I went through the motions of picking out a dress in her favorite color for her to be buried in. I attended the funeral, and sat shivah with my father and brother. And I thought about all that I had learned from her.

My mother was a thrifty and extremely competent person. She taught me not to be wasteful and not to shy away from trying anything I might conceivably be able to accomplish. I was going off to college in the fall, and I spent the summer remaking many of her clothes to wear in my new life. I still have a few of them, now half a century later.

But it took a year for me to actually mourn her passing. It took a year for me to cry. I was riding my bicycle at school on an especially beautiful day the following spring when it suddenly hit me—my mother would never again experience a magnificent day like this one. And finally I could cry. I cried for all that she was missing and for all that I was missing because she was gone. I like to think she somehow knows that I started my job at *The New York Times* on her birthday.

What to Say When Someone Dies

A few years ago I was sent a little book with one of the all-time best titles: *Don't Ask for the Dead Man's Golf Clubs: Advice for Friends When Someone Dies.* The book was written by Lynn Kelly, a mother of three who was widowed at age thirty-four. The title was inspired by what some of her brother's friends asked of his wife, Lianne Enderton of Alberta, Canada, following his untimely death.

People are often uncomfortable and insecure when talking to the bereaved, and in those awkward moments they sometimes say things they don't really mean or that come out sounding unsympathetic, like "Don't worry, you'll have another baby," to the mother of stillborn twins.

Here are some other examples of the "darndest things" people have said when attempting to comfort the bereaved:

To a sixty-year-old recent widow: "Don't worry, you're young and attractive, you'll find someone else."

To a woman whose husband died of lung cancer: "You have to meet this man. His wife also died of lung cancer."

To a man whose twenty-six-year-old daughter died of AIDS: "If she hadn't been that way, God wouldn't have struck her dead with AIDS" and "It was just a purification thing."

To a woman who suffered a miscarriage: "It is probably for the best."

To a woman whose twenty-five-year-old son was killed by a drunk driver: "At least you have four other children."

To a man whose elderly mother died: "Oh well, seventy-nine."

To a young man whose nineteen-year-old brother died of cancer: "I know how you must feel losing a brother."

And to the boy's mother: "I know it's not the same, but I really empathize because I lost my dog."

To a woman whose husband committed suicide: "Are you going to get a dog now?"

And to Marta Felber, whose husband died of cancer: "Remember, it could be worse. He could have lingered longer" and "Joe is waiting for you over there. Some day you will be with him." Ms. Felber is a counselor and author of *Grief Expressed: When a Mate Dies*, a road map to recovery for the bereaved and a guide to those who wish to express sympathy and offer comfort and support.

A few other no-no's: "It was probably for the best." "He lived seventy-five years and had a very good life." "She's in a better place now." "You'll feel better once you get back to a normal routine."

In a search for better suggestions on how to comfort the bereaved, Ms. Kelly interviewed survivors ages seventeen to ninety throughout the United States and Canada who had lost husbands, wives, children, fathers, mothers, brothers, sisters, and grandparents. She asked each person she interviewed what did and did not prove helpful while they were grieving their losses. Here are some things she warns against:

- Don't judge the way people grieve. Those who don't cry can be just as devastated as those who can't stop crying.

- Don't assume the death was for the best, even if the person was old, deformed, or very ill.

- Don't assume that because a person has other children, the pain of losing one child is lessened.

- Don't say "I know how you feel" to those who are grieving. No one knows how they feel.

- Don't make comparisons to the loss of a pet, which suggests, for example, that a lost spouse could be replaced with a dog.

- Don't say, "Don't worry, you'll get married again" or "You'll have another baby" or "It's God's will."

Probably the most universally appreciated expression of sympathy is a hug and three little words: "I'm so sorry." Ms. Felber said that in the beginning when her greatest need was to talk, she was always grateful to find a good listener—someone not in a hurry who held her hand, did not interrupt or give advice, and seemed comfortable when she said nothing or just cried.

Talking about the person who died helps to keep them alive in the minds of the bereaved. Carole Crewdson of Brooklyn, New York, who lost her husband, Frank, said, "Some people were afraid to mention Frank because they thought it would upset me. But what I appreciated most were the people who told little stories, little personal connections about themselves and Frank. And the people who brought pictures. They made me feel good."

Marge Druckman of Potomac, Maryland, echoed Ms. Crewdson's sentiments. "It's great to hear stories about the person who died and to have friends let you know how much they liked and appreciated your loved one."

The same goes for grieving children, who may fear they will forget the person they lost because they are so young. Tell them stories about the person who died; give them happy memories they can treasure forever.

If you did not know the person who died very well or at all, you can always say something like, "I'm so sorry for your pain," "I'm here to help you in any way I can," "I'm told he was a dear man, and I know you're going to miss him."

Remember, too, that even if the deceased was very old or very ill, he or she was loved by someone who will be grieving. When you lose someone you loved, it hurts no matter what the circumstances.

And, as Ms. Kelly emphasized, "Be honest. If you don't know what to say, don't be afraid to say so. Saying nothing is okay too. Your very presence can be an adequate expression of sympathy."

At the very least, and especially if you live far from the bereaved, you can send a sympathy card or note of condolence. But be sure to add a personal message to whatever may be printed on the card.

Whatever you do, *don't do nothing*. Dr. Jennifer Schneider, whose daughter, Jessica Wing, died of cancer at age thirty-one, said many people she knew deliberately avoided her for months afterward. When at last she encountered these people, they were clearly embarrassed and expressed regret, saying something like, "I didn't say anything to you earlier because I didn't know what to say." But as Dr. Schneider put it, "All they needed to say was, 'I'm so sorry for your loss.' Anything would have been better than nothing." When nothing is said, the bereaved feel isolated and abandoned at a time when most people need emotional support and understanding.

What You Can Do to Help the Bereaved

When a drunk driver left Margaret Kramer a young widow with four small children, her Minnesota friends and neighbors pitched in with ready-to-eat meals, took turns mowing the lawn and baby-sitting, and a year or so later surprised her by painting the outside of her house when she and the children were away on vacation.

When Ms. Crewdson's husband died, a friend asked, "Tell me what needs doing," and proceeded to clean the refrigerator, which had suffered serious neglect during the months Frank was ill. Other friends investigated cremation arrangements, brought frozen packets of homemade soup, and took her shopping. When things quieted down a bit, friends took her out to lunch, to the movies, and even on a short trip.

If you choose to bring food, which is nearly always a welcome gift, try to use disposable containers that don't have to be returned. Or, if that is not feasible, let the bereaved know that you will pick up the container at a later date—and don't forget to do so. Label packaged meals as to contents and directions for reheating.

If you have expertise that can be useful to the bereaved, consider offering your help. Possibilities include home repairs and legal or financial matters. Ms. Crewdson was the beneficiary of efforts by several able friends. One fixed a broken door knob and light fixture, another wrote up a list of needed house repairs, a third advised her on legal matters, and a fourth helped her figure out her finances.

Ask what needs to be done, and if the person can't answer, look around to see how you might help, perhaps by doing the laundry, getting the car serviced, caring for pets or plants, chauffering children or taking them on an outing or away for an overnight or weekend, babysitting, cleaning the house, tending the garden, even helping to sort through the deceased person's clothing and other personal effects.

If nothing seems obvious, consider saying, "I can do this, this, and this. I would like to be helpful. Tell me what I can do to help." But don't promise to do something and not follow through. If you say you will invite the bereaved for dinner or a weekend in the country, do it. If you tell children you will take them to a ball game or a show or movie, do it. Those who are grieving do not forget such promises, and failing to fulfill the promise just reinforces their feelings of abandonment.

As Joel Bershok of Littleton, Colorado, who was nine years old when his father died, told Ms. Kelly, three men from a volunteer organization offered to help. The boy poured his heart out to one man, who was never seen again. The second moved away before he could do anything helpful, and the third never called after the initial contact. The boy, now a man, never forgot their empty promises.

And don't do things without asking, as happened to the Newton family of Englewood, Colorado, after his seven-year-old daughter died in an accident. As Sam Newton told Ms. Kelly, "Somebody— we don't know who—came in right away and cleaned out our little girl's room and took away all of her things. We really didn't want that."

Memorial gifts to an organization cherished by the deceased are always appreciated. Consider gathering donations for a memorial fund in memory of the deceased, say, to establish a scholarship, plant a tree, or erect a plaque or bench in a place important to the deceased or the bereaved. For Mickey Martinez, a man who was passionate about tennis, a family friend started a tennis scholarship in his memory and raised thousands of dollars to support children who could not otherwise afford tennis lessons.

Continued contacts with the bereaved are also important. Ms. Felber was especially appreciative of a friend who called long-distance every evening for the first ten days she was alone. "I'm just calling to hear about your day and tuck you into bed," the friend would say. Another called often to say she was going shopping and did Ms. Felber want to come along? Still another kept writing notes to her long after everyone else had stopped.

And don't be discouraged if your grieving friend or relative turns down invitations. Ms. Felber wrote that many people wanted to keep her busy after her husband died. But what she most wanted was time alone to grieve. So at first she said no to invitations to pot luck suppers, bridge club, a computer class, jazz concert, singles group, and a long trip. However, activities like these could be very enjoyable at a future time when the pain of a loss is less acute, so keep the invitations coming.

Ms. Crewdson, too, often vacillated when an invitation was issued. She said one of the most valued contributions from her friends was their willingness to "put up with my mood changes and sudden changes of plans."

Finally, keep in mind that holidays, anniversaries, birthdays, and other such occasions are especially difficult for people who are grieving. Try to make sure they are not alone at these times, but be prepared for the possibility that they may refuse company or be unwilling to participate in celebrations. Be understanding, and whatever you do, don't take a refusal as a personal affront.

FOR FURTHER READING

Didion, Joan. *The Year of Magical Thinking*. New York: Alfred A. Knopf, 2005.

Felber, Marta. *Grief Expressed: When a Mate Dies*. Cincinnati, OH: LifeWords, 1997.

Kelly, Lynn. *Don't Ask for the Dead Man's Golf Clubs: Advice for Friends When Someone Dies*. New York: Workman, 2000.

Kübler-Ross, Elisabeth, and David Kessler. *On Grief and Grieving: Finding the Meaning of Grief through the Five Stages of Loss*. New York: Scribner, 2005.

Tatelbaum, Judy. *The Courage to Grieve*. New York: HarperPerennial, 1980.

PART 3

LIFE AFTER DEATH: WHAT YOU LEAVE BEHIND COUNTS

Perhaps there is no greater salve to hearts pained by the death of a loved one than to know that the person's life in some way goes on—through donation of the deceased person's organs to save the lives or sight of others, through autopsy of the deceased to answer survivors' questions and help future generations cope with inherited health risks, and through treasured memories or life lessons left for present and future generations to hear or read.

"Not much in the way of hard assets, I'm afraid, but he did leave some highly desirable organs."

CHAPTER 16

Organ and Body Donations: A Gift of Life

Mumtaz Bari-Brown's brother, Abdul Brown, died of a stroke at age forty-three, and the family elected to have his healthy organs and tissues donated. She said, "To know that one person's organs and tissues can help more than fifty people made us sure it was the right decision. He is still helping people, and that brings me comfort as I continue to grieve and to mourn him."

When nine-year-old Tiffany Gunaratne was declared brain dead after being hit by a car outside her family home in Staten Island, New York, her liver and kidneys were transplanted, prolonging the lives of three strangers, one of them just seven years old. Her heartbroken mother, Surangni, said the ability to pass on Tiffany's healthy organs to others in need gave her solace. She now wears a rubber wristband that says "Donate life."

Forty-year-old Laurie McLendon had prearranged to have her organs donated. When she suffered a sudden, fatal cardiac arrest and was taken to New York–Presbyterian Hospital / Weill Cornell Medical Center, two women got her kidneys, the hospital's burn center got her skin, the Eye Bank of New York received her corneas, and a sixty-one-year-old pediatric oncologist, Dr. Michael Harris of Englewood, New Jersey, got her liver. Dr. Harris had contracted a hepatitis C infection years earlier from an accidental needle stick while treating a patient and his liver had now failed. Without a transplant, and soon, he was doomed.

Two years later, he said, "I realized that someone needed to die for me to survive. I feel a tremendous responsibility to the McLendons and to Laurie's memory. I think of that every day, that she is part of me now." In November 2006 Laurie's parents were guests at the wedding of Dr. Harris's daughter, an event he would not have been able to attend if not for the transplant.

A Need Unmet

In 2006 a total of 29,000 solid organs were transplanted, three-fourths of them from deceased donors. But as of June 2007 there were 97,000 people on waiting lists for organs because their own had failed or were invaded by a deadly disease. The need for organs grows daily, five times faster than the rate of donations. In 2006 more than 40,000 people were added to the national transplant waiting list.

People typically wait three to five years for a donated organ, and each year 6,700 of them die waiting even though a single organ donor could save as many as eight lives. At the same time, more than 20,000 organs that could have been transplanted are buried or cremated each year. In a society that now commonly recycles paper, glass, plastic, and aluminum, losing those life-giving organs can be considered an unconscionable waste.

Organs that can be donated are the heart, kidneys, pancreas, lungs, liver, and intestines. Tissues that can be donated are corneas, skin, bone marrow, heart valves, and connective tissue. To be viable for transplantation, all organs and tissues must receive blood until they are removed from the donor, which may require placing the donor on a breathing machine temporarily or providing other treatments to sustain the viability of a donor's organs.

However, because of the effects of illness or accident, only about

1 percent of people who die in hospitals each year are judged to be suitable donors.

In the United States, as well as in many European countries, when people renew their driver's license, they also decide whether they want to be organ donors. But while most Americans approve of organ donation, only about one in four has so indicated by signing a form. In Europe where you are considered a potential organ donor unless you expressly indicate that you do not want to be one, more than 90 percent of people are organ donors.

Studies have shown that when stories appear about organ donations from people like Abdul Brown, Tiffany Gunaratne, and the McLendons, more of them are motivated to register as organ donors. Unfortunately, such increases don't come close to meeting local, regional, or national needs.

A shortage of donated organs is particularly severe among minorities. Organ transplants are most successful when done within ethnic groups because the genetic backgrounds of donor and recipient are more similar. Among those awaiting transplants, 27 percent are black, but blacks make up only 12 percent of both the total population and the pool of potential donors. Kidneys are in especially short supply for blacks, who account for 35 percent of those awaiting kidney transplants, owing in part to high rates of diabetes and hypertension among blacks.

Mrs. Gunaratne decided after five days to remove her daughter from life support and pass her useful organs on to others in dire need through the intervention of a new kind of health professional, a family services coordinator named Kathleen Atkinson employed by the New York Organ Donor Network. As of 2007 twenty family service coordinators worked for the network fulltime, offering whatever practical or emotional help a grieving family needs at the same time as they make a pitch for organ donation. The result in New York has been an increase in donors from 199 in 2001 to 319 in 2006.

When a hospital has a brain-dead patient who might be a suitable organ donor, it alerts its regional procurement group. That organization then sends a nurse to assess the potential donor and to make sure necessary steps are taken to keep the patient's organs working. The family service coordinator then takes over.

Families throughout the country may encounter such coordinators when a potential organ donor hovers between life and death. About half the members of the National Association of Organ Procurement Organizations now have family service coordinators who are trained to provide whatever a family needs. As Ms. Atkinson put it, "We connect them with social workers, clergy, anything they need, and we go to funerals and keep up with them afterwards. We had a family from Mexico who needed family members to get here, and we worked with the consulates."

As you can see, in addition to increasing the number of organs available for donation, the family service coordinator can be a great friend for the family in a time of great need.

Misconceptions Abound

Hesitancy to become an organ donor has its roots in several misconceptions about the process and its effects. People with an underlying distrust of the medical system may fear that a person's death may be unnaturally hastened to obtain donor organs, or that organs may be removed even before the person has died. The facts are different; there are clearly written national rules defining death and governing organ procurement from a dead donor. *Donors are not "killed" for their organs.*

When people are severely injured or suffer a potentially fatal disease, the only goal of the doctors caring for them is to try to keep them alive and restore them to health. Considering such patients as potential organ donors comes only after there is clearly no hope for meaningful survival. No doctor who is in any way involved in the procurement or transplantation of organs can declare a person dead or be present during the removal of that person's organs.

Most donor organs are obtained from people who are declared

brain dead, as might happen following an accident, stroke, or heart attack. But only 1 to 2 percent of patients who die in hospitals are declared brain dead, so the pool of potential donors is not that large if this is the only source of donations from the deceased.

In past generations, stoppage of the heart and spontaneous breathing was considered necessary to declare a person dead. But since 1968 the absence of electrical activity in the brain has been the official definition of death. The vital organs of many such individuals can be maintained by providing artificial respiratory support, that is, by placing them on a ventilator, and by giving them drugs or other measures that support blood flow throughout the body. The longer a brain-dead person is maintained on a ventilator, however, the less healthy the person's organs are likely to become, which can make them unavailable for donation.

In most cases, it is up to the next of kin of a brain-dead person to okay the removal of life support and make that person's organs available for transplantation. When no next of kin can be located or contacted, doctors must rely on a signed driver's license or possession of a donor card stating that the person had joined a state or national organ donor registry. Searching for such documentation can waste precious hours or days, during which people most critically in need—those at the top of the transplant waiting list—may die. Also, donor cards and signed driver's licenses are not usually legally binding. Thus, it is best if you list your intent to be an organ donor in your advance directive and notify your next of kin, health care proxy, or durable power of attorney (see chapter 3) of your desire to donate your organs when you die.

Donation Following Cardiac Death

A small but growing number of organ donations come from people experiencing cardiac deaths, considered by transplantation experts to be the best hope for increasing the pool of donors. In 2006, the 645 victims of cardiac death accounted for 8 percent of all dead organ donors, up from 182 in 2002. But very few of these organ do-nations come from people who suffer unexpected fatal heart attacks; usually too much time elapses between a person's death outside a hospital and the ability of doctors to obtain viable organs.

Rather, cardiac death in patients who become organ donors occurs after the removal of life-supporting measures from someone who is not brain dead and whose heart still beats but who may have sustained an injury or illness that is incompatible with life, such as an irreversible neurological or high spinal cord injury or end-stage pulmonary disease or a musculoskeletal disease like amyotrophic lateral sclerosis (ALS, or Lou Gehrig's disease). In such cases, consent from the legal next of kin is necessary before life support is stopped and organs removed for transplant.

Timing is critical, because once life support is discontinued, there is a narrow window of opportunity to obtain organs that are still healthy enough to be transplanted. So potential donors are transferred to the operating room while still on life support and while they are still alive. The blood-thinner heparin is administered to prevent clots from forming and damaging vital organs. After life support is removed and the patient's heart stops, doctors must wait for up to five minutes before declaring the patient dead to be sure the heart does not resume functioning on its own.

However, if the patient's heart and respiratory function continue unaided for more than an hour after life support is disconnected, end-of-life care is resumed and all plans for the donation of organs are canceled. This happens in about 20 percent of cases.

According to Dr. Francis L. Delmonico, a transplant surgeon at the Massachusetts General Hospital in Boston and medical director of the New England Organ Bank, "If donation after cardiac death—once the only form of transplantation from deceased donors—were pursued as diligently as donation after brain death, the number of organs available for transplant could rise significantly."

He added that too often it is the doctors, rather than families, who limit the availability of donor organs after cardiac death: "As long as a segment of the medical community stands in the way of donation after cardiac death, lives will be lost unnecessarily. And families of potential donors, at a time of enormous grief, will be deprived of the comfort of knowing that their loved ones' organs can be used to save lives."

The success of organ transplants following a cardiac death is as good as those following brain death, but timing is critical. For the liver to be useful, it must be removed and perfused with a cold preservative solution within thirty minutes of the heart stoppage. Doctors have a little more time with kidneys and pancreas; with these organs the preservative solution must be perfused within sixty minutes. But in all cases, the faster the process, the healthier the organ and the more likely a transplant will survive.

Age and Health Are Not Limiting Factors

Another common misconception about organ donation is the thought that older people are not useful donors. In fact, there is no age cut-off. Only the donor's physical condition is considered. Organs have been transplanted successfully from people in their seventies and eighties. There have been successful donors as old as ninety-two. And patients who received hearts from donors fifty years old and older have done just as well as those whose hearts came from younger donors. Parental or guardian consent must be given for people under eighteen to be organ donors.

Nor must the donor have been in perfect health at the time of the fatal event. Someone with end-stage liver disease, for example, may have lungs or a heart suitable for transplantation. It is up to medical professionals at the time of a person's death to determine whether organs are healthy enough to be donated.

There is no added cost to the decedent's heirs for organ donation, nor do they receive payment for agreeing to the donation. All transplantation costs are borne by the recipient. However, the donor's family is still responsible for funeral expenses.

Finally, as with an autopsy (see chapter 17), the donation of organs and tissues does not preclude an open casket at the person's funeral. The body is stitched up just as it would be after surgery. If the eyes are donated, artificial eyes are inserted and the lids closed. If a bone is donated, a rod is inserted in its place.

Whole Body Donation

Medical students still require real human bodies to study, and researchers sometimes need them to better understand disease. Some people, including both of my sons, would prefer to donate their bodies after death to a medical school. This would preclude the possibility of organ donation, since students need an intact body if they are going to learn what they must.

For those who do not care to have their dead bodies on view at a funeral service or who might otherwise choose cremation, donating one's body to medical research is an excellent option. It has the added advantage of eliminating the cost of a funeral or burial, although once a medical center is finished with the body, the remains can still be returned to the family for burial or cremation.

However, such donations must be arranged for in advance. If there is a nearby medical school or center that you would prefer to have your body, contact the facility, obtain the necessary forms, and complete and return them, keeping copies for yourself and your health care proxy.

YOUR WISHES ABOUT ORGAN AND TISSUE DONATION

The Commission on Law and Aging of the American Bar Association suggests that people make clear their wishes about organ donation and autopsy well in advance of their death. Here is what the organization suggests you complete.

1. Do you want to donate viable ORGANS for transplant? *(Circle one)*
   Yes
   Not sure
   No
   If **Yes,** check one:
   _____ I will donate any organs.
   _____ Just the following: _____

2. Do you want to donate viable TISSUES for transplant? *(Circle one)*
   Yes
   Not sure
   No
   If **Yes,** check one:
   _____ I will donate any tissues.
   _____ Just the following: _____

If you circled **Yes** for either of the above questions, be sure to write this into your health care advance directive. You may also fill out an organ donor card or register as an organ donor when you renew your driver's license. But be sure to tell your proxy and loved ones. Make sure they support your wishes. Even with an organ donor card, hospitals will usually ask your proxy or family to sign a consent form.

3. If you do not donate organs or tissues, you may choose to donate your WHOLE BODY for medical research or education. Would you like to do this?
Yes
Not sure
No

If you circled **Yes,** you must contact a medical institution to which you are interested in making this donation. This kind of donation must be accepted by the medical institution. Note that total body donation is not an option if you also choose to be an organ or tissue donor.

CHAPTER 17

Autopsy: Valuable Lessons from the Dead

On a calm August morning my father-in-law, age sixty-six, disappeared while fishing alone in a rowboat on a Minnesota lake he had known since childhood. He had never learned to swim and was presumed to have drowned. His body was found three days later when, bloated with gases, it floated to the surface. The local coroner, who was not a medical doctor, told my mother-in-law an autopsy would not show much. And so none was performed.

I was appalled. I had mistakenly assumed that all accidental deaths from an unknown cause were automatically a coroner's case, to be examined by a pathologist to determine the true cause of death. And so we are never to know why Daddy died in that lake. Did he have a heart attack or a stroke? Was he the victim of foul play or perhaps a teenage prank? Or did he just lose his footing, fall into the lake, and drown?

When you complete a medical history in a doctor's office, you are usually asked—or you *should* be asked—whether your parents are still alive and, if not, what was the age and cause of their death. Your family's medical history is important because it provides a sneak preview of your medical future—your inherited risk of developing certain potentially fatal diseases, especially heart disease, stroke, and several common cancers, as well as other disabilities that can have a hereditary component, like osteoporosis, dementia, and osteoarthritis.

And so I am left wondering, not only why my beloved father-in-law drowned but also what medical issues my husband and my sons may face in the future and how they might protect themselves, for example, through changes in lifestyle and/or screening tests of one sort or another.

In retrospect, many survivors find themselves facing similar quandaries, including the children of a physician in his forties who died suddenly while playing tennis. It was assumed their father had suffered a fatal heart attack, but without an autopsy they really don't know. Now they wonder about their own vulnerability. The doctor's wife also has regrets about not requesting an autopsy. She

"He's one tough cookie. I've never seen anyone bounce back from an autopsy before."

realized afterward that knowing why her husband died might have helped her accept what had happened. Not knowing what happened at the end is like reading a mystery novel from which the last chapter is missing.

You see, the *apparent* cause of death is not always the *real* cause. And determining the real cause can sometimes make a big difference to the survivors. Here are some examples:

- A Roto-Rooter operator collapsed and died while working on a drain. The assumption was he'd suffered a heart attack. But the autopsy showed that he had been electrocuted, a finding that could save the lives of others using the faulty equipment. It also resulted in double-indemnity insurance for his survivors.

- A seemingly healthy baby died in his sleep. The baby was assumed to have succumbed to sudden infant death syndrome, or crib death. The autopsy findings were far more ominous. The baby had succumbed to previously undiagnosed bacterial meningitis, prompting protective vaccinations of other children in the family and in the neighborhood.

- An elderly Kentucky woman, known to have malignant-looking lesions in her brain, died before undergoing exploratory surgery. The assumption was she'd died of metastatic cancer. In fact, the autopsy found no cancer. Rather, the lethal lesions in her brain were abscesses resulting from an advanced case of untreated periodontal disease.

- A forty-three-year-old Connecticut man with shortness of breath, a cough, multiple clots in his lungs, and a positive skin test for tuberculosis was assumed to have died of tuberculosis, or TB. The man may, or may not, have had TB. But what killed him, the autopsy revealed, were not clots but rather tumors in his lungs that had spread from a previously undiagnosed and fatal pancreatic cancer.

However, the rate of autopsies in the nation's hospitals has been declining for decades. In the 1940s and 1950s about half of all deaths were autopsied. The decline, which began in the mid-1960s, accelerated after 1970 when the Joint Commission on Accreditation of Healthcare Organizations (now the Joint Commission) decided to drop its requirement that hospitals perform autopsies in at least 20 percent of deaths. Today in many institutions, the autopsy rate is so low—perhaps only 5 percent of deaths, if that—that it is no longer possible for the living to learn from the dead. The autopsy rate in nursing homes is even lower; at most 1 percent of deaths result in an autopsy. And many newer hospitals never bothered to include an autopsy room in their construction.

When a death occurs suddenly or results from unusual or violent circumstances outside of a hospital or nursing home, in most states it is up to the county coroner or medical examiner to decide whether an autopsy is warranted, although some states mandate that autopsies be performed in certain situations. About half of unusual or suspicious deaths turn out to be due to natural causes, a finding that can provide emotional relief and medical benefit to the survivors.

When an autopsy is not legally mandated, the physician who performs it must first obtain consent from the survivors, which in some states includes the spouse and all surviving children. It may be helpful, then, for families to consider this issue in advance of a death.

A Difficult Decision

The matter of autopsy comes up at a time when emotional turmoil is usually greatest for the very people who must request and consent to it—the survivors of those who have just died. Families often feel that their loved ones have "suffered enough" and view the procedure as a further injury or indignity. However, an autopsy cannot increase the suffering of someone who is already dead.

Families may be afraid that their loved ones will be disfigured when in fact the incisions made by the pathologist are discreet and would not be apparent to anyone who views the deceased in an open casket. Families can even request that any internal organs that are removed for diagnostic purposes be replaced before the incisions are closed. An autopsy does not interfere with embalming and does not have to delay a funeral by more than a few hours.

In some families, religious objections are the issue. An autopsy is viewed as a violation of the body of the deceased. However, when foul play is suspected or the deceased may have committed suicide, legal requirements to determine how and why the person died necessarily override religious issues.

Joan Didion, whose husband of forty years died suddenly, "actively wanted" an autopsy done. "I needed to know how and why and when it happened," she wrote, explaining that until she read the autopsy report she persisted in deluding herself that she might have been able to do something to save him.

Too often, both physicians and families assume incorrectly that, since patients have often been examined by such advanced diagnostic tools as CT scans, MRIs and PET scans, nothing more of value can be learned from an autopsy. But, as the case of the Kentucky woman with brain abscesses showed, no test can replace the accuracy of "seeing for yourself," which is the literal meaning of the Greek-derived word *autopsy*.

Sometimes physicians are the obstacle. They may be reluctant to request an autopsy for fear that the findings may result in a lawsuit. But the statistics show that autopsies are much in the doctor's favor, since in 95 percent of cases, a good autopsy dispels any notion of malpractice suspected by the family, and more lawsuits are thrown out because of autopsy findings than are won.

Finally, there's the matter of cost. Autopsies are expensive—usually in the range of $2,500 or more—and the expense, which once was borne as a general operating expense by the hospital in which the person died, is now typically borne by the family (although there is no charge in some leading hospitals). And, since the person is dead, the fee is not covered by medical insurance. When added to the costs of a funeral, the expense of an autopsy may be more than the family can or wants to bear—unless, of course, they recognize in advance the potential value of what an autopsy may reveal and how it can help the survivors.

Many Benefits of Autopsy

Physicians who perform autopsies are known as forensic pathologists, now frequent characters on popular crime shows like *CSI Miami* and *Law and Order*. Real-life forensic pathologists can relate numerous tales of missed diagnoses, missed diseases, and wrong assumptions. Any of these, if undetected, can undermine the quality of future medical care and/or leave survivors racked with guilt, deprived of deserved compensation, or vulnerable to preventable diseases.

A man who dies in an automobile accident may have suffered a heart attack before he lost control of the car, a finding that would alert his siblings and children to a possible increased risk of heart disease and inspire them to pursue heart-healthy living habits.

In many cases, what is recorded as the cause of death on a death certificate is far from the truth. For example, in a Connecticut study of 272 randomly selected autopsies and their corresponding death certificates, in 29 percent of the deaths there was a major disagreement between the true underlying cause of death and the category of disease listed on the death certificate. Another 26 percent of deaths were incorrectly attributed to a disease within the same category. And in 14 percent of cases, had the right disease been diagnosed while the patient was still alive, it could have led to a change in treatment that might have resulted in a cure or prolonged survival.

Another study showed that autopsies detected major unexpected findings that, if they had been correctly diagnosed during the patient's life, would have improved survival in 11 percent of patients at a university hospital and 12 percent at a community hospital. And a study conducted at the Cleveland Clinic Foundation, a state-of-the-art medical facility, found that one death in five that occurred in the medical intensive care unit had been misdiagnosed, and in nearly half these cases a correct diagnosis would have resulted in different treatment.

"A good autopsy uncovers the true disease process," said Dr. Gregory Davis, a forensic pathologist at the University of Kentucky. "In 20 to 40 percent of cases, the autopsy finds a diagnostic discrepancy between the medical diagnosis and the actual disease," which can help improve the care of future patients.

One study found, for example, that doctors who treat elderly patients often overlooked the presence of a fatal blood clot in the lung. The finding prompted the researchers to recommend that doctors who care for patients in nursing homes pay more attention to prescribing leg exercises, the wearing of compression stockings, and other measures that can reduce the risk of blood clots forming in the legs that can travel to the lungs and cause sudden death.

In addition to the potential health benefits to survivors that I've already described, an autopsy can remove guilt feelings among family members or others who may erroneously believe that they somehow contributed to the person's death. This is especially important when a child dies, even more so when a child dies unexpectedly. Parents may be plagued with "what ifs"—"Why didn't I check on the baby before I went to bed?" "Why did I let him go on that camping trip?" "Why did I send her to camp instead of taking her with us?" "Why didn't I take him to the doctor when he complained for two days that he had a bad headache?"

More often than not, the autopsy will show that there was nothing the parents might have done to prevent their child's death. In one study of suspected crib deaths, one in ten of the babies turned out on autopsy to have had a previously unrecognized inborn error of metabolism. Such a finding could, through prenatal diagnosis, help prevent future births of affected children to those parents.

When a man dies while shoveling snow, his wife may berate herself for not hiring someone younger and stronger to clear the walk. But when the autopsy reveals that the husband had an advanced heart condition that could have caused his death at any time—even while carrying groceries or a grandchild or having intimate relations with his wife—her guilt will be much assuaged.

Furthermore, the autopsy findings may result in the dropping of a criminal charge of child abuse, neglect, or manslaughter. In one such case a fourteen-year-old boy who refused to stop roller-skating in the lobby of his apartment building was slapped by an exasperated doorman. The boy collapsed and died, and the doorman was booked on a homicide charge. But he was released when the autopsy found that the boy had suffered a brain hemorrhage from a ruptured aneurysm, a condition that had preexisted and could have caused the boy's death at any time, even while he was asleep.

Autopsy findings can establish the correct diagnosis and may even reveal instances of medical malpractice or result in higher insurance awards. Even following a lengthy hospitalization, the recorded cause of death is wrong in a surprisingly large percentage of cases. Nearly half of presumed cardiac deaths turn out to have other causes. When a teenager dies unexpectedly, the first thought is likely to be drugs. In a case painfully familiar to me, the nineteen-year-old son of a neighbor died in his sleep. The boy was known to have used drugs, and the police officers called to the bedside scene presumed he had died of a drug overdose. However, an autopsy revealed that the boy had suffered a skull fracture and cerebral hemorrhage, the result of a mugging that had occurred two weeks earlier. The hospital where he was treated for his head wound had failed to take an X-ray, which would have revealed the fracture, and his parents won a sizable malpractice award.

An elderly man with known heart disease stumbled on a table, fell across his bed, and died. His physician tentatively listed the cause of death as a heart attack. Nonetheless, he convinced the man's wife to consent to an autopsy, which showed that the man had died from a ruptured spleen caused by his accidental fall. The wife then received double the insurance benefit that would have resulted from a natural cause of death.

An autopsy may disclose a previously unrecognized genetic illness that can affect the life decisions of the survivors. For example, a child may have succumbed to a congenital defect that could influence the parents' decisions about future childbearing or provide an opportunity for prenatal or preimplantation screening to eliminate this risk in future offspring. Or a parent's early cardiac death may have resulted from an inherited abnormality in serum cholesterol that warrants strict preventive measures by the person's siblings and children if they, too, are found to have inherited the same abnormality.

Sometimes an autopsy can lead to the detection of an environmental hazard that could cause further deaths. When a fifty-year-old woman died on the eve of an operation that she had been dreading, the cause of her death was assumed to have been an overdose of the sleeping pills the doctor had prescribed to help her relax before surgery. On autopsy, a high level of carbon monoxide was found in her blood. Further investigation uncovered a defective gas refrigerator as the source of the poisonous gas. Seventeen other apartments were found to have the same equipment, and removing these appliances spared the occupants a similar fate.

Through autopsies, Legionnaire's disease and AIDS were discovered, and the so-called café coronary was revealed to be a choking death that could be prevented by using the Heimlich maneuver when food or a foreign object lodges in the trachea and blocks the flow of oxygen. Autopsies of crash victims have led to improved safety standards in cars and planes. Autopsies have also alerted public health officials to growing threats of infection or drug addiction. And sometimes car "accidents" are discovered through autopsies to have been suicides or even homicides.

In light of these many benefits, families should insist on an autopsy when a loved one dies, assuming they can afford the expense if there is one.

FOR FURTHER READING

Amatuzio, Janis. *Forever Ours: Real Stories of Immortality and Living from a Forensic Pathologist.* New York: New World Library, 2004.

Baines, Barry K. *Ethical Wills: Putting Your Values on Paper.* New York: Da Capo, 2006.

CHAPTER 18

Lasting Legacies: Leave Memories and Life Lessons

When people die, they typically take with them a treasure trove of information and wisdom—memories, facts, life lessons that can have infinite value and interest for those left behind and for future generations not yet born.

You may think you're just an ordinary person with nothing to tell that would be especially interesting to anyone. But chances are you're wrong. As the growing number of programs that foster life story writing by elderly persons has clearly shown, *everyone* has a story to tell, a story that may amaze, enlighten, or inspire others. And writing or recording that story can also enrich the lives of those who tell it.

There's been an explosion of memoir writing in recent years, not just by former presidents, actors and actresses, and professional athletes, but also by ordinary people you might meet on the street or encounter at work. Once they get to thinking about it, many people discover that their lives had more meaning and interesting details than they had previously realized.

As June C. Hussey, who has worked for two decades in and around retirement communities, wrote in the *Journal on Active Aging:* "I met lots of people who were, by all accounts, *ordinary,* yet I found their lives rich and storied. One of them was Howard.

Howard was the youngest of 10 children. His family homesteaded in the Arizona desert outside of Phoenix around 1910, long before the days of air conditioning. His family was in the business of raising turkeys. He told me of the time his father, with shotgun, foiled an attempt by rustlers to steal his family's livelihood. He told me of boyhood escapades, such as swimming in irrigation ditches to get out of the heat. Once he latched his bicycle to the bumper of an unsuspecting Ford Model T driving up a mountain towards Prescott. Halfway up the hill, Howard discovered a Chinese man, bound and gagged in the backseat, who was being smuggled as a slave. Shortly afterwards, the driver discovered Howard. The boy was sworn never to tell a soul about what he had seen, lest he be punished for bike-hitching."

Legacies to Treasure

In his book *Dying Well,* Dr. Ira Byock wrote: "Whether we are rich or poor, the valuable gift we can give to our children, grandchildren and those yet to come are the treasures of our memories, our stories, our values, insights and special wisdom." A study conducted in 2005 for the Allianz Life Insurance Company of North America found that "non-financial leave-behinds [were] 10 times more important" to their potential heirs "than the financial aspects of a legacy transfer."

But fewer than 6 percent of Americans currently alive have taken the time to record their legacies, a statistic that speaks to an enormous loss not only to their families and friends but to future generations and the society at large.

In the 1990s Erin Tierney Kramp, age thirty-two, wife of Douglas and mother of one-year-old Peyton, was working as a venture capitalist when she was diagnosed with breast cancer. She learned a year later that the disease had spread to her spine and that the cancer would ultimately be fatal. She didn't know just how much time she had left, but she and Doug chose to use part of the time that remained to write an extraordinary little book aptly titled *Living with the End in Mind.* One chapter describes the why and how to leave a legacy for the people you love. With coauthor Emily P. McKhann, they wrote, "Even if you are strong and healthy, by creating legacies, you can give your loved ones gifts that they can treasure for years and generations to come." These are some of their most valuable suggestions:

- Organize your photographs into albums and record audiotapes to be played along with them.

- Create a "remember" book in which you recount your earliest memories, most memorable teachers, favorite childhood and adult activities, most inspiring books or movies, and important life lessons.

- Select personal treasures—jewelry, heirlooms, furniture, items you made, sports equipment, and so on—that you would want certain friends or family members to have after you die.

- Write a letter or create a videotape that expresses your love and encouragement for the people you care about.

- If you are a parent or grandparent, write or record the values and traits you would like to instill in your children or grandchildren. Help them to answer such questions as whom to talk to about their problems and how to decide what to do with their lives.

I know that Erin Kramp left ample legacies for her young daughter to cherish as she grows up, but perhaps the greatest legacy of this incredible woman is the book she coauthored, a treasure she chose to share with the world. It contains something for everyone, regardless of one's religious or secular persuasions, age, or state of health. You might be able to find a copy on the Internet; try www.amazon.com.

My sister-in-law, Muriel Cashin, was neither chronically or

acutely ill. But she has spent her retirement years writing down memories from her youth growing up in rural Minnesota. The stories, often funny, sometimes sad, but always interesting, tell of a life gone by that not only preserves a history but also fosters great appreciation for the fortitude and ingenuity of the family's and community's forebears. Here is an excerpt from one of her voluminous writings:

HOME

Fog swirled around my ankles as I walked to the bus in the morning. Each foggy morning I expected to see the mummy looming up before me or hear him dragging behind. We all had nightmares as a result of having seen a horror movie double-feature. Years later my dad wrote a letter in which he apologized for taking us to those movies. I was terrified for years when I walked through a foggy swamp.

The corduroy road on which I walked passed by a swamp. Perhaps it should be called a marsh rather than a swamp. A corduroy road is built on unfirm land. Railroad ties are laid adjacent to each other the entire length and width of the roadbed until it reaches solid ground. Dirt is filled in, around and over the ties, to create a reasonably smooth surface which is then covered with gravel.

The east side of the corduroy road had two different areas. One area was peat and was not used at all. One spring a fire started in the peat and smoldered all summer. The north end of the east side of the road was a pasture. Jacks-in-the-pulpit, trillium, and purple violets bloomed, as well as mayflowers and hepaticas.

A neighbor kept cows in the pasture and drove over morning and evening from April to October to milk them under the spreading elm tree, the home of squirrels. We walked over to watch the neighbor milk his cows. We must have been in-

trigued with cows because the conversation, if I remember correctly, consisted mainly of "yep," "nope," and "izzatso?" from the neighbor. He wasn't a farmer, he was a bricklayer, but he liked farming. He laid brick for a living and farmed for fun. That was an interesting concept, I thought. My dad hated farming so much he quit farming and became a truck driver. That neighbor liked farming so much he farmed for fun.

Watercress choked a creek which ran through the marsh and pasture, and through two tunnels, eventually ending at the St. Croix River. We waded in the creek to the end of the second tunnel where the water fell about thirty feet into solid rock. My dad cleared some watercress and built a small dam where he kept his minnow bucket.

We didn't own the land our house stood on. The land was owned by the railroad company. We paid rent for the lot and personal property taxes on the house. There was no basement, no foundation, and no sewer. The house stood on wooden posts and railroad ties which needed replacing periodically. When the ties decayed, the house dipped a little in places. When we put a marble on the floor, if it rolled across the room, it was time to jack up the house and replace the wooden ties.

The well was near the back door and was only ten feet deep. The water got murky occasionally. We took buckets to the spring a half block away and carried spring water until the well water cleared up again. We used many gallons of water each day for drinking, cooking, bathing, washing clothes, scrubbing floors, etc. Of course, it had to be heated on a stove fueled by wood, gasoline, kerosene, fuel oil, or coal, all of which were carried in from separate storage places.

The living quarters were upstairs, up a flight of seventeen steps. My great-uncle Hjalmer, on his only visit, stopped halfway up and said, "If I knew it was so far, I would have brought a lunch."

The rooms were attractive and cozy, but not unique. They resembled a compact and fairly modern bungalow, without *the modern conveniences. However, the kitchen sink had a convenient device, a hose through a hole in the floor, which allowed it to drain into the garden.*

The bathroom [which doubled as a store room and laundry] had a real cast-iron bathtub. We heated the water on the stove, carried it to the tub, and poured it in. It, too, drained into the garden.

The toilet was outside, of course. There was no plumbing. The outhouse was owned by the railroad company, for the use of railroad personnel and passengers. We used it also. It wasn't attractively decorated with old calendars and cute pictures like most outhouses. We didn't decorate it because it belonged to the railroad company. It did have a Sears Roebuck catalog, as well as real toilet paper. My dad threatened to put in a box of corncobs, such as they had on the farm, but he never did. Of course, we didn't farm, so we didn't have corncobs anyway.

There was no electricity. We had Coleman gasoline lamps and lanterns and good kerosene lamps. As the only family on the road, we would have been required to pay to build an electric line and we could not afford to do so. When I was twenty-one years old, the county finally built the line and we got electrified. It was nice to have electricity, but, in retrospect, it wasn't wonderful. We lost the charm of the kerosene lamps and the novelty of being unique. We still didn't have running water, indoor plumbing, or central heating.

I remember the day we moved in, April 1, 1938. The key broke off in the keyhole, so we left it there and never locked the door.

Of course, it is best to follow Muriel's example and not wait until you are near death or diagnosed with a fatal illness to write or dictate into a tape recorder the tales that are unique to your life and being. But sometimes it is the knowledge that one's days are numbered that inspires people to, as the saying goes, put pen to paper.

One such person was Eugene O'Kelly. He was fifty-three years old, chairman and CEO of a major corporation, the accounting firm KPMG, living a joy-filled and productive life, when he learned in May 2005 that he had an incurable brain cancer and three to six months of life remaining. What would he do with that time, which turned out to be a mere one hundred days? He chose to share his thoughts about his life and approaching death and how receiving a prognosis of impending death had transformed his life. With the aid and encouragement of his wife, Corinne, this culminated in the book, *Chasing Daylight,* in which he revealed that his life's accomplishments mattered less to him than the human and spiritual bonds he had forged and the experiences he had shared with those he loved.

Dr. Christina Puchalski, a geriatrician who specializes in obtaining spiritual histories, was asked to visit a mother of several children who was dying and appeared to be very depressed. Instead, Dr. Puchalski found, not depression, but a feeling that the woman's life had no purpose and she had nothing more to do in the time she had left. Her biggest concern: "My two-year-old daughter is not going to remember me." So the doctor helped the woman compose a written legacy for her daughter, telling the child about herself as a person and mother, her values and experiences, and what her hopes and dreams were for her daughter. In addition, one of the nurses videotaped the mother, and the document and videotape became a permanent legacy for her daughter. The woman's "depression" lifted right away, without any medication, Dr. Puchalski said.

Sometimes one's legacy is not a life story but an accomplishment that can have a life of its own long after the creator has died. Jessica Wing was only twenty-nine years old when she received a diagnosis of metastatic colon cancer. Though she hoped for a different outcome, she knew too well that her disease could not be cured, only controlled for a limited amount of time. Jessica was an extraordinarily talented young woman, and she was writing an opera, ultimately called *Lost,* loosely based on the story of Hansel and Gretel. She wrote the very last notes of *Lost* the day before she died, just two years after her diagnosis. The opera was performed off Broadway to much acclaim three weeks after her death. I was privileged to see and enjoy it and to know that Jessica had left behind a body of work and evidence of her talents that would live on long after her.

Jessica left behind another "gift" that she never knew about. While a student at Stanford University, she donated her eggs to a fertility clinic. It has since been discovered that at least five children were born to two very happy families using her eggs. The children are beautiful and brilliant, as was Jessica. Someday I hope they will have the chance to learn about their origins and the marvelous young woman who was their biological mother.

Overcome Your Resistance

As you can see, you don't have to be a genius, a world leader, or a famous person to have memories, thoughts, ideas, passions, actions and reactions, and pearls of wisdom that are worth sharing with others. There are numerous programs available to get you started. Several are available on the Internet. For example, The Remembering Site, at www.therememberingsite.com, is a nonprofit effort that allows people to write, publish, and add to their personal histories over time for a nominal, onetime registration fee. LifeBio, at www.LifeBio.com, can help to get you started by asking life-probing, thought-provoking, memory-stimulating questions.

If for some reason you are unable or unwilling to write, you can speak your thoughts into a tape recorder. Or perhaps a family member—son, daughter, grandchild—or a friend can interview you, asking pertinent questions and writing down or recording your answers.

If you are reluctant to participate in this grand adventure, June Hussey has apt responses to help you overcome your resistance. Here is how she would respond to some people's natural reticence:

- *"It's not polite to talk about myself."* It's not really about you; it's about those who follow you and how your life experiences and lessons can help shape them.

- *"My children don't want to know about my life."* They do.

- *"My children already know all about me."* They don't.

- *"I don't have children."* So what? Everyone's life matters to someone.

- *"My life is too insignificant to write about."* No one's life is insignificant. Beauty is often camouflaged by the ordinary and mundane.

Waste no more time. Get started today. You never know which day will be your last and how much you can accomplish before that day comes.

FOR FURTHER READING

Albom, Mitch. *Tuesdays with Morrie.* New York: Broadway, 2002.

Kramp, Erin Tierney, and Douglas H. Kramp, with Emily P. McKhann. *Living with the End in Mind.* New York: Three Rivers Press, 1998.

O'Kelly, Eugene, with Andrew Postman. *Chasing Daylight: How My Forthcoming Death Transformed My Life.* New York: McGraw-Hill, 2005.

Pausch, Randy. *The Last Lecture.* New York: Hyperion, 2008.

Victoria Roberts

"*Uncertainty, Sylvia, is life's big draw.*"

EPILOGUE:
From the Start Consider the Finish

No sooner had I completed the manuscript for this book than I learned of another, the title of which fully captures the essence of my message: *From the Start Consider the Finish*. It was written by two registered nurses and former hospice volunteers, Susan Riker Dolan and Audrey Riker Vizzard, and published in 2007 by Outskirts Press in Parker, Colorado. Susan and Audrey are a mother–daughter team who had firsthand experience with excellent end-of-life preparation and care.

The title of their book comes from the slogan of the paint and coatings company that Susan's husband's grandfather, V. J. Dolan, had started in 1924 and passed on to his son, Bill Dolan. As Susan recounts the story of Bill Dolan's last days on earth, he lived the motto of his company. One day, out of the blue, Bill suffered a massive stroke. A decision had to be made quickly about whether to put him on a ventilator to help him breathe, though he was never expected to regain consciousness. As painful as it was to lose the man they loved, the decision was a no-brainer because Bill had made it easy for his large family.

As the authors describe him, Bill "was the poster child for excellent end-of-life planning. He had decided how he wanted to be treated if he were ever in a position where he was ill and could not speak for himself. He had documented his wishes in advance and he had discussed those wishes with his family. There were many conversations over the years. He left no doubts: 'Let nature take its course. No extraordinary measures. Keep me comfortable and let me go.' Because of his careful planning, the family knew exactly what to do."

With his mother's blessing, Bill's son, John, said "no ventilator." Instead, he asked the doctor to order hospice services and write a "do not resuscitate" order to prevent any attempts to revive him should his heart or lungs stop working completely. By that evening all eleven of Bill's children and their spouses had gathered by Bill's bedside to say good-bye to a man they loved and greatly respected. Bill's wife, Fran, reassured the children that by accepting hospice she was honoring her husband's explicit wishes.

"Dad gave us an invaluable gift; he told us exactly what to do in this situation: *no extraordinary measures*. We will abide by his wishes." At the same time, Bill had taught his children and their spouses how to live well and, equally important, how to die well. Less than twenty-four hours after suffering a stroke from which he could never recover, Bill Dolan died without having to endure "aggressive, futile treatment [that] would have robbed the family of a natural and deeply moving process," the authors wrote.

In their introduction to *From the Start Consider the Finish*, the authors point to why so many Americans fail to experience a peaceful death unhampered by tubes, needles, and machinery that only prolong the agony and create untold misery for both the dying and those who love them.

"When it comes to death and dying, most people report they avoid conversations about their own demise and fail to make plans for it. Most of us choose to ignore death or at least stay as far away from it as possible. So unwelcome are thoughts of dying in our culture that we have developed a sturdy shield of denial to protect us from the knowledge and experience of what is a normal, natural life event."

They recommend, as do I, that "the best time to have these conversations and complete your advance directive is before you become ill. Taking the time to plan and prepare now makes it reasonably certain that your wishes will be honored and last-minute conflicts between family members avoided. *From the start consider the finish.*"*

Please, for your own sake and the sake of those who love you and will be left behind, do it. *Do it now!* Your loved ones will thank you for it, and I assure you that you won't live to regret it.

JANE E. BRODY

* An expanded version of *From the Start Consider the Finish* is now available as *The End-of-Life Advisor* (New York: Kaplan, 2009).

ACKNOWLEDGMENTS

How does one say thanks to people who have died? But that is what I'm about to do. Thanks to each and every one of the scores of people I have known and loved who have preceded me in death and left me with life lessons—lessons in both living and dying—that have helped to shape me and the words in this book, which I hope will help to shape you, the reader. People like my mother-in-law, Anna Engquist, my friend Mickey Martinez, Jessica Wing, the winsome daughter of a college friend, my neighborhood friend Jan Jeffrey, and countless other people who have shared their experiences with me either directly or indirectly through their families and friends.

Instead of having to reinvent the wheel with each person's passing, we can all benefit from the lessons learned by those who have gone before us, as well as those who have attended them, like Dr. Diane Meier, who gave so generously of her time and wisdom and has done so much to foster the field of palliative care that can benefit all of us, those who will live as well as those who will soon die.

I have benefited, too, from the dozens of authors who, before me, took pen to paper to record their personal and professional experiences, not only with death and dying, but also with living as if each day could be the last. I adopted this approach to life at seventeen when my own mother died at the tender age of forty-nine and have pursued it as best as I could for the next half century. I recommend it highly and expect to continue along this line until my own death ends it.

Thanks, too, to Nancy Miller, who gently pursued me and encouraged me to write this book when she was an editor at Random House. Thanks to my special friend Gail Godwin, who introduced me to Nancy and never let up on her enthusiastic endorsement for this project. "We all need this book, Jane," was her constant refrain. And thanks to Marnie Cochran, the young editor who took up the project when Nancy moved on, for her diligent, caring, and sensitive attention to this work and her recognition of its potential value to people of all ages. The assistance of three other Random House editors, Jennifer Hershey, Lea Beresford, and Christina Duffy, was also invaluable, as was the enthusiasm of everyone at Random House who has had a role in bringing this book into the hands of readers.

Finally, thanks both to my husband, Richard Engquist, for his periodic advice and expertise and for putting up with so many months of catch-as-catch-can meals, and my agent, Wendy Weil, whose patience with me is nothing short of remarkable.

JANE E. BRODY

INDEX

ILLUSTRATION AND PERMISSION CREDITS

ILLUSTRATION CREDITS

Sam Gross, "Grandma's going to Florida." Copyright © 2007 Sam Gross, from *Last Laughs*.

Lee Lorenz, "Leaving desirable organs." Copyright © 2007 Lee Lorenz, from *Last Laughs*.

Mike Twohy, "Bounce back from an autopsy." Copyright © 2007 Mike Twohy, from *Last Laughs*.

Victoria Roberts, "Life's big draw." Copyright © 2007 Victoria Roberts, from *Last Laughs*.

PERMISSION CREDITS

ABOUT THE AUTHOR

JANE E. BRODY began her career as a science and medical writer for *The New York Times* in 1965 and became the *Times*'s Personal Health columnist in 1976. Her widely read and quoted weekly column appears in dozens of other newspapers. She also lectures frequently on health issues to both lay and professional audiences around the country. She has written scores of magazine articles, won numerous awards for journalistic excellence, and appeared on hundreds of radio and television programs.

Ms. Brody is the author of ten books, including two bestsellers: *Jane Brody's Nutrition Book* and *Jane Brody's Good Food Gourmet.*

Ms. Brody graduated with high honors from the New York State College of Agriculture and Life Sciences at Cornell University, where she majored in biochemistry. She has a master's degree in science writing from the University of Wisconsin School of Journalism.

Ms. Brody is the proud mother of twin sons and grandmother of four boys, including a pair of twins. She is a prodigious knitter and crocheter and enjoys trips to foreign lands and daily exercise indoors and out. She resides in Brooklyn, New York, the town of her birth, with her husband.

ABOUT THE TYPE

This book was set in New Caledonia, a typeface designed in 1939 by William Addison Dwiggins for the Merganthaler Linotype Company. Its name is the ancient Roman term for Scotland, because the face was intended to have a Scotch–Roman flavor. New Caledonia is considered to be a well-proportioned, businesslike face with little contrast between its thick and thin lines.